ALL THOSE IN FAVOUR?

ALL THOSE IN FAVOUR?

AN ACCOUNT OF THE
HIGH COURT ACTION
AGAINST THE
ELECTRICAL TRADES UNION
AND ITS OFFICERS FOR BALLOT-RIGGING
IN THE ELECTION OF UNION OFFICIALS

(Byrne & Chapple v. Foulkes & Others, 1961)

———

PREPARED FROM THE
OFFICIAL COURT TRANSCRIPT
BY
C. H. ROLPH

WITH A PREFACE BY
JOHN FREEMAN

ANDRE DEUTSCH

FIRST PUBLISHED 1962 BY
ANDRE DEUTSCH LIMITED
105 GREAT RUSSELL STREET
LONDON WC1
PRINTED IN GREAT BRITAIN BY
THE GARDEN CITY PRESS LIMITED
LETCHWORTH, HERTFORDSHIRE

CONTENTS

PREFACE

IN years to come students of British social history may remember and quote the case of *Byrne and Chapple v. Foulkes and Others* in the same way as we refer today to the Taff Vale judgment and even the trial of Oscar Wilde, first for its importance in the case-book of trade union law and secondly for the total collapse of individual reputation with which it ended.

The ETU case, as it has come to be known, is of special interest in trade union law because of the particular way in which its circumstances skirted—and by a hair's breadth avoided—the difficult question of whether a trade union can be sued in tort by its own members and because, against all the accepted conventions of trade union intercourse, the Plaintiffs (themselves working trade unionists) invoked the law of conspiracy against the officers of their own union for actions undertaken in the course of official duty.

C. H. Rolph's lucid, fair and tightly-written summary of this mammoth case picks out the relevance and importance of these two legal points with impeccable clarity. He also unravels the complicated skein of plot and counter-plot with a logic and simplicity which few if any other legal journalists can command. Indeed, the real importance of this book is not to lawyers—who can after all have access to the full transcript—but to the public, who were the ultimate sufferers from the corruption of power in the ETU and who are only too likely to have lost the thread of fact in the seemingly interminable exchanges of the Court.

What happened in this case, said Mr Gerald Gardiner, QC, leading counsel for the Plaintiffs, was 'the biggest fraud in the history of trade unionism'. And there you have it. This was a civil action. No criminal charge was brought against any of the Defendants. The case was fraught with legal complexity and baffling conflicts of evidence. It is easy to conclude that the issues which were being tried were themselves complex, baffling or even academic. They were not. They were fraud, lies and conspiracy. The men who lost this action failed in a civil court. Yet, when Mr Justice Winn found against them, he found both explicitly and implicitly that they had deliberately cheated and defrauded their own members and, in most cases, lied to cover their guilt.

The Judge's definition of their various degrees of falsehood varied from 'Honest John' Hendy and Sam Goldberg, who gave 'materially untrue evidence to the court', through the pathetic Frank Foulkes, who (like Frank Haxell) was a man 'prepared to prefer expediency to truth', to Haxell and John Frazer, who put forward to the Court 'puerile mendacities'. But the sum of it all was, in the Judge's words, that none of the Defendants (i.e., of the ten whom the defence chose to put into the witness-box, and of course excluding Messrs Rengert and Shipman, who were discharged from the case at an early stage) was frank or truthful: all of them incurred discredit by their evidence. Seldom have parties to a civil action emerged with so much individual discredit as did the losers in this case. Foulkes subsequently applied for legal aid in order to appeal against the Judge's findings, but his application was refused. The Executive Council of the ETU thereupon decided with outstanding generosity to offer Foulkes a sum from the Union's funds in order that he should be able to appeal, but his appeal failed.

How have the Communist leaders of the ETU reacted to the loss not only of their case but also of their personal honour? Since the judgment, elections to the Executive Council have been held and the Communists have been overwhelmingly defeated. The new Executive took office on January 1, 1962, and within twenty-four hours took decisive action to consolidate their position. They sacked Robert McLennan, who, though found by the Judge to be both a conspirator and a liar, had retained the post of Assistant General Secretary, and they invalidated certain last-minute rule changes made by the Communist Executive in the hope of maintaining their hold on at least some of the levers of power. It can, I think, fairly be said that power in the ETU has now been put back into the hands of its members. But even now the Communists have not given up. A determined attempt is being made to rehabilitate the reputations of 'Honest John' Hendy (who gave materially untrue evidence to the court) and Frank Foulkes (who is 'prepared to prefer expediency to truth'). Both these men have considerable personal charm, and the story is being industriously put about that they (unlike the rest of the Defendants, who seem to have been written off by the Communist Party) were the victims of circumstance and never privy to the malpractices. A careful study of the evidence in the pages following reveals nothing which materially substantiates this claim. Nevertheless, the signs are that the Party tactic is to rebuild Communist prestige in the ETU round the figures of Foulkes and Hendy and hope that by appeals to sentiment, coupled with as much local trickery as Communist branch secretaries are allowed to get away with, they may be able to make an electoral comeback in two or three years' time.

The Communists' second, and related, response to the exposure of their malpractices is to protest that the case against them was trumped up by the 'capitalist Press' and was really an attack on their socialist leadership. A brief roll-call of those who played the leading parts in marshalling the case against them provides the best answer to that.

At the head of the list I must put Mr John Byrne, the principal Plaintiff in the action and now General Secretary of the ETU. Byrne was the first of the nationally known figures in the ETU to challenge the Communist leadership—at a time when his fellow plaintiff, Frank Chapple, and others who subsequently played important parts, were themselves still members of the Communist Party. Year after year he plugged away, brave, pertinacious and regardless of his health, until finally (and with rare justice) it was he who had the distinction of laying Foulkes, Haxell and company by the heels.

Frank Chapple, the second Plaintiff in the action, left the Communist Party in 1956 after Hungary and since then he has not spared himself in working to redress the wrongs that were committed in his name. He remains a left-wing socialist by political conviction.

One name you will find seldom mentioned in this book—Les Cannon. Cannon, like Chapple, left the Party after Hungary and in 1957 he beat John Frazer in an election for a seat on the Executive. Since he was no longer acceptable to the Communist clique, the election results were falsified and Frazer was declared the winner. This particular fraud was perhaps the beginning of the end for the Communists. Cannon resolved to let nothing stand in the way in his efforts to see justice done in the ETU, and I think no one who has seen him at work will deny that since 1957 his almost super-human refusal to accept defeat, coupled with extraordinary knowledge of the ETU and its rules, have been an inspiration to his comrades. Chapple and Cannon are, of course, far less well known to the public than Byrne. But when the time comes for Byrne to give up, they and those who carried on the fight with them represent, in my view, the ETU's best hope for wise and honest administration in the future.

Apart from members of the ETU—and they, of course, have at all times provided the impetus for the whole campaign—one journalist appears to me to merit special mention. As early as 1956, Mr Woodrow Wyatt, MP, in an article in the magazine, *Illustrated*, exposed the falsification of ETU elections. A year later he prepared and took part in the first two of the BBC's four *Panorama* programmes, which played a vital role in alerting the trade union world to what was going on. He followed these with an article in the *New Statesman* which formed the effective brief to which many others subsequently worked.

Persons apart, I think it true to say that the *New Statesman* has played a special role, beyond that of other organs of the Press. Ever since 1957, the *New Statesman* has consistently exposed the operations of the Communist clique and urged both the rank and file of the ETU, and the TUC, to take action to remove a scandal which, allowed to go unchecked, would bring grave discredit on the whole trade union movement. Of course other papers played reputable roles, especially in the later stages. But it was the *New Statesman* (not then under my editorship) which from 1957 onwards provided the main platform from which the reformist case was argued.

Now the significant thing to me about that roll of honour is that every single name on it is fully identified with the Labour movement, while Chapple and Cannon (like most members of the new Executive) can fairly be described as well to the left of centre. The Communist conspiracy in the ETU had to be smashed because its crookery and corruption were a denial of everything that socialism ought to stand for. The battle was planned, directed and finally won by a group of dedicated trade unionists who are far, far better socialists and truer representatives of their fellow-workers than the liars and cheats they ousted. That is the answer to the Communist smear that the case was trumped up in the capitalist Press.

Now that the battle is won, it remains to say one more word. The ETU may not have been the only case of fraud and corruption in British trade unionism—though it was beyond doubt the most shameful. And the Communist Party may not be the only organisation prepared to cheat its way to power. The one effective safeguard is the constant vigilance of ordinary trade unionists against all forms of jobbery and double-dealing, above all at branch level. The real importance of this trial, I wrote earlier, is to the public rather than to the legal specialists. But some ten million of the British public are trade unionists. I would like to hope that this admirable book, bought or borrowed, might be read by every one of them, so that those who pay the piper of British trade unionism may realise how great was the evil in the ETU and how much was accomplished by the handful of brave, energetic and resourceful men who had the guts to fight it.

JOHN FREEMAN

INTRODUCTION

LORD BACON said at the close of a trial: 'This case bristles with simplicity. The facts are admitted. The law is plain. And yet it has taken seven days to try—one day more than God Almighty took to create the universe.' *Byrne and Chapple v. Foulkes and Others* (1961) did not bristle with simplicity. But the trial started with an admission by the Defence that the announced Byrne-Haxell election result was invalid—which was to have been one of the main issues in the action. The law about conspiracy was at least fairly plain, though this was its first application to a trade union election. And yet this non-jury case took forty-two days to try. The statistically minded may be further excited by the information that about 1,365,000 words were spoken (at the rate of about 32,500 a day) and that the documentary 'exhibits' weighed rather more than a ton.

Each side maintained that the length of the trial was the other's fault: the Defendants' for being so dilatory in producing the documents needed, and the Plaintiffs' for wanting them. Certainly there can seldom have been a High Court action so precariously dependent on the Defendants' day-by-day self-incrimination. Its progress waited on the slow-moving production of tell-tale letters, schedules, books, and minutes, which the Plaintiffs (as Mr Justice Winn said), 'not being able to see the end of the road, had to use as paving material as they advanced'.

Where did it all begin? You have to imagine a trade union 'branch meeting', held as a rule in a back room at a pub after a day's work. Perhaps twenty-five or thirty men are there, though the branch membership may be 600, 750, or 1,000. Though they are not necessarily of a quality tougher than or superior to that of their absent and seemingly apathetic colleagues, they are the active heart of trade unionism; they are there because the others will never come. They are the kind of men who, in the nineteenth century, established the building society, the friendly society, the working men's club, industrial life assurance and what we now call 'adult education'. There are relatively few among us who are not enormously in their debt, though the respectable majority of us have contrived to forget it. In the very nature of things, these activists are men 'of the Left'; and at *their* extreme left are those who too often gain the leadership because there is none to gainsay them. A few of these men will use any means for their cherished ends, even going so far as to deceive those whom they represent, and the great mass of the membership is satisfied so long as wage claims are well fought.

Some trade unions, of which the ETU is a perfect example, are always preoccupied with elections. They elect nearly everyone whom they will require or expect to do anything in their name. To read their Rules (duly and gravely deposited with the Registrar of Friendly Societies) may give you the sensation of being lost in the lunatic shouting-fringe of a newly articulate democracy. If you are wiser, you will know that you are reading the literate expression of the fears, hopes, and 'solidarity' of a hundred hard-working generations of men.

'Democracy substitutes election by the incompetent many,' Bernard Shaw said, 'for appointment by the corrupt few'. It can also, by the proliferation of dimly understood and loosely drafted rules, enthrone the demagogue in a position of power (as it did with Adolf Hitler) from which he can be dislodged only by violence —or sometimes, in Britain, the Commonwealth, and the United States, by 'going to law'. In 703 branch meetings of the Electrical Trades Union, in pubs and clubs and British Legion headquarters and cafés and village halls, the ETU men gradually came to see that only the High Court could rescue them from the control of a handful of dedicated sea-lawyers who belonged to the Communist Party as well as to the ETU. Most of them, probably, had never much minded (even if they knew) that their Union leaders were Communists, for those leaders presented at least an appearance of skill and success. But now at last there were forces at work that professed to see better than the membership what was good for them—and, what was more important, saw grave danger to the country in a Communist domination of the trade union movement.

The Communists, for their part, held before them the famous exhortation from Lenin himself:

> The leaders of opportunism will resort to every trick to prevent Communists from getting into the trade unions. It is therefore necessary to agree to any and every sacrifice and even, if need be, to resort to all sorts of stratagems, manœuvres, and illegal methods, to evasions and subterfuges, in order to penetrate the trade unions and to remain in them, carrying on Communist activities inside them at all costs.

Here, in the opening words of Mr Gerald Gardiner, QC, is how the Defendants were alleged to have achieved their main object— the 'rigging' of elections.

1) By arranging that there should never be more than one candidate offering himself for election in any given position;
2) By arranging who that candidate was to be;
3) By ensuring that the candidate was proposed by as many branches as possible;
4) By sending 'national officers' (employees of the Union) to branch meetings just before an election, ostensibly on some official business, but really to canvass for the Communist candidate;
5) By making trivial charges against prominent non-Communists, so that they could be disqualified from Union office for a period of years;
6) By 'disqualifying' non-Communist branches, using the impossibly complicated Rules as a source of reported irregularities in election procedure, and condoning the same irregularities at Communist ones;
7) When all else had failed, by altering the returns of voting sent in by branches.

In the 1959 election for the office of General Secretary of the ETU, when the candidates were Mr John Byrne, a non-Communist, and Mr Frank Haxell, a Communist, the racket was carried just too far. 'The Defendants,' said Mr Gardiner, 'not only adopted all their usual methods, but actually excelled themselves. There was, as usual, only one Communist candidate, and as was customary they arranged for as many nominations from the branches as possible—there was more canvassing than ever. They had already

trumped up a charge against Mr Chapple, a non-Communist. They
thereafter had an extra 26,000 voting papers printed and sent to
Communist supporters, these votes being simply fraudulent votes.
They altered some of the branch returns. But even so, in spite of
these practices, they found when the votes came in that Mr Haxell
had plainly lost the election—Mr Byrne had won by a substantial
majority. There was only one way out left, and that was to disqualify as many non-Communist branches as possible.'

That was the essence of the story.

In the first five minutes of the trial there was a surprising
development.

I MR GERALD GARDINER, QC,
OPENS THE CASE

'IN this case, my Lord,' Mr Gardiner began, 'I appear with my learned friend, Mr Sofer, for the Plaintiffs, and my learned friends Mr Neil Lawson, Mr Ralph Millner, and Mr Bernard Marder appear for the Defendants. My friend Mr Lawson has told me that he is anxious to make some statement about the nature of his case, and I thought that as a matter of courtesy he should have the opportunity to do it now.'

Mr Lawson then said that the Defendants 'did not now seek to uphold the validity of the election, and agreed that a new election must be held'. It had come to their knowledge, he said (and you could have imagined that it had only just come), 'first of all, that owing to mistakes made by the branch secretaries in their returns to the Head Office of the number of members entitled to vote, a large number of papers were issued by branch secretaries to persons who were not entitled to vote, and secondly that a substantial number of members who were entitled to vote were not issued with ballot papers at all'. Furthermore, in the course of the election scrutiny 'irregularities occurred which make it impossible for the Defendants to contend that the Rules were observed . . . Since the Rules of the Union make it doubtful whether the Union can declare the election void because of the lapse of time, it may well be that your Lordship will at some stage make the appropriate declarations.'

'It comes as a complete surprise to me,' said Mr Justice Winn. 'It occurs to me that perhaps the affairs of this Union cannot be administered properly until those matters are cleared up. It would seem, on what you have said, to be extremely doubtful who is the properly elected Secretary of this Union.' Counsel should get together, he said, and agree on declaring someone Secretary.

'What matters very much more, my Lord,' Mr Gardiner submitted, 'is the purpose for which the action has been brought, namely that after due investigation in open Court it may be decided whether or not elections in this Union have for some time been rigged. It is essential that members of the Union should know by a hearing in open Court whether these charges are well founded. From the Plaintiffs' point of view, if Mr Haxell were to step down and Mr McLennan, the Assistant General Secretary, were to take his place, I don't know that that would make very much difference.'

The Judge then repeated his hope that the parties might agree on the provisional appointment of some new General Secretary; but what seems to have happened, at least for the duration of the trial, is that Mr Frank Haxell carried on as before, fitting his secretarial duties into the intervals between his attendances at Court.

Meanwhile Mr Gardiner proceeded with the opening of the Plaintiffs' case.

'As your Lordship knows,' he said, 'the action is one for conspiracy, and for certain declarations and other relief; it being alleged, first, that the Defendant, Mr Foulkes, as General President of the ETU—a trade union of some 241,000 members and 703 branches, of which 241,000 members only about 37,000 take the trouble to vote at elections—is and was at all material times a member of the Communist Party; that the second Defendant, Mr Haxell, was until the disputed election in 1959 the General Secretary, and also was at all material times a member of the Communist Party; that Mr McLennan, the Assistant General Secretary, was and is a member of the Communist Party; that the Defendants Foulkes, Haxell, McLennan, Cosby, Davies, Feathers, John Frazer, Hendy and Sell, who, quite apart from the officers of the Union, constitute nine out of the fourteen members of the Executive Council, are all members of the Communist Party.'

Secondly, said Mr Gardiner, the Defendants had conspired together, by breaches of the Union Rules and by various frauds, to prevent non-Communists from being elected to any Union office and to procure the election of Communists.

Thirdly, they all belonged to Committees of the Communist Party made up of members of the ETU.

Fourthly, they had rigged certain elections (in the several ways set out on page 15).

'Now, the position of two ordinary members of a trade union suing the union and its principal officers, my Lord, is not an easy one. Financially the two Plaintiffs in *this* case satisfied a Legal Aid Committee, and this is a Legal Aid case. But of course the Defendants had possession of all the documents. The writ in the action was issued on May 10, 1960; and in July a Judge in Chambers granted a certificate for a speedy trial. In October the trial was fixed for February 27. Then it unfortunately proved necessary to move for contempt of Court against the Defendant Haxell, and the Defendant Scott, for attempted intimidation of witnesses by issuing a circular which said that it would be wrong for members to give any information to the Plaintiffs' solicitors. In the Divisional Court recently, the learned Lord Chief Justice presiding, the view was expressed that there had been a clear contempt of Court, warranting imprisonment, but that as this would only have delayed the trial the Court was content to impose only a penalty of costs.

'On February 13—a fortnight, your Lordship will observe, before the date fixed for the trial—an application was made to delay the hearing until June, it being said that the Defendants couldn't possibly be ready for trial on February 27. They said they were employing a special staff of fifty men working day and night, whereas my instructing solicitors had only an assistant solicitor and five typists and *could* be ready in time. Mr Justice Barry fixed today for the hearing and said that the trial must begin then.

'I shall be calling a number of branch secretaries who will tell your Lordship on what date they posted their returns. I don't know exactly how many I *am* going to call because, immediately the Defendants obtained their adjournment, nearly all my intended witnesses received a summons to Head Office.' (What happened there was, at this stage of the trial, left open to conjecture.)

'My clients were anxious, as were other members, for a special Delegate Conference to be called, at which a thorough internal enquiry could be made into these allegations. But the Defendants would have none of that. The TUC were prepared to hold a judicial enquiry, and also invited Mr Haxell to take proceedings for defamation against those who made these allegations; but he wouldn't do either of these things.'

Mr Gardiner explained why, with all the evidence he was proposing to call as to the 'overt acts' of individuals, he was suing for conspiracy. 'First,' he said, 'where there is *in fact* a conspiracy, so that an allegation of conspiracy is properly made, acts done by *any* Defendants pursuant to a conspiracy by *all* the Defendants would be acts for which all the Defendants would be liable. If the Haxell election stood-alone with no plea of conspiracy, there might be difficulty in proving what act was done by which Defendant. (My two clients cannot know exactly what is going on in the Head Office of the Union.) And if there were no plea of conspiracy, Mr Haxell might at the end of the case be able to say: "All you've proved is, either McLennan or I did it; you haven't proved which." And Mr McLennan might make the same submission.'

Mr Gardiner then went through the many aspects of the evidence he was going to call. Its salient features appear, for the most part, in the witnesses' own words in the pages which follow. It should be observed, however, that both Mr Gardiner's speech and the examination of witnesses included the reading out of enormously long letters from Mr Haxell to importunate and suspicious branch secretaries, to the TUC, and to 'trouble-makers' like Mr Chapple; and for these, and the lesson they afforded in articulate democracy, the reader is referred to the official Court transcript, where they occupy space of the order of 100,000 words. A further 50,000 consisted of extracts from the transcripted tape-recordings of ETU Executive Council meetings; and these, as will to some extent be seen, provided evidence of so damning a character that the skilled electricians who installed and operated the machines contributed unwittingly but powerfully to the ultimate rescue of their own Union.

Late on the third day of Mr Gardiner's speech he had what appeared to be a narrow escape from having the whole case adjourned for yet another six months. Mr Lawson intervened to ask the Judge's leave to 'amend the Defence'. He wanted to collect evidence that would refute Mr John Byrne's claim to have won the 1959 election. He repeated that many members had voted without being eligible, while many others, though eligible, had been unable to vote because they had never received ballot papers. This made the whole election a nullity, which was why he had conceded at the start of the trial that Mr Haxell wasn't really the General Secretary. But to *prove* that it was a nullity (the only way of keeping Mr Byrne out), one would have to go through the branches' 'contribution ledgers'* (for about a hundred branches) and work out which of the 30,000 members of those branches were entitled to vote on the relevant date. The Plaintiffs already had photostat copies of a number of the branch contribution ledgers, and of these Mr Gardiner remarked that whereas the ledgers themselves were kept in red, black and green ink (the colours having a varying significance about the status of a member), the photostat copies did not reproduce the colours and were therefore quite useless.

Mr Gardiner's answer to Mr Lawson's argument was, in effect, that Mr Lawson had already tried twice to get this 'permission to amend', once from a Master and once from Mr Justice Buckley; and had failed. Indeed, Mr Justice Buckley had said: 'If the case from the beginning has always been that Mr Haxell was validly elected, how can you at one and the same time ask leave to make this amendment?' This, suggested Mr Gardiner, was the *real* reason why Mr Lawson, on the very first morning of the trial, had got up and admitted that the election was a nullity.

'If I granted the application,' said Mr Justice Winn, 'I should adjourn the case until October—I say *if* I did. I think the Defendants, who have had these contribution ledgers available to them ever since the action began' (i.e., since May 1960, when the writs were issued) 'have waited far too long for leave to amend the Defence. I therefore reject the application.'

So the trial went on. 'Then I will call my first witness—Mr Keill,' said Mr Gardiner in a general atmosphere of lessened tension.

* These vast and complicated tomes are understood only by the branch treasurers, and are of a kind to make the strongest accountant turn pale. —*Editor.*

II THE PLAINTIFFS' EVIDENCE

1 The Substituted Envelopes

THE first of the Plaintiffs' ninety-seven witnesses was Mr Richard Cecil Keill, of Gillmos, Liverpool, a member of the ETU for twenty years, Branch Secretary at Gillmos for eight and a half years, Shop Steward since 1951, and a delegate to the Union's Annual Policy Conference from 1953 to 1960. He told Mr Gerald Gardiner that the ballot for General Secretary was held at his branch's quarterly meeting on Monday, December 21, in the Hare and Hounds Hotel, West Derby village.

'Is it right,' asked Mr Gardiner, 'that there voted one hundred and fifty-four for Mr Byrne and twenty for Mr Haxell?'—'Yes.'

'Did you post the return to Head Office yourself?'—'Yes.'

'When did you do it?'—'Roughly eleven p.m. on the same evening,' said Mr Keill.

Mr Gardiner then read to him a letter he (Mr Keill) had received from Head Office dated January 8:

> The national scrutineers at their last meeting decided they could not accept your branch quarterly documents in view of an infringement of Rule 21, Clauses 65 and 74. (The effect of these two Clauses is summarised on page 31.) In arriving at their decision the national scrutineers took into consideration the fact that your branch had infringed the Rule governing ballots on a previous occasion.

To this Mr Keill had replied on February 16 as follows:

> We vigorously protest at the decision of the national scrutineers, and appeal against their decision. We demand the production of the date-stamped envelope containing the documents. The date-stamp will show that it was collected by the GPO at 8.30 a.m. on December 22, having been placed in the post-box about 11 p.m. the night before, December 21, one hour and forty-five minutes after the branch quarterly meeting finished.

Our appeal is based on Rule 21, Clause 64, and you can rest assured that our members do not accept, under any circumstances whatsoever, the ridiculous and farcical excuse of the national scrutineers that our returns arrived too late.

To this Mr R. G. McLennan, Assistant General Secretary of the ETU (and one of the Defendants in the trial) had replied with a request, or indeed a summons, to Mr Keill and his Branch Chairman (Mr McGann) to 'be in attendance at this office at 3.30 p.m. on Wednesday, March 9, for the purpose of examining the documents referred to'. They went; and they were received by Mr McLennan and Mr J. N. Frazer, a member of the Executive Council (and also a Defendant).

'Did they produce to you,' asked Mr Gardiner, 'an envelope which they were asserting was the envelope in which your return had been received?'—'Yes,' said Mr Keill.

'What did you say?'—'The actual words I can't remember off-hand, but briefly it was that, as I saw it, it wasn't our envelope. I said to the Chairman' (i.e., to Mr McGann) 'it's all right to sign the form, because this is just an envelope.'

'They produced a form for you to sign?'—'Yes,' said Mr Keill, and the contents of the form were then read out:

We the undersigned attended at Head Office on Wednesday, March 9, 1960, in connection with the December quarterly documents, 1959. We examined the documents in question, and agree that the date-stamp on the envelope showed that it had been stamped at Liverpool '1.15 p.m. January 2, 1960', and that the date-stamp as being received at Head Office was 'January 4, 1960'.

'Were you agreeing,' asked Mr Gardiner, 'that that was the date on the envelope produced to you, or that that was the envelope in which your returns had been sent?'—'That was the envelope that was shown me. It had that date on it—one-fifteen p.m. January the 2nd, Liverpool. I said it just couldn't possibly be our envelope.'

'Where were you at eleven-fifteen on January the 2nd?'—'I was on stand-by duty.'

'Where?'—'At the English Electric Company.'

'How far away is that from the place where the envelope was

supposed to have been posted?'—'The nearest post-box that would bear a local postmark would be about five miles away.'

Then Mr Keill confirmed that he wrote to Head Office on May 6:

> After scrutinising the ballot returns for December quarter and having studied the Secretary's report in respect to the posting of the envelope containing the ballot returns for Gillmos Branch, our members are still not convinced that the ballot for General Secretary was not rigged. Our members urgently request the views of the Executive Council on this matter.

The word 'rigged' had thus at last made its way into the correspondence. There was no reply for five weeks, and then—

> . . . the delay in replying (wrote Head Office on June 10) has been occasioned by the necessity of having to consult the Union's legal advisers. Arising from that consultation, I sincerely regret to have to inform you that no further correspondence can be entered into on this matter, as the question is now *sub judice* in view of the writs which have been issued against members of the Union and the Union itself.

'Mr Keill,' said Mr Gardiner very deliberately, 'have you any doubt whatever that you posted those returns *on the night of the meeting*?'

'No doubt whatsoever,' Mr Keill repeated; and his cross-examination by Mr Neil Lawson, QC, then began.

'Mr Keill, you were removed by the branch from your post as Secretary, were you not, some time last year?'—'This year,' said Mr Keill.

'Your branch is not a Communist branch, as it has been described, is it?'—'I wouldn't say so.'

'It's right, is it not, that while you were Secretary your branch had been disqualified on a previous occasion for a late return?'—'Correct.'

'You also, I think, have unfortunately lost branch documents, have you not?'—'They weren't lost. They were stolen.'

'Did you report the theft of them to the police?'—'Yes—to the Chief Constable of Liverpool.'

'When did that happen?'—'June the 13th, 1960, at roughly half-past ten on a Monday night.'

Mr Lawson didn't pursue this.

'There was a good deal of criticism,' he said, 'by members of the branch, concerning your conduct in relation to the December 1959 election, was there not?'—'No.'

'Didn't the branch members complain to you that they didn't get their ballot papers until December the 19th?'—'I received no complaints whatsoever,' replied Mr Keill emphatically.

'How far is it from the place where the branch meeting was held, the Hare and Hounds, to the place where you live?'—'I have to get two buses. It would take me, say, varying on the buses, half an hour or forty minutes.'

'Did you post your returns near the place where the branch meeting was held or near your home?'—'Near my home.'

'About what time did you *get* home that night?'—'Roughly half-past ten.'

'And the meeting had finished when?'—'I believe it was nine-ten or nine-fifteen.'

'You have no specific reason, have you, to remember an actual posting on the same day as the branch quarterly meeting?'—'I don't understand,' said Mr Keill, after a pause.

'You have no specific recollection of having posted on the same day as the branch quarterly meeting, have you?'

But he had. 'This was the first time I had ever done it. I normally posted them the following night, and they were always accepted.'

Mr Lawson went on to the matter of the postmark.

'You don't know how the envelopes you post from your home area to other people are postmarked, do you?'—'Yes.'

'How do you know? Do you see the envelopes?'—'Yes, I've seen quite a considerable number, because all the people I work with are in our branch, and they've often brought mail in to me with that stamp on.'

'You didn't say anything when you were at Head Office, did you, about the envelope not being the one you posted?'—'I *did* say.'

'What I suggest you did was to sign the document which said: "We the undersigned agree that the date-stamp as being received at Head Office was January 4, 1960." Both you and Mr McGann signed that?'—'In actual fact he *wouldn't* sign it, and I asked him to because I thought it was only about an envelope with a date-stamp on it.'

But besides the envelope there were forms involved—a scrutineers' return form and a scrutineers' declaration form. The former is signed by branch secretaries after elections, but not the latter, which (Mr Keill said) is 'in the full control of the scrutineers—they handle all those ballot papers, not me.' Mr Justice Winn examined the 'declaration form'.

'There doesn't appear on the face of it,' said his Lordship, 'to be a space for the secretary to sign.' He turned to the 'scrutineers' return form'.

'As Branch Secretary sending in the scrutineers' return form to Head Office,' he went on, 'the one that you sent on the evening of December the 21st, had you any particular practice about marking any document before you dispatched it?'—'No, my Lord, because all the years I had been Secretary I had always been able to trust Head Office and never had any complaints. I never marked anything.'

'I want you to be very careful about this. Are you quite sure, thinking about it, that you didn't put any personal identification mark of any kind on any document before posting it to Head Office?'—'None whatsoever.'

The Judge repeated his question twice in different forms, and it was clear that he thought Mr Keill's evidence must stand or fall according to the true answer to it. 'You haven't had a chance to look at this, Mr Gardiner?' he said.

'No, my Lord.'

'You and your learned junior should look at that—not only at that which is immediately visible as you glance at it, but raise the tear-off flap where one opens the envelope.'

'I won't express any opinion,' said Mr Gardiner, after looking at it, 'because sometimes original documents get marked, which ought not to be marked, as a matter of convenience'.

'Let me look again,' said the Judge. 'You didn't write "Gillmos" on that?' he asked Mr Keill.

'No, my Lord.'

'With a line across from the one part of the envelope to the other?'—'I wrote absolutely nothing. All that went on that envelope was a stamp.'

'My Lord,' said Mr Gardiner, who had been conferring with Mr Hooberman, the Plaintiffs' solicitor, 'I understand that on *all* the envelopes somebody has put the names of the branches.'

'Well, it will be easy enough, if it was done by the solicitors, for the handwriting to be identified. The peculiarity which I have remarked upon is that the line runs across, which is one well-known method of determining whether one portion of paper attached to another has been removed at any time . . . The principal object of that set of questions was not so much to ascertain *who* had written the name on, but whether it had been written on *by this witness*. Then it would have destroyed his evidence completely.'

That was the end of Mr Keill's evidence.

But 'may I ask,' said Mr Gardiner first thing the next morning, 'whether the Plaintiffs' solicitors may be at liberty to inspect, forthwith, all the original envelopes? They have never been inspected because the Master originally ordered that the Defendants' solicitors should supply photostat copies. Photostat copies were supplied of the *fronts* of the envelopes, but it didn't occur to anybody that there might be something on the back.'

'Have you any objection, Mr Lawson?' asked Mr Justice Winn.
'No, my Lord.'

Then came Mr Keill's wife, who was at the Hare and Hounds with him on the night of the election. She said that her brother, Mr Robert Lennon, another member of the ETU, took them both home in his car after the meeting, and that her husband, immediately he was home, said, 'Let's not have any discussion now, until we get this form in the post. It's most important.'

'So we just sat around and he did it,' she said. They then went immediately in the car to post it, and she saw it posted—on the same night, December 21.

When Mr Lawson cross-examined her she said that she saw her brother 'at times, on and off', that he lived in the same postal district as herself (Liverpool 11) but about three or four miles away, and that he came to her house 'over Christmas'.

'On Christmas Day or Boxing Day?' asked Mr Lawson, who

was concerned to prove that the election return was not posted until January 2.

'I don't know. Christmas Day, probably.'—'Don't you remember?'

'Christmas Day I think it must have been—that's the usual day when all the family get together.'—'I suggest you are mistaken about the date when this document was posted. Did you get out of the car when your husband posted the letter?'—'There wasn't any need. The post-box was a yard from the pavement, or half a yard; there was no need for us all to get out.'

Mr Robert Lennon didn't remember, either, whether it was on Christmas or Boxing Day that he went to his sister's; and he told Mr Lawson under cross-examination that she and her husband came to visit him during the week that included New Year's Eve, but he was not certain that it was in fact New Year's Eve. He didn't think he took them anywhere in his car during the New Year holiday, but had a recollection that 'about Christmas time' he went with them to the ICI Club on the East Lancs Road, which they all frequented regularly.

'Have there been other occasions,' asked Mr Lawson, 'on which Mr and Mrs Keill have posted anything while they have been given a ride in your car?'—'I don't think so.'

'Do you think it may ever have happened?'—'Football coupons, perhaps, I don't know. Nothing I can remember. Nothing appertaining to the Union.'

'You see, I am bound to suggest to you that you are mistaken about the posting which you saw take place on this particular night. I suggest that the posting took place on a later occasion.'—'I'm absolutely certain it was that night,' said Mr Lennon.

The first of the date-stamp episodes had thus been dealt with. There were many to follow, and their striking similarity makes it unnecessary to recount them all here; but it affords an excuse to glance around the Court and take note of the setting . . .

We are in Divorce Court 4, which was once intended to accommodate the Court of Criminal Appeal (but has never done so). It is the largest court room—it would seat perhaps two hundred packed-in people—in the Royal Courts of Justice, that mock-Gothic assembly in the Strand which architects deride, lawyers love, prudent citizens fear, and socialites use as a background for snapshots at the frequent cross-roads in their lives. Divorce Court 4 is unused to trade union rule books and rigged ballots. It has a dock, a jury-box, and an atmosphere. If, in the present case, you could stand behind the Judge you would look down upon the two camps of litigators entrenched behind their lawyers: to your right Mr Gerald Gardiner, QC, and Mr Jonathan Sofer, his able junior, with Mr Ben Hooberman, the Plaintiffs' solicitor, who has done so much to bring this conspiracy into the light of day. Behind them the two Plaintiffs—Mr John Thomas Byrne, white-haired, comfortable, self-composed, and ample, and Mr Frank Chapple, young, dark, thick-set, and self-assured, a former member of the Communist Party, disenchanted with it by Kruschev's merciless repression of the Hungarian 'white collar' rising in 1956. With them—the only man to be in attendance throughout the trial—sits Mr Leslie Cannon, formerly head of the ETU Education College at Esher, one of the few men to whom most of this story is already well known. Around these three sit friends, supporters, and the interested onlookers, who in these particular Law Courts (but in no others that I have seen) seem able to come and go as the mood or whim pleases them, to a constant flip-flapping of the swing doors at both sides of the Court Room. These seats, which are like church pews and run the entire length of the Court, have no division down the middle: and yet they might as well, today, have a curtain of iron or asbestos dividing the people just described from the Defendants' lawyers and friends. Here, to the Judge's left, are Mr Neil Lawson, QC, and Mr Ralph Millner and Mr Bernard Marder, his juniors; and behind them the Defendants—Mr Frank Haxell, usually with a faintly sardonic smile, Mr Frank Foulkes, never with any kind of smile, Mr McLennan, Assistant General Secretary of the ETU, Mr J. Humphrey, its Office Manager, Mr J. N. Frazer, Mr John Hendy and all the others. Every seat on this side of the Court (but not on the Plaintiffs' side) is occupied; and there is standing room for those prepared to place one foot on top of the other. But it is among the standing partisans here that the strongest separation shows itself.

The Court officials are using a rubber-wheeled trolley to manipulate the vast bulk of documentary 'exhibits' in this case—

massive joint product of Hollerith machines, Communist dedica-
tion and midnight oil. The standing listeners get in its way.
Repeatedly they are asked by the ushers to move; almost as often
their attention is directed to the empty seats in the 'Plaintiffs' half'
of the Court Room. Won't they go and sit there? They will not. It
is defilement to be in the same Court Room, the same building
even, as the Plaintiffs. This implacable hostility is patent to everyone in Court. (To the Judge, even? Mr Justice Winn misses
nothing, literally nothing.) It would be amusing if it were not
tragic. But it is tragic to anyone with any sense of trade union
history and of what has been achieved in the dark days by
'solidarity', mutual trust, and the desperate, shared courage of
adversity. Will the result of this case dissipate the clouds? Everyone knows it won't. These reluctant litigants are not film stars or
tap-dancers who, at the end, will leave the Court hand-in-hand
and tell the Press that they are 'just good friends'.

We must hear the evidence of Mr Alexander Sinclair, of Silloth,
Cumberland, a member of the ETU for nine years and secretary
of its Silloth Branch for three. A Silloth quarterly meeting took
place on December 15, 1959, he says, and the voting was: Byrne
24, Haxell 1. He posted the returns the following evening in the
pillar-box outside Silloth post office.
  'Are you quite sure of that?' Mr Jonathan Sofer asks him.
  'I am dead certain.'
  'Did you have any reason for being meticulous about the posting
of this return?'—'Well, I know for a fact that on a previous
occasion we had been warned about late posting, and I took
special care on this occasion to see that it was not so.'
  Mr Sinclair was shown the envelope he had posted at Silloth on
December 16, 1959, and was asked about the postmark on it.
  'The postmark is Carlisle,' he said, 'and January the 1st'.
  'Could you have been in Carlisle on January the 1st?'—'No. I
was in Scotland, for the Hogmanay festivities.'
  His family were with him, he said; he did not have with him
any ETU documents, and he was in Scotland until January 3.
Then, in response to the same kind of invitation as had reached
the last witness, Mr Keill, he went to the Union's Head Office at

Hayes, in Kent, and was shown the envelope bearing the Carlisle postmark and the date January 1. He said that it could not be his.

'I want to read the branch correspondence to you,' said Mr Jonathan Sofer, and the following letters, which merit careful attention, were read out. Mr Sinclair had written to Head Office on January 12:

Our branch has never had any notification of the results of the elections held on the September and December quarter nights. Could we have a copy for our information?

Not until February 8 did he get a reply:

The national scrutineers at their last meeting decided they could not accept your branch quarterly documents in view of an infringement of Rule 21, Clauses 65 and 74. In arriving at their decision, they took into consideration the fact that your branch had infringed no Rule governing ballots on a previous occasion.

Rule 21 of the Electrical Trades Union spreads itself over seventy-five somewhat involved clauses and sub-clauses and typifies the English working man's love of constitution-making; a habit which is based on a rational desire to know exactly where you stand and a belief that you can achieve this in writing if only you go on long enough. Clause 65 says that branch secretaries must send electoral nomination forms to the Head Office so that they reach it 'at the latest by the first post on the fifth day following the branch meeting making the nomination'; and Clause 74 says that after an election the 'branch scrutineers' must open the envelopes, count the votes, fill in a 'scrutineers' return' showing how the voting went, and ensure that it too reaches the Head Office not later than the first post on the fifth day after the branch quarterly meeting at which the voting took place.

Mr Sinclair had challenged the ruling that his returns went in too late, a fact which had been communicated to the branch by the *Daily Express*:

Our Branch [he wrote on February 29] would like to deplore the fact that it should be possible for a newspaper reporter to inform the Branch that our votes had not been accepted, three days before we had any official notification on the subject. This reporter called on myself to ask my views on the throw-out of the Branch votes. I informed him that I had no information on the subject, and in any case I could make no comment. According to the Rules, we can make no appeal on this matter until the minutes of the meeting are published . . . We did our very best to see that as far as possible no rule was broken . . . We are not in favour of the publicity being given to the matter by the Press, TV, etc., and feel that these matters are definitely inter-Union and should be respected as such.

Six weeks had then elapsed, said Mr Sinclair. Then came a letter (on April 19) from the Head Office to say that the nomination and scrutineers' forms had not reached them within the prescribed five days from the quarterly meeting, and that the information given to the Press 'must have come from someone present at that meeting'. On June 2 came a letter declaring that the branch had no right of appeal, but that if a special meeting was convened 'a representative of the Executive Council' would come to it and join in the discussion. It was arranged that Mr Haxell himself should come.

'Mr Sinclair,' said Mr Lawson, QC, in cross-examination, 'there were irregularities at your quarterly meeting?'—'There was an irregularity.'

'The Branch Chairman acted as scrutineer?'—'Yes, that is correct.'

'And the other irregularity was that the other scrutineer was a new member, whose membership had only been accepted from December the 1st, 1959?'—'This is the first I've heard of it, but that may be so.'

'And the only other members present were members of the Branch Committee?'—'That is so.'

'Do you know what newspaper the reporter was representing?'—'The *Daily Express*.'

'You weren't surprised at the fact of being disqualified, were you?'

Mr Sinclair had not been surprised, but, he said—'We were open about the matter. We thought that would be better than trying to forge anybody's signature or do anything underhand.'

Mr Lawson was sceptical about the posting of the voting returns. He elicited from Mr Sinclair that his home at Silloth was about twenty-two miles from Carlisle, where the letter was posted.

'You would probably agree with me about this,' said Mr Lawson, 'that if somebody was pretending that this envelope contained the returns of the Silloth Branch, it was rather a crazy thing to post it from Carlisle?'

'There are crazy people,' said Mr Sinclair. But he agreed that he had gone up to Scotland by road on the New Year's Eve, and went through Carlisle.

'You see,' Mr Lawson persisted, 'what I suggest to you is this—and just think about it for a moment, will you?—that you may have delayed posting your December 1959 returns until you were on your journey to Scotland on December the 31st.'—'No. I *know* I didn't. If I had been going to forget, I wouldn't have remembered on that evening.'

'I don't know whether this has ever happened to you—it has happened to most of us in our lives—that one has got a letter in one's pocket to post and one finds it there a few days later unposted?'—'It's something I've heard of, but it has never happened to me yet.'

And Mr Sinclair concluded his evidence by giving Mr Jonathan Sofer, in re-examination, the previously omitted information that in elections held at the Silloth Branch of the ETU there was no postal voting whatsoever. Other branches might have a majority of postal votes, but it was a feature of the case against the Defendants that in 1959 the postal voting was suspiciously heavy.

Then followed a procession of witnesses with almost identical stories about the fraudulent manipulation of posting dates, an examination which was to occupy seven whole days of the trial.

There was Mr Jack Varty, Secretary of the Kendal Branch, who posted his voting returns on December 19 (the day after the election) at Windermere post office, in an envelope which then somehow acquired the postmark '9.30 a.m. January 2, Westmorland', and which did not reach ETU headquarters for sixteen days, until January 4. The voting was Byrne 49, Haxell 9, and it was disqualified. To all Mr Varty's subsequent letters disputing this—and demanding to be told the *town* named in the alleged January 2 postmark—either Mr Haxell or Mr McLennan returned replies as long and verbose as they were evasive.

Mr Ernest Veitch, Secretary of the ETU branch at Billingham, County Durham (Byrne 43, Haxell 12), had the same experience, though Mr Lawson was able to shake him a little because his memory as to the place of posting was unreliable, and because his wife often posted letters for him and *might* have inadvertently delayed it.

Mr Edward Henderson, Secretary of the ETU branch at Stanley, County Durham, posted his return—Byrne 64, Haxell 9—on December 24 outside Catchgate post office. It (or another envelope exactly like it) was postmarked December 31, and the branch's vote was disqualified.

'You would agree with me, I expect,' said Mr Lawson in cross-examining him, 'that it's unlikely that anybody who wanted to pretend they hadn't received a return in due time, when they had in fact received it, would have *kept* your letter of December the 24th?'

Mr Henderson thought about this.

'Would you repeat that?' he said at last. 'I am a bit confused with this.'

Mr Justice Winn interposed. 'I don't think you need bother,' he told the witness. 'It's an attempt to treat me as a jury. You need not bother.'

'I am sorry,' said Mr Lawson, 'if your Lordship thinks I am trying to make "jury points".'

'Mr Lawson, it's *always* done. I'm not blaming you. It is perfectly natural, no irritation resulting. But I think, if you will allow me to say so, it's neither strictly necessary nor worth taking up time with.'

Mr William Boyle, Secretary of the North Shields Branch, posted his voting return at seven-fifteen in the morning on December 23 (the voting took place on the 21st); and yet, according to the ETU Head Office, the envelope was postmarked January 1, 1960. (Rule 21 (64), be it noted, says that the postmark governs the question of when a letter is posted.)

Then came Mr Frank McMenemy of the Galashiels Branch (Byrne 53, Haxell 13), with a similar tale to tell. Mr James Petterson of Ayr (Byrne 101, Haxell 4), the next witness, had used some pungent phrases in his letters to Headquarters:

> The motive for the non-acceptance of my Branch's documents is perfectly obvious to me . . . I will say no more until my Branch has the chance of discussing this revolting decision by

(as you phrase it) the national scrutineers . . . If I don't get complete satisfaction I will not hesitate to use a copy of this letter as I think fit . . . (*Later*) Your infamous note to this Branch was discussed at the last meeting. It would be impossible to convey to you some of the expressions of disgust at the decisions you claim were made by the national scrutineers . . . Perhaps you will enlighten me how to post returns to reach you in time, since posting them on the night of the meeting is not time enough.

I will be interested to know just how to get ballot returns at a meeting and post them before the meeting takes place. The returns of this Branch were posted as per rule and I defy you to prove otherwise.

These extracts from the Ayr Branch Secretary's letter of protest are given here because they typify much of the correspondence that was read out in Court and dispel any suggestion of docile acquiescence in the attitude of at least some of the branches.

The next witness was Mr William Fairlam, of the Doncaster Branch (Byrne 114, Haxell 26), whose return was rejected as being late, though he had posted it the day after the meeting. Doncaster's complaint led to a visit from Mr Leslie Cannon—but not at the instance of the Executive Council: Mr Cannon, who had left the Communist Party in consequence of the Soviet action in Hungary in 1956, was one of the men chiefly responsible for the exposure of the whole ballot-rigging conspiracy, and at this time, with leave of absence from his job in the electrical industry, he was working closely with the firm of solicitors representing the Plaintiffs. Cross-examining Mr Fairlam, Mr Lawson wanted to know in what capacity Leslie Cannon had paid his visit to the Doncaster Branch.

'As a visitor,' said Mr Fairlam.

'Did he indicate that he was managing clerk employed by the Plaintiffs' solicitors in this action?'—'He did not, and I don't think he was at that particular time.'

'There is no secret about this, that for several years past Mr Cannon has been a very, very bitter opponent of the General President, the General Secretary, and a lot of members of the Executive Council? There's no secret about that, is there?'—'No, I don't think so.'

'Had you been following the warfare that was going on between these two sections in the Union with some interest?'—'I wouldn't say following it. I was aware of it.'

'Had you met Cannon when he was in charge of the Union's College?'—'No, I never attended the College when Mr Cannon was in charge.'

'You knew this, did you not, that until some time I think in 1957 Mr Cannon was a very active member of the Communist Party?'—'One was aware of that, yes.'

'And little opportunity was lost to *make* you aware of it?'—'What do you mean by that, make *me* aware of it?'

'Make everybody aware of it?'—'That's better.'

The Judge intervened. 'I'm not quite sure I follow, Mr Lawson. Is one of the issues in this action whether or not one should automatically discredit any witness who talks with someone who has been a member of the Communist Party? Or is this cross-examination directed to the suggestion that anybody on either side, if one probes back a bit, will be found to have been a member of the Communist Party? Is it the latter?'—'Yes, my Lord.'

'So I have to consider, have I, with regard to almost every name that is mentioned, whether that individual at some time was a member of some Communist Party, so as to be able to deal with the issue whether the Communist Party was controlling the Union?' —'No, my Lord,' said Mr Lawson, 'I wouldn't put it quite in that way. One can use the phrase "poachers turned gamekeepers", or the other way round.'

'Which are the poachers?'—'Whichever way your Lordship likes to put them to me.'

'Then that doesn't help me. I am wondering, as between the two of you, you and Mr Gardiner, what your respective positions are going to be with regard to any connection I may find existed between any individual and the Communist Party. It may be we can save a couple or three weeks, or a month, of this action, if I ask you at once: Is it common ground that the various individuals named in the statement of claim were at times members of the Communist Party and of committees of the Communist Party?'

Mr Lawson replied that they were all members of the Party but not of committees of it. (The question of committees became important later in the trial.)

'What I am exploring,' said the Judge, 'to see if I can ascertain briefly from you, is this: Is the true issue (a) were those persons members of any body or organisation properly to be called a committee? Or is it (b) whether, accepting that they were, that committee exercised any control or influence over the affairs of the Union?'

'My Lord,' said Mr Lawson, 'both are in issue'.

'Then I have saved no time,' said Mr Justice Winn, adding wryly, 'which is usually the result of judicial intervention. I thought, if it had only been the latter, then I could really ignore the question of who had been a Communist at any particular time. Let me make it clear: I am not prepared to equate the word "Communist" with any kind of pejorative significance. It means no more to me than Conservative or Liberal. The importance is not whether a man has that adjective attached to his name, but whether he has, by reason of, and through the function of, membership of that political party, in a committee or otherwise, brought to bear on the affairs of this Union influences and forces belonging to that political party.'

'As I understand my learned friend's opening,' said Mr Lawson, 'the case is put bluntly on this ground: "You conspired together to rig elections by fraudulent practices".'

' "Because you were motivated to do that by allegiance to a political party, overriding your allegiance to your Union." Isn't that right?'

'I suppose that is the way my learned friend would put it.'

'Tell me why in this particular case,' said the Judge, 'this witness is being asked whether someone else called Cannon was at some time or other talking loudly and heedlessly about his affection for the Communist Party? Why am I interested? If I am, tell me, because I want to follow it.'

'No doubt your Lordship will be hearing Mr Cannon in the witness-box in due course. It will be my duty to take a certain line in relation to his evidence.'

'I follow. Well, I will see later, always remembering that I have made it quite clear—and I mean it, it's not just a façade—that I am not prepared to have the adjective "Communist" used pejoratively in this case, nor am I prepared to allow any attempt to be made to influence my mind to suppose that because a man is a Communist he is not to be believed on oath, or trusted to conduct affairs honestly and straightforwardly. It may coincide, but it is not the reason for it.'

Then came Mr Arnold Bedford, of the Barnsley Branch (Byrne 43, Haxell 4), who remembered posting his letter to Head Office at three-fifty p.m. on Boxing Day. This clarity of recollection was due to his having bought sixty cigarettes from a slot machine at the same time (because all the shops were closed) and also some automatic-machine chocolate for his little daughter. The whole of his cross-examination by Mr Lawson was designed to show that this story was a lie, and previous discrepancies in his clerical work for the Union were called in aid to show that he would be un-likely to remember anything so clearly as he was saying he did.

'I suppose,' said Mr Justice Winn, looking at the Barnsley Branch contribution ledger and other books and documents, 'that you chaps who are branch secretaries have really quite a lot to do in working time as well as keeping all these?'—'Quite a lot, my Lord,' smiled Mr Bedford.

'You've got your families to support and a job to do?'—'Yes.'

'It's easy enough, is it, to make a few odd mistakes?'—'It's quite easy.'

'Whatever did happen about these, you have done your best on it?'—'Quite true, my Lord.'

'One of the things I'm beginning to wonder is how anybody in this Union has time to earn his living, and how the Union have time to collect enough money to be able to pay their members to go about and spend time on matters of this sort. However, that is comment.'

'You appreciate,' said Mr Gerald Gardiner to the witness, 'that it's being suggested to you by Mr Lawson that your evidence about posting the return at the same time as you bought the cigarettes, and your little girl being there, is a complete invention? (If that is not the suggestion, no doubt my friend will correct me.)'

'It *is* true that I posted the documents on December the 26th, 1959,' said Mr Bedford firmly.

Then came Mr Horace Peer, of the Halesowen Branch (Byrne 19, Haxell 3); Mr Robert Swift, of Huddersfield (Byrne 47, Haxell

5); Mr Derek Parsons, of the Pontypool Branch (Byrne 26, Haxell 8); Mr John Middleton, of the Seaham Branch (Byrne 25, Haxell 4); Mr Alfred Goodson, of Boston (Byrne 36, Haxell 3); and Mr Edmund Challis, of Cirencester (Byrne 16, Haxell nil); all of whom had posted their 'voting returns' within one day or at the most three days after the branch election meetings, and all of whom had been told by Head Office—after many weeks of silence—that their returns had come in 'too late'. It was noticeable, too, that the degree of lateness was always about the same—nine or ten days. It is fair to say that all of them had, in previous years, failed in one way or another to comply strictly with the ETU Rules governing elections, though it would probably be difficult to find a branch of the ETU (or of any other trade union) of which the same could not be said.

But by now the trial was in its fifth day; and at this point Mr Gardiner asked permission to call a witness 'out of the intended order' because he had just arrived on subpoena and wanted to be released as soon as possible. This was Mr Norman Swift, of Stockport, joint managing director of the Express Printing Company Ltd, of Manchester, printers for many years to the Electrical Trades Union. The High Court had subpoenaed him to 'give evidence and also to bring with him all printer's copy instructions, invoices, orders, dispatch sheets, correspondence, books of account, all the memoranda and notes of telephone conversations relating to ballots and all other matters between the Defendants and his company between January 1, 1957, and June 30, 1960'.

Mr Swift's evidence about the printing and dispatch of surplus ballot forms was of the utmost importance in itself, but it was the occasion of a disclosure that caused great surprise in Court and must have had a considerable influence upon Mr Justice Winn's developing view of the case. The surprise was the more complete because no preparatory statement had been obtained from Mr Swift (i.e., no 'proof of evidence'), and no one knew quite what he was going to say.

Mr Swift described how he always asked the ETU for an estimated quantity of ballot forms required. 'It's quite a big job,' he said, 'and if we were to wait until all branch returns' (i.e., figures of qualified voters) 'arrived at Head Office stating definitely how many ballot papers they required, the job would be so late go-ing out. We ask for an estimate to be put in to facilitate the print-ing.' He said that the ballot forms were printed in sheets of four at a time; so that, in the case, to take one example, of the Belfast Central Branch, for which Head Office had estimated for 591 forms, he printed 600 because that was four times 150, and there would thus be a surplus of nine. He sometimes made a further allowance for 'spoilage' by defects in the machinery and so forth. In the event, Belfast Central wanted only 502, which left him with 98 still in his possession. But in any such transaction he never dealt with ETU branches—always with Head Office.

It was from Head Office that Mr Robert Oliver, then Office Manager (and predecessor in that capacity to Mr J. Humphrey, one of the Defendants), came to see him about the printing of additional ballot papers. He 'brought the amended sheets with him because he superintended the dispatch of this ballot'. He retained those sheets in his possession, *giving Mr Swift the amended figures by word of mouth only*. Subsequent or lesser changes would be conveyed to him by telephone from the ETU Head Office.

After Mr Robert Oliver's visit in November 1959 the surplus papers were parcelled up, labelled according to the branches for which they were supposedly destined, and dispatched by rail—whither?

'Could you give us the date or dates of dispatch to the Head Office?' Mr Swift was asked by Mr Gerald Gardiner; and then, *almost* as an afterthought: 'That *is* right, is it—to the Head Office?'

'They were actually sent,' said Mr Swift, 'to St Pancras Station. They were marked "to be called for".'

'Was that on Mr Oliver's instructions?'—'That is right.'

And at this point Mr Lawson made an unexpected contribution to the emerging picture.

'If I can help about this,' he said, 'I am prepared to agree that on November the 10th, 1959, four parcels were dispatched to Head Office—to St Pancras—to be called for; that on November the 11th four further parcels were dispatched by this witness's company in the same way; on November the 12th three parcels; on November the 13th two parcels; on November the 16th three parcels; on

November the 17th two parcels, and on November the 18th nine parcels.'

'I take it,' said Mr Gardiner, 'they were all sent to St Pancras, to be called for?'—'Yes,' said Mr Lawson.

'But addressed to the Union?'—'Yes,' said Mr Lawson, who now seemed almost to be under cross-examination himself.

'Mr Swift,' Mr Gardiner then resumed, 'in relation to the additional voting papers sent to branches, when you were instructed to send additional voting papers were you given any information as to why they were wanted?'—'No. That was really no concern of ours.'

'Was it suggested that you had been at fault in not sending the proper number in the first place?'—'Sometimes that has been suggested, yes. The counting is very strictly supervised and checked when they are actually making the parcels up on dispatch, but mistakes can occur.'

'Do I gather there were occasions when that suggestion was *not* made, but you were merely asked to send additional voting papers?'—'Yes.'

A little later Mr Gardiner came back to the subject of the papers sent to St Pancras Station.

'When Mr Oliver asked you to send the surplus ballot papers, addressed to Head Office, to St Pancras Station to be called for, did he give you any reason for that?'—'No reason whatsoever,' replied Mr Swift. 'As far as my men on dispatch are concerned, *he* was running the dispatch of those ballot papers. He didn't necessarily give those instructions to me; he could have given them to the foreman.'

'I was asking you whether, according to your best recollection, he gave any reason why the Union wanted them?'—'Only from a security point of view, that they wouldn't be left lying around anywhere.'

Mr Gardiner now sought to find out what had happened in previous elections.

'I have called for the schedules relating to earlier elections,' he said with special deliberation and with a glance at Mr Lawson, '*and none of them has been produced*'.

Mr Lawson stood up. 'By "schedules",' he said, 'I suppose my friend is meaning instructions to the printers similar to those which have been produced in the case of the December 1959 election?'—'Yes,' Mr Gardiner said.

Mr Lawson's answer was, to say the least, unexpected. 'I think this is the first time, in all the preparations for the trial, that those matters have been mentioned.'

'I am not quite sure what is involved,' said the Judge. 'Calling for documents merely means that secondary evidence may be tendered' (i.e., evidence of their contents may be given by witnesses who did not actually compile them) 'if they are not produced. I do not quite know what point is being made here.'

'The point is this,' said the unruffled Mr Gerald Gardiner. 'It will either be produced or not. If it is not produced I cannot give secondary evidence because I haven't got it. I call for the surplus voting papers which, according to this witness, were returned to Head Office in respect of the election for General Secretary which took place in December 1959, and which have not been included in the Defendants' affidavit of documents, either as documents they have, or as documents they ever have had in their possession or power. *I now call for them.*'

It was one of the dramatic moments in this long trial. What had happened to the 26,000 missing ballot papers? Let us briefly reconsider what they were and how they came into existence. For the Byrne-Haxell election the ETU Head Office compiled a list of the numbers of ballot papers to be sent to the branches for the election, and sent that list to the printers. It was a rough figure, an estimate. When the final 'indents' came in from the branches, the figures were of course lower, mainly because the estimated number needed by certain branches had been deliberately inflated, with the object of creating a surplus for fraudulent use.

In fact, when the final figures came in, they totalled 26,833 less than the original Head Office estimate. Head Office nevertheless told the printers to go ahead and print the original number, and send the 26,833 papers to St Pancras 'to be called for'. (They were called for, in November of that year, by Mr Humphrey, a Communist who had been appointed by the Executive Council—not elected—to the job of Office Manager. He took them in his car to the Head Office at Hayes and locked them away in a small office, the key of which was held by him alone.) Their disappearance, and the extreme reticence of the Defence about their mere existence, were central to this trial.

'I now call for them,' said Mr Gardiner.

'They are not produced,' Mr Lawson replied.

The Judge leaned forward. 'I wondered about this some little time ago,' he said. 'This is a matter of non-disclosure. Those documents, on the evidence as it stands, were at some time in the possession of an agent of the Union.'

'Yes, my Lord,' said Mr Lawson, unabashed, 'and yesterday, I think, so admitted'.

'That being so, their history must be accounted for, must it not?' —'Yes, my Lord, I respectfully agree. So far as disclosure is concerned, I must concede that there was a serious omission in this respect in the Defendants' "disclosure".'

'Would you like an opportunity for a "further affidavit" to be sworn disclosing these documents, and accounting for their whereabouts or subsequent destruction?'

Mr Lawson took the hint. 'May I deal with the matter in that way? I am not trying, as your Lordship knows,' he went on, 'to avoid anything. In the normal course one would have expected an application for "specific discovery" in relation to this matter; and in such circumstances, of course, one would have been obliged to make an additional affidavit. I can only tell your Lordship that those instructing me, and I myself, realise that this was an important omission in the affidavit, but your Lordship may feel there is some expiation in this sense—'

'I think everybody has had an appalling time,' interrupted the Judge kindly, 'and it would have been a miracle if all the procedural matters had been in order. But where does this lead to? I have the same powers as a Master would have had a few weeks ago. Is there any reason why I shouldn't order a "further and better affidavit"?'

'No reason at all, my Lord,' said Mr Lawson.

'Then may it be done ... Of course, experienced solicitors of great knowledge, such as those instructing you, must have known that they had to inform themselves, in order to inform you, what had happened to these surplus ballot papers.'

'I wish to say no more at all about the matter and submit to the order your Lordship has made.'

Mr Gardiner brought the emphasis back to the area from which it seemed to him to be moving. 'Of course, as your Lordship appreciates,' he said, 'my clients have been faced with Mr Scott's repeated statement to branches' (this was Mr George Scott, ETU national officer) 'that Head Office had never had any ballot papers. And that was consistent with the Defendants' affidavit of documents.'

'It may be they disappeared,' said the Judge. 'Some unfortunate sneak thief thought they were Bank of England notes. We will see what the explanation is in due course.'

And they did. Meanwhile, it is fair to say that the suggestion that spare ballot papers should be sent from the printers' works to the ETU Head Office came from Mr Swift himself, as he declared when Mr Lawson cross-examined him:

'It was in fact your suggestion that one of the ways round the security problem, anyhow so far as your employees were concerned, was that any surplus ballot papers should be sent by your firm to Head Office?'

'Well, we don't allow any unauthorised persons in the works at any time, but of course there's always the possibility—especially if we have casual labour—you just can't be everywhere and watch everything; but I think I am right in saying that the suggestion was put forward (and probably by myself) that if any surplus *was* sent to Head Office, they would then know that we hadn't any remaining on the premises.'

Before the December 1959 election, said Mr Swift, if there were any surplus ballot papers they remained at the printers and were eventually destroyed. But in September 1959 the suggestion was adopted that the printer should work to estimates of the number required, so that all could be ready at shorter notice when the elections came round. The final figure was always smaller than the estimate: hence the surpluses—and the danger.

Back now to more evidence of 'out of date' election results from the branches. Mr James Brown, of Cambuslang (Glasgow) Branch —Byrne 49, Haxell 17—was the next of these witnesses. He was communicative, and he ran into difficulties over the rule of evidence excluding 'hearsay' (though the hearsay evidence he wanted to give was about as innocuous as you could imagine). He described how he put the election results in his brief-case at the end of the quarterly meeting, set off for home, and arrived about eleven p.m.

'My wife looked at me,' he said.

'Don't tell us what she said,' broke in Mr Sofer rather anxiously. 'Tell us what *you* did.'

'I flopped down in the big chair in front of the fire, threw the brief-case down at my side and said, "Thank God, that's done". She said, "What happened?" I said, "We've had a hell of a night". My wife said, "The coffee's ready", and I said, "Let's have it—" '

'I believe,' said the Judge wickedly, 'that Mr Lawson is about to object. This doesn't offend against the hearsay rule unless it is tendered as evidence to prove the conversation.' (The conversation seemed not to matter much.) 'You can always say "My wife looked at me and smiled", or "My wife looked at me and dropped down in horror", or even "My wife looked at me and said, 'I've never seen you look so ghastly' ", provided it is not a fact that is an issue in the case.'

Mr Lawson thought otherwise. 'With great respect, my Lord, I *must* quarrel with your Lordship this time.'

'What is the objection then?'—'The witness was telling your Lordship what he was telling his wife. That, in my submission, must on any view be inadmissible.'

'I'm not proposing to exclude it from my mind except in so far as it has some bearing on the facts.'

'I would ask your Lordship,' persisted Mr Lawson, 'not to say that'.

'If you don't want me to let the witness give his evidence in a natural way, then you *must* make your objection. The little experience I've had of listening to evidence has convinced me that a witness should be allowed his head up to the point where he begins to say something which the law of evidence properly excludes because it may be tendered as evidence when it has no evidential value. I much prefer to let them talk in their own way. If the objection is that he must not say what he said to his wife—'

'On the ground that it is not admissible, my Lord.'

'Well, I suppose on a strict view of the rules of evidence that is so.'

There was really no doubt of it—though the next week Mr Justice Winn brought the subject up again, and said that there was never much point in getting a witness to say that a *conversation* had taken place if he wasn't to be allowed to say how the conversation went. Mr Brown's response to his wife's announcement that the coffee was ready was in all strictness, however, inadmissible in the trial of a conspiracy to wangle a trade union election. Mr Lawson, having won his point, sat down; and Mr Sofer continued his examination of Mr Brown:

'You can tell his Lordship what *happened*, as you wish, without saying what you said to your wife and what she said to you.'

And Mr Brown thereupon, still rather more informally than other witnesses and with some vivid background material, told the familiar story about allegedly late arrival hotly but fruitlessly denied by the officers of the Cambuslang Branch.

He was followed by Mr John Cleminson, of Bishop Auckland (Byrne 100, Haxell 15), whose evidence, more or less identical with that of all his predecessors in the witness-box, and supported by his wife who actually posted the letter and remembered it, brought the first week of the trial to a close—with an interesting observation from Mr Justice Winn.

'It seems to me,' said the Judge to Mr Gardiner and Mr Lawson, 'subject to anything either of you may say, that there are only three explanations of late arrival, if there was late arrival.

'One is that the person who tells me that he or she posted it on Day x really didn't post it until Day x plus one, two, three or four.

'The second is that that evidence, from such persons, is accurate, but that between the physical entry of the package into the postal-box and the time when the date-stamp was put upon it, a very unusual period of time elapsed owing to some post office oversight of some kind.

'The third explanation is that the postmarks that have been produced here have been fraudulently prepared, which would presumably mean that after the arrival of the actual packages posted the whole contents would have to be removed, the old envelope destroyed and a further envelope, by some method or other, posted thereafter in more or less the same area.'

(This was what the Plaintiffs believed had happened; and later they were to call evidence showing how it could have been done.)

'I would be greatly helped,' the Judge continued, 'if at some later stage either of you could suggest any other explanation. There may be embellishments of *those* explanations, but I can't see any other than those three categories; and therefore I don't think we need waste a great deal of time on the sort of comment which you, Mr Lawson, have quite rightly made, namely that these witnesses did not leap to the *third* explanation but thought the second the most probable, in order to reconcile their beliefs with the evidence produced.'

'Subject to this, my Lord,' interposed Mr Lawson, 'that the force of the observation, when it comes to be made, is that it also goes to some extent to test the recollection of the witness'.

'That is another matter. I don't want to shut out at this stage, or ever, any comment or argument either of you wish to address to me. I only want to indicate from time to time those matters with regard to which I feel that the expenditure of public time and money is not commensurate with the effect likely to be made upon what is sometimes known as the judicial mind.'

On Monday, April 24 the story of 'late arrivals' through the post was taken up by Mr Arthur Hamlin, of the Leicester Branch (Byrne 65, Haxell 5), who prolonged the correspondence with the Head Office right into July 1960, when Mr McLennan was able to put a stop to it by announcing, simply, that 'writs have been issued against certain members of the Union . . . and as the matter is now *sub judice* the request of your branch members cannot be complied with'. Then came Mr Duncan Bishop, of Peterborough Branch (Byrne 59, Haxell 9), and Mr Ronald Edwards, of Rogerstone, Monmouthshire (Byrne 40, Haxell 11).

After Mr Edwards, the Judge called for some elucidation about 'postal votes' and what system there was of verifying that such votes had been either dispatched by the voting member or received by the branch. 'I am struggling hard to understand these Rules,' said his Lordship, 'and I *would* like a little help from time to time. Which is the Rule that regulates postal votes?'

'Rule 21, Clause 68, my Lord,' said Mr Lawson.

'Does that mean that members have to be unable to attend, or that they don't care to attend?'—'I don't know, my Lord. I venture to think we should approach the construction of that on the basis that they are under no obligation to attend.'

'And it means, does it, that anyone who doesn't in fact attend has to incur postal charges in order to vote at all?'—'Or he can do it through his money steward or shop steward, if the shop steward is a member of the same branch.'

'Or if in fact there *is* such a steward,' put in Mr Sofer—'in some cases there might not be.'

'And to what address are they to be sent?'—'I suppose to the branch secretary's address, though the Rule doesn't say so.'

'Then does it mean being put in the post in the hope that it will reach its destination?'—'I don't know, my Lord,' admitted Mr Lawson.

'I don't know what most of these Rules mean,' said the Judge. 'However, there it is. It all augments the revenue of the Post Office, I suppose.'

At this point Mr Lawson put in the 'affidavit of documents' about the fate of the 26,833 surplus ballot papers referred to in the evidence of Mr Swift, the printer (see page 41). The Judge asked to be reminded why it was that none of these ballot papers had been sent by the printer to Union branches but were all sent to Head Office.

'Because,' said Mr Lawson, 'branch *membership* returns were received late—in other words, were not received in time to dispatch to the printers'.

'But they did have *some* ballot sheets?'

'Well, all the branches who sent in branch membership returns had ballot papers. Eleven branches had no ballot papers.'

'Those were all destroyed?'—'Yes, my Lord.'

Before the taking of evidence was resumed, Mr Jonathan Sofer took the opportunity to mention a matter arising out of the new affidavit. He pointed out that in the original 'pleadings' on which the whole trial was based there appeared the statement: 'The Defendant Haxell has failed to account for the extra ballot papers in his affirmation of documents and on discovery.'

'ex among magibate ?'

'As appears from the printer's dispatch sheets,' said Mr Sofer, 'the Defendant Haxell had ordered more than 26,000 ballot papers in excess of those bespoken by branch secretaries from him for direct dispatch to them by the printers. There were thus available at the Head Office of the Union ballot papers bearing the appropriate code-marking of each branch of the Union, for distribution to Communist members of the Union if required for fraudulent voting. The Defendant Haxell has failed to account for those extra ballot papers. Now, in the affidavit we have got this morning, Mr Haxell says: "The facts are not within my personal knowledge but have been ascertained from members of the Head Office staff of the Union." One wonders whether your Lordship would not think it proper to order a "further and better affidavit" from whichever of the Defendants *can* give the information—some of them *are* members of the Head Office staff of the Union—as to who is said to have disposed of these ballot papers.'

But, 'I think perhaps that had better be left to your learned leader,' said the Judge (Mr Gerald Gardiner was not in Court); and the evidence of the 'late arrivals' proceeded.

Mr Harold Sparkes, of the Yeovil Branch (Byrne 117, Haxell 14), was followed by Mr George White, of Neath (Byrne 86, Haxell 35). They both told the now familiar story of promptly posted election results rejected as 'too late', and an ensuing correspondence of growing acerbity ending (for the branches) in total frustration. And then the Judge made an important request.

'Mr Lawson, you were good enough to tell me that you had a record, I gather kept by Mr Oliver, of previous breaches, which would show breaches of the rule regulating time of delivery.'

'Yes, my Lord—I haven't seen the original myself, but I have a copy ... The general nature of the infringements is shown and the letters are given. For example, *NC* means Not Complete, *TL* means Time Limit, that is to say Too Late, *N* means Wrong Meeting Night, and *S* means a defect in relation to scrutineers.'

'The task I have to perform in this case,' the Judge continued, 'is really an extremely difficult one, and it is right in everybody's interests that I should have assistance in bringing the issues into concrete form. I am minded to request the parties to prepare for me certain documents. If either one of the parties is not prepared to accede to my request, then I think I should obtain for the assistance of the Court a scientific adviser such as an actuary or a mathematician to carry out certain calculations for me. They appear to me, however, to be of a very simple kind, and it's only because they involve quite a lot of physical work that I am not at all minded to do it myself. I would add, so as to acquit myself of mere indolence, that I would always hesitate to rely on any mathematical or other purported accurate work which I did myself.'

His Lordship then revealed that he had drawn up a list of his requirements—a list of the branches which (according to Head Office records) had committed breaches of the election Rules *before* the 1959 election, a list of those whose votes had therefore been rejected, the percentage of them which voted for Byrne in 1959, and some explanatory graphs.

And then came Mr Harold Nancarrow, of the Cwmbran Branch (Bryne 56, Haxell 11), whose story, precisely similar again, afforded the Court another small opportunity to glimpse the conditions under which the Plaintiffs' lawyers were having to work. Mr Nancarrow had possessed two postcards from Head Office acknowledging the particulars he had supplied about nominations and scrutineers. Months later (when the trouble was warming up?) he received a circular letter from Head Office saying that 'all correspondence relative to the December ballot should be returned to Head Office'. So he returned the two postcards.

'I call for those two receipts,' said Mr Sofer.

'I don't think any notice to produce has been given,' Mr Lawson replied without looking up.

'There has been,' said Mr Sofer.

'Not produced,' Mr Lawson said tersely.

The importance of this was that Head Office, in disqualifying the Cwmbran Branch's vote, had referred to 'the envelope' in which the two documents were received, and had said that 'it' was postmarked 'Cwmbran, Jan. 1'. Not only was the posting date *December 19*, however; there were *two* envelopes, and for each of them a receipt was (belatedly) forthcoming. 'This is a fact which we can prove,' wrote the branch to Head Office, 'beyond any doubt— we have the two official receipts... The branch draws its own conclusions, bearing in mind the manner in which the branch voted' (Byrne 56, Haxell 11).

Mr Walter Coldwell, of Nuneaton (Byrne 37, Haxell 3), was one of many who got as far as being interviewed at Head Office about their complaints that the voting was rigged.

'When you got to the Union's headquarters,' Mr Sofer asked him, 'did you see a Mr Tarlo, of the Union's solicitors?'—'Yes, I did.'

'And did Mr Tarlo ask you questions?'—'Yes, he asked me about the posting.'

'For how long were you being questioned?'—'Roughly half an hour.'

'And at the end was a statement produced for you to sign?'— 'He called it a statement. That was the first time the word was used, when he asked me to sign it. He had it typed out, and asked me to wait in his office, and I signed it.'

'Did you read through it before you signed it?'—'Yes.'

'Did the statement contain what you had, in fact, said in the course of that questioning?'—'Yes, *some* of the points. He took it down in longhand, asked me various questions, and where the answers were not favourable he crossed them out. Then he read it into a tape-recorder.'

'Were you given a copy?'—'No. I wrote after a copy, but I received no reply to my letter.'

In cross-examination, Mr Coldwell was asked no question on this. He was followed by Mr Peter Osborne, of Rochdale (Byrne 36, Haxell 6), whose wife had posted the results on the day after the meeting, and who learned, as all the others had, that they arrived long out of time.

The fifth day of the evidence (and the ninth of the trial) began with Mr James Fleming, of the Eastleigh (Hants) Branch (Byrne 89, Haxell 14), who got into a slight muddle over his posting date, but only as between December 19 and 20. Somehow or other, at all events, his envelope (or one like it) had acquired the date-stamp December 30. The usual acrimonious correspondence ensued. So it did in the case of Mr James McBain, of Newport (Byrne 94, Haxell 13); of Mr Norman Glentworth, of Brigg, Lincolnshire (Byrne 45. Haxell 13); of Mr Arthur Brown, of Croesyceiliog, Monmouthshire

(Byrne 16, Haxell 2); of Mr Wilfrid Thomas, of Wallingford, Berks (Byrne 26, Haxell 3); of Mr David Rabin, of South Ascot (Byrne 38, Haxell 1); of Mr John Campbell, of LSE 18 (or London Station Engineers 18), which voted Byrne 63, Haxell 50; and of Mr Richard Allum, of Reading (Byrne 47, Haxell 34).

Then Mr Sofer called Miss Adrienne Cousins, a clerk in the office of the Plaintiffs' solicitors, Messrs Lawford & Co, 9 Gray's Inn Square, London. She said that she opened letters received at that office, and produced a bundle of letters said to have been posted to the firm by a private enquiry agent in the course of a tour round the towns whose ETU branches had been disqualified for lateness. She read out their towns of origin and the date-stamps on them.

'The whole question really is,' the Judge said to Mr Sofer, 'whether all these discrepancies between the time of posting and the postmark are similar in kind but not in degree to those which, apparently, you are going to prove.'

'If your Lordship pleases.'

'I really don't know where I am going to be at the end, except speculating about how the Post Office works at Christmas time, which will be very difficult.'

It became even plainer, as the trial proceeded, that the discrepancies between the dates of posting and the alleged dates of delivery were not destined to play so large a part in the Judge's view of the whole case as the Plaintiffs had hoped. It will be seen from his remarks in the final judgment (page 227) that he placed greater reliance upon other details.

Mr Sofer resumed the calling of 'branch' witnesses. Mr George Nixon, of Staines, entered the witness-box to say that his branch voted Byrne 18, Haxell 16, but it transpired that, although he was reasonably sure that he posted his return on December 23 or 24, 1959, the envelope postmarked December 31 *might* have been in his handwriting—and he had not, he agreed, used the official ETU envelope.

'Well,' said the Judge, 'I assume that you would wish to take the earliest opportunity of withdrawing the allegation in relation to *that* envelope—that it was fraudulently substituted?'

'Certainly, my Lord,' replied Mr Sofer; and the fifth day of the evidence for the Plaintiffs was over.

On the sixth day, April 26, Mr Charles Saunders, of Bassett, Southampton, Secretary of the Woolston Branch (Byrne 48, Haxell 11), introduced to the Court the strange story of the Southampton ballot forms.

They came by post to his own private address from the printers. He examined the parcel to ensure that it had not been tampered with, then counted the contents—175 ballot forms—and found all correct. His job as Branch Secretary was then to get them into the hands of the members.

'And they then either post them back to you,' Mr Sofer asked him, 'or bring them to the shop stewards?'—'Yes, or bring them to the branch meeting.'

On Sunday evening, December 13, 1959, Mr Saunders took all the ballot papers round to the house of Mr Sullivan, the Branch Treasurer, who had already written up all the envelopes from his register of members. Together they counted the forms again—175. Then they made two separate piles of envelopes relating respectively to those who were entitled to vote and those who were not. Into both piles they put notices calling the quarterly meeting, and into the voters' envelopes they put envelopes addressed to the scrutineers who would in due course count the votes.

When that was done there remained eleven spare ballot papers. (Mr Saunders kept these, and later handed them to Mr Scott when, in January, the latter conducted an enquiry into allegations that the election was rigged.)

The next morning, Monday, December 14, Mr Saunders was at work by seven-thirty a.m.—before the first postal delivery. He got home at seven p.m. that evening, and found six letters waiting for him. Two concerned routine trade union matters, but the other four obviously contained votes—completed ballot papers.

'I was half-way through the cooked meal my wife had prepared for me,' he told the Court, 'when it suddenly struck me—the physical impossibility of my receiving them back so quickly.'

'What did you do?'—'I examined them—purely from the outside—and I checked the date-stamp; I realised that they were *not* envelopes I had handled, because I had all the envelopes at seven forty-five the evening before, and these were postmarked six forty-five.'

In fact, he then agreed with Mr Sofer that he had left all the legitimate envelopes at the Branch Treasurer's house at nine-fifty that evening. He wrote at once (on December 15), to Mr Haxell, a letter which was one of the outstanding documents of the whole trial:

> I am writing you urgently on a very serious matter affecting the ballots of this branch. I have received four envelopes, exact duplicates of this branch's issue, prior to my members having received the official ones from me. Our treasurer and myself checked and filled envelopes to our members last Sunday, December 13, finishing at around ten p.m. They were then posted, together with quarterly meeting notices for Tuesday, December 22, for collection nine a.m. Monday, December 14. [Mr Saunders later assured the Judge that they were all in *sealed* envelopes, though it had once been the practice merely to tuck the flaps in and post them at printed paper rate.]
>
> At seven-thirty a.m. on Monday, December 14, I received four ballot envelopes (sealed, 3d stamp) postmarked Southampton, 6.45 p.m., December 13. Our meeting tonight decided to open these envelopes, and found that they each contained a vote for Bro. Haxell—apparently by the same person, as they were similarly crossed with identical type markings. I am prepared to swear on oath that I have not previously seen or handled these ballot envelopes prior to receiving them individually by post last evening. The branch number of both envelope and ballot paper completely corresponds with this branch's official issue, and we are at a loss to understand how it came about. The branch feels that the fullest possible investigation should be made, as there appears to be a deliberate attempt by a person or persons yet unknown to carry out a forgery. Will you please advise me as soon as possible on this matter, as I am proceeding with our proper ballot in the normal way. Meanwhile, these faked ballot papers are being held, and have been signed (as witnesses) by each member present tonight—on the decision to open them as being extraneous to this branch's issue. We feel sure you will regard this as a serious matter in view of recent publicity on this Union's ballots.

In response, Mr Haxell dispatched Mr Scott from Hayes to enquire into the 'allegations'. Mr Scott met the seven members of the branch's committee in Southampton. They repeated their story to him, and tried in vain to ascertain from him how the extra ballot papers came into existence. Mr Scott then compiled a report to

Mr Haxell which reads like a copy of Mr Saunders' original letter of complaint, and which goes on to say that the number of ballot papers to be printed is always a matter for arrangement *between the printer and the branch.*

But Mr Sofer had a question to ask about this.

'Did Mr Scott tell you anything suggesting that the printer had been asked to print about twenty ballot papers more than you had indented for?'—'He may have done,' said Mr Saunders. 'Quite possibly he did.'

'Did he tell you, by any chance, that some twenty-six thousand ballot papers had been sent by the printer to St Pancras Station and that perhaps there might be some leakage from St Pancras Station?'

'No,' was the reply; but Mr Lawson, not unexpectedly, had decided that this witness was being too pointedly 'led' by Mr Sofer's questions.

'Is that not a little leading, with respect?' he said moderately.

'Yes,' said the Judge at once.

'If your Lordship pleases,' said Mr Sofer, and led no more. He turned instead to the Head Office decision that the Woolston Branch election results were invalid because they had been 'interfered with' (i.e., by the opening of the four bogus envelopes). This had struck the branch members as bad enough, Mr Saunders told him, but when a letter came from Head Office saying that the returns were also disqualified through late posting—'that', said Mr Saunders, 'seemed about the last straw'. Mr Sofer took him then to the minutes of the Union's Executive Council Meeting on July 2 and 3, 1960, and read out for his approval, by way of showing that there had never been the merest mention of 'late arrival', the following passages from the remarks of Mr Foulkes and Mr Goldberg:

'In each case' (Mr Foulkes was speaking of the three Southampton Branch elections, of which Woolston was one) 'they kept those particular ballot papers out of the ballot, didn't they? They conducted the rest of the ballot—well, they conducted their ballot in accordance with the Rules.' Then Mr Goldberg: 'I was going to say that. It seems to me we can't possibly invalidate the returns of the three branches for this reason. But it does raise a very serious matter, because all the evidence shows that someone in the Southampton area, from which all these three have been sent, is underwriting an attempt to cast suspicion on the entire ballot—not merely in that area. I read the report in the *Express*, and it made it perfectly plain that if four false or fake ballot papers had been sent to every branch secretary (i.e., every branch in the country) then Brother Haxell would be returned by four times six hundred, namely 2,400 majority.' Then Mr Foulkes: 'And who told the newspaper man to stand on the branch doorstep because there might be something happening that night?'

Then Mr Haxell: 'Well, if you'll take my advice you'll just decide whether or not in your view there has been a breach of the Rule, and if there has, whether or not the ballot should stand.'

Then Mr Goldberg: 'I think the ballot should stand.'

'My Lord,' said Mr Sofer, interrupting his reading, 'that is Woolston, Hythe and Southampton Central.' Then Mr Foulkes—

'Sam moves that the ballots of the three branches should stand. Somebody second?'

Mr Haxell: Well, I think all you need to do is to note the report, in which case it'll be included in the returns. You don't decide *not* to invalidate something.

Mr Foulkes: You accept the report? Moved by Brother Goldberg, seconded by Brother Davies. All those in favour? Against? One against, one abstention.

Mr Chapple: Aren't you going to record it?

To this Mr Chapple got no satisfactory reply.

'My Lord,' Mr Sofer continued, 'I am not going to comment on this at length, but it is quite clear that the Executive Council at that time were under the impression that the only matter that was being investigated was Scott's report. *There was no mention there of any lateness.*'

Before cross-examining Mr Saunders, Mr Lawson produced the list giving particulars of the branches whose spare ballot papers were sent to St Pancras Station to await collection. ('Your Lordship remembers that I asked Mr Swift about it, but I didn't put the details to him.') Then he turned to Mr Saunders:

'When did you first know that the same sort of thing as has happened with you' (i.e., the receipt of bogus postal votes) 'was also said to have happened in two neighbouring branches, Southampton Central and Hythe?'—'I had no knowledge at all until I read it on page two of the *Daily Express* on Thursday, December the 17th.'

'One of these envelopes doesn't look as though it has been through the post at all, does it?'—'No, sir,' said Mr Saunders. 'We remarked on it at the time, but it was definitely received in my letter-box with the three other envelopes at the same time, according to my wife.'

'There's no cancellation mark on the stamp, and no postmark on the envelope, is there?'—'I've known that happen before, sir. I've received envelopes on more than one occasion where the machine has not franked the envelope.'

Mr Saunders then said that he received the ballot papers from the printers about three weeks before the eventful Sunday December 13, but that he did *not* tell the Branch Chairman or the Treasurer, or anyone except his wife, that they had arrived—there was no need to make any special mention of it, he said. (Mr Lawson was seeking to establish that there were people who knew the ballot papers to be in Mr Saunders' house.) He opened the parcel the day it arrived, counted the papers without taking the rubber rings off the several separate packages, locked them in a box and hid the key in a place known only to his wife and himself. He was sure that thereafter no one saw them, though he was not prepared to swear he had no visitors during that time. Mr Lawson pressed him repeatedly on this, and then—

'I'm not troubling you about your wife because I assume that she knew, and in a sense probably co-operates with you?'—'My wife has the fullest respect for my union.'

'Please don't think for a moment that I'm attacking Mrs Saunders.'

'I am not quite certain,' interposed Mr Justice Winn, 'whom you're attacking, if anyone, Mr Lawson. You are just testing the witness's memory?'

'Does your Lordship feel that I am cross-examining this witness improperly?'—'I didn't say that, Mr Lawson. Only when you said that you were not attacking Mrs Saunders, as though you were excepting her from a category, I just wondered.'—'I thought that was a right thing to say to the witness, my Lord.'

Mr Saunders said that on December 13 he took the parcel of ballot papers to the Treasurer's house on his bicycle, having some difficulty in getting the parcel into his saddle-bag. His cross-examination then took him all through the events of that Sunday evening again, and established for the first time that he had posted his own ballot paper to himself.

'Are you sure about that?'—'Yes.'

'You actually put it in the post-box and posted it to yourself?'—'I didn't, the Treasurer did.'

'I wish you would be careful, because I thought you said you hadn't posted anything. When did you receive the ballot paper which was addressed to yourself?'—'On the Tuesday morning.'

'Before you went to work?'—'No. It came during the morning while I was at work.'

'And you received it when? Was it on the Tuesday evening?'—'Actually in my hand, yes.'

And as Mr Saunders reached the end of his long session in the witness-box, the Judge said:

'So that there shall be no possibility of an oversight, before I let this witness go—there has been no challenge of his evidence that he posted his return at the head post office at Southampton on December the 23rd?'

'No, my Lord,' said Mr Lawson. And there hadn't.

2 The Communist Party 'Advisory Committees'

The trial now moved on to a new stage.

The next witness, Mr William Blairford, of Edinburgh, who had been Assistant Secretary and Chairman of the Edinburgh Branch, as well as a member of an Area Committee and a trades council, and a delegate to the Confederation of Shipbuilding and Engineering Unions, told the Court about the much-discussed committees by which the Communist Party controlled or influenced the affairs of certain trade unions.

'In 1946,' he said, in answer to Mr Gerald Gardiner, 'the decision was taken by rule to have this "Policy Conference", and I have been at all those conferences, except two, up to the present date.' He was a member of the Communist Party from March 1942 until the time of the Hungarian rising; and from 1946 onwards he used to go to meetings of the Communist Party's 'National Advisory Committee' in King Street, Covent Garden, in company with Mr Haxell, Mr McLennan, Mr Frazer, Mr Humphrey (all these being Defendants in the present trial), as well as Mr Cannon, Mr Gregory, Mr Vetterlein, Mr Maitland and Mr Elsom. These meetings discussed Communist Party policy.

'It was our responsibility,' said Mr Blairford, 'to have that policy implemented throughout the various branches we were members of, and trades councils, and so on ... We had discussion about elections that were coming along. If it was a very important election, the National Advisory Committee might meet and decide on a nominee, and we wouldn't have any say in that respect.'

'Apart from committees, did you attend any conferences of the Communist Party?'—'Yes. The last one was where the late Harry Pollitt referred to the exposures which had taken place with regard to the cult of the individual in the Soviet Union—that is, Stalin. I think they were every two years, and I think I attended altogether about four or five. They were called the National Congress or National Conference, and they were open to anyone who was a member of the Communist Party.'

Mr Gardiner then asked him: 'Have you ever discussed questions of elections and ballot papers with Mr Haxell?'—'Yes. I wondered how it was possible for certain branches to have big returns, as far as ballot papers were concerned. I discussed this with several people who were members of the Communist Party and the Union. They were very tight about the thing. They weren't prepared to make statements. So I asked Mr Frazer how it was possible. I said the only thing I could see was that they must be getting ballot papers from Head Office ... I met Mr Haxell privately at a Trades Union Congress in the late 'fifties, and I was advised by him that I should tell the Communist Party members of the ETU who were branch secretaries that if they wished to indulge in this, all they had to do was to send a notification to the General Secretary saying they were short of ballot papers. I've seen them receive these papers with the General Secretary's compliments.'

When he was cross-examined Mr Blairford said that the Communist Party did have committees 'with regard to certain industries', and that internal Union questions were discussed by them. 'For example, when it was a question of Mr Byrne standing, well, it was necessary (since he was one of the biggest opponents) that it be made clear that everything had to be done to see that our candidate defeated Mr Byrne.' But the lengths to which he himself was at that time prepared to go were elicited from him by the persistence of Mr Lawson, who wanted to know much more about the conversation with Mr Haxell 'at a TUC in the late 'fifties'. It turned out that this probably took place at Southport in 1955, in the bar of a public house; that Mr Foulkes was there too, but that Mr Haxell had spoken so that he couldn't hear; and that Mr Frazer, though not present, knew the purport of the conversation because Mr Blairford had already talked to him in the same way in a café.

'What do you say you said to Mr Frazer?' asked Mr Lawson.

'I discussed this question about the elections.'

'I want to know what you said.'—'Well—*you* know—I'd come to the conclusion that ballot-rigging had been procured, because you couldn't possibly get that return in votes.' He added that he was 'after a situation where it would be possible to get more votes on to the branches, which I was very anxious to do in my particular area'.

'Let me see if I can understand it,' said Mr Lawson, a phrase by which lawyers infallibly betray that they understand only too well and propose to do some knife-twisting. 'Were you saying: "Tell me how I can get some additional ballot papers, so that the votes in my area can be boosted up?" Was *that* the object of it?'

There was a considerable pause.

'That,' said Mr Blairford rather unhappily, 'was the meaning of the point'.

'The idea being that you were going fraudulently to use these ballot papers?'—'Yes.'

'And are you telling my Lord that Mr Frazer said to you: "You mustn't ask me about it—you go and speak to Haxell"?'—'He said he would try and arrange a meeting for me with Haxell, to discuss it . . . Mr Frazer was in the Communist Party at that time, and he was the one through whom we made contacts with Mr Haxell.'

'You see,' said Mr Lawson, 'I suggest that your evidence on this matter is false; that you never had a conversation of this kind with Mr Frazer, or Mr Haxell. You understand that?'—'I'm telling the truth.'

(When he delivered judgment, Mr Justice Winn observed that at this moment in Mr Blairford's evidence he thought that the witness's voice and face carried conviction while he spoke of the *occurrence* of the conversation and its substance, whereas they betrayed lack of confidence and some confusion while he was giving details such as time and place. He is not a practised liar. Throughout his evidence he made a good impression as a straightforward witness'.)

'I want to make it perfectly clear what I suggest to you ultimately,' went on Mr Lawson, 'about what you have called the National Advisory Committee. Firstly, that that was *not* an organised committee of the Communist Party. Would you agree?'—'*Of course* it's an organ of the Communist Party.'

'Secondly, that it was merely a coming together of people who were members of the Communist Party, from time to time?'—'They were members of the ETU. It was an ETU Advisory Committee organised by the Communist Party.'

(Mr Haxell himself, when he gave evidence later, totally denied its existence.)

'It has been suggested to you,' said Mr Gerald Gardiner in re-examination, 'that this conversation with Mr Frazer and Mr Haxell is a complete invention. Do you know—of your own knowledge—whether after that conversation any branch secretaries in Scotland received additional ballot papers?'—'I know of three. There is William Coyle, Secretary of East Branch, John Boyle, Secretary of Rosyth Branch, and John Warwick, Secretary of Central Branch. I don't think any of them are now secretaries.'

'Thank you,' said Mr Gardiner. Mr Blairford's evidence had ended after all on a challenging note—without being further challenged.

Another former Communist, Mr Dick Reno, still a member of the ETU at Putney, then gave evidence that he once belonged to the 'South West group' of the Communist Party and took part in the election of representatives to its London Advisory Committee, which was the policy-forming body for the London area. He, too, had a gruelling time under cross-examination. Mr Lawson asked him about the 'South Western group'.

'Was it really concerned with general political and industrial questions affecting the country as a whole?'—'No, it mainly concerned itself with pressing Communist nominations through the branches, discussing the opposition to them, and generally pressing policies through the trade union branches of the Communist Party.'

'You felt it was in the interests of the Union that these policies should be pressed through?'—'At that time I did misguidedly think that way. We met regularly at 100 Rochester Row, which was the headquarters then of the Westminster Branch of the Communist Party.'

For fifteen years Mr Reno was a member of the Fulham Branch; but on February 22, 1960, a member of that branch 'made a charge' against him for a breach of the Rules.

'The Fulham Branch,' he told Mr Lawson, 'unconstitutionally and against the rules of the Union, tried the case themselves—the procedure should have gone to the Area Committee. But Fulham tried the case, found me guilty, and *then* presented the case to the Area Sub-Committee, every single member of which is a sympathiser with the Communist Party. I protested to the General Secretary, but, as on other occasions, he upheld the breaking of Rules against me.'

'What happened was this, was it not, that on February 22, 1960, there was a discussion in the branch concerning two appearances that you had made on television?'—'Originally I was asked to explain statements I had made on the radio. They were enlarged, I believe, on the television, but they more or less repeated themselves.'

'At the conclusion of that discussion it was moved, was it not, that you be charged for breach of the Rules?'—Mr Reno said that the local Press had reported that he was to be expelled from the Union. The charge was heard by a thirteen-man Sub-Committee.

'Two of that Committee were members whom I had laid accusations against on the radio and television and in public, so it was heavily prejudiced ... I was not heard, because I refused to state my defence before the Committee because of its political composition. They did try the case, without my defending myself.'

'They held that the charge was proved?'—'I don't see how they could do anything else, being, as they were, a hundred per cent Communist-controlled.'

'You were disqualified from holding office in the Union for ten years?'—'Yes.'

'And you were fined ten pounds?'—'That is correct.'

'When you were in the Communist Party, did you know of the existence of such "advisory committees' as, for example, the Economic Advisory Committee, the Building Advisory Committee, and Electricity Supply Advisory Committee, and committees of that kind?'—'I knew there were advisory committees in existence, yes.'

'Their function, as far as you knew, was purely advisory?'—'In the days when I was in the Communist Party it was. It took on a different character, and that was the reason I came out of the Communist Party. Advisory committees took on dictatorial power. They didn't take their instructions from the membership. They issued their directives, and that forced me out of the Party.' (Later the Judge said that he did not altogether accept this story, since he thought Mr Reno to be 'prone to bitterness and exaggeration', but that he felt it contained more than a grain of truth.)

When Mr Gardiner re-examined, he gave Mr Reno an opportunity which brought him into conflict with the Judge. 'Is there anything else you want to add with reference to the charge made against you?'

There was. 'That, I maintain,' began Mr Reno, 'is the second conspiracy. We've been told that a second group operates in the ETU and that its intentions are to knock out the leadership by any means at our disposal. Unfortunately that is not true. If there *were* such a group I would be a member of it. The conspiracy is against members like Mr Cannon and myself, who have been viciously handled by the Communist Party, because they maintain that we were challenging their power. I am very convinced by what I have heard in this Court and in the papers the last week—'

'Please don't attempt to usurp my function,' interrupted the

Judge very sharply. 'It is for me to decide what the evidence convinces anybody of. I don't want any comment from you as to what the evidence establishes. You were asked by Mr Gardiner whether you wanted to say anything more by way of explanation about this order made against you by the Area Sub-Committee.'

'I was expelled because of my menace to the Communist Party position in the Union. Many other members in the Union, my Lord—'

'Very well,' said the Judge with an air of finality.

The Judge was clearly getting a little tired of listening to evidence that was extraneous to the extent, at least, that it merely ventilated private feuds and feelings. When the next witness, Mr J. R. Thomas, Secretary of the Luton Branch of the ETU, was detailing his many trade union and former Communist Party posts, Mr Lawson rose to ask what it was all relevant to.

'It puzzles me,' the Judge assured him, 'what relevance this and a lot of other evidence has to any issue, but how can I possibly tell yet, Mr Lawson? He was asked whether he had knowledge of any advisory committees of the Communist Party in his area, and he starts, as most of the witnesses do, in the Garden of Eden or some such remote starting point, and he will, ultimately, come to the point about the area committees.'

'I'm sorry, my Lord,' said Mr Thomas, 'to be a little bit long-winded'.

'It's all right,' the Judge said resignedly. 'Everybody is.'

Mr Thomas described, rather as Mr Blairford had done in relation to Mr Frazer, how he met Mr Batchelor in a Luton café when the 1954 election was imminent. Batchelor said to him: 'It's a pity we couldn't get hold of a branch stamp,' referring to the Luton Branch; and he replied that it might be possible. 'Oh, is that so?' Mr Batchelor had said, adding that there might be some way also of getting extra ballot papers.

'He then asked me how many the branch could handle. I left the figure to him. He suggested fifty or a hundred spare branch ballot papers. From that moment on, I refused to have anything to do with it.' (No one said so, but it seemed as though Mr Thomas had been specially repelled by the ambitious quantities suggested.)

Later, referring to Mr Foulkes' candidature for the Presidency of the ETU in 1959, Mr Thomas described a meeting with him in an hotel at Stevenage. Mr Foulkes was continually urging him (and others present) to do what they could to ensure that as many ballot papers as possible came into the branches in support of his own candidature. 'He also said, and turned round to me personally, "Joe, is there a pub in your area for sale, because it looks as though I shall be out of a job very shortly?" Those are his exact words.'

Mr Thomas was going on to retail other snippets of pre-election conversation, when the Judge intervened.

'I wonder whether, out of mercy to me, the question which I have asked Mr Lawson once or twice might be answered by you, Mr Sofer? To what allegation, issue, or cognate matter has that last phase of the evidence any relevance?'

'My Lord,' said Mr Sofer, 'the point here is that it is alleged that in various elections there had been ballot-rigging. The point is the advance knowledge, before the results had been announced by one of the candidates (who is a Defendant), of the results as they were coming in. Some five or six days before the election results are announced, one of the candidates is saying that the election is running badly against him and that he is very worried.'

'I suppose,' said the Judge, 'you have never had to hold the hand of a Parliamentary candidate in his constituency as polling day arrives? Quite apart from having seen any of the actual ballots that have perhaps by that time come in, the candidate and his agent are usually in a state of depression.'

'I would respectfully agree,' Mr Sofer began, 'that on polling day—'

'No—I said *without* any knowledge of ballots that had come in. There is a cyclothymic syndrome, if you follow me; first, way up in the clouds with optimism, and then depressed. Frankly, at the moment, this conversation on the whole seems to me to amount to precisely nothing. And I say that to Mr Lawson. Let me just make it clear. I am anxious that (a) we should keep as near the real issues as possible in this case, but even more important perhaps that (b) casual remarks and conversations should not be used merely for vituperative purposes, in order to blacken general character and credibility. I am going to ignore this matter altogether, this hotel conversation. You need not trouble with it therefore, Mr Lawson. It will not be taken against you.'

'I am much obliged to your Lordship,' said Mr Lawson, but he proceeded to cross-examine on the question whether the results of the Stevenage election *were* known at the moment when Mr Foulkes was saying that he 'looked like being out of a job'. Mr Lawson urged that they were, but the witness didn't remember. However, on the question whether Mr Batchelor had really asked for a Luton Branch stamp, Mr Lawson was in the difficulty that Mr Batchelor was ill at home. 'I am not in a position to take instructions,' he told the Judge; and the further cross-examination of Mr J. R. Thomas as to his 'hearsay' account of conversations with Mr Foulkes (which the Judge had hinted was superfluous) was therefore postponed.

The next ETU witness, Mr Thomas Vetterlein, a member of the Communist Party from 1924 until he resigned from it in 1958, and a member of the ETU Executive Council from 1949 to 1957, was present 'on subpoena'—that is, under compulsion. In the course of his evidence it became clearer than ever that (at least among the half-hearted, the fellow-travellers) the various committees of the Party were not called committees, but 'advisories'. There was something less sinister, or at least less committed, about the term 'advisory' used as a noun. These advisories met at the Communist Party District Office in Great Ormond Street, at Cremer Street, at Clerkenwell Green, in 'a café off the City Road', at Marx House, at the *Daily Worker* offices in Farringdon Road, at the Garibaldi Café in Rosebery Avenue, at a Communist Party District Office in Greek Street, Soho, and at King Street, Covent Garden. They discussed Communist policy for the trade unions, wages policy, the World Federation of Trade Unions, 'problems like Malaya and Kenya', the placing of 'under-cover' men in the Labour Party, and who should be 'run' for election to office in the unions.

'Do you know,' Mr Gerald Gardiner asked him, 'whether these Communist advisories are still in existence?'—'I am certain they are,' said Mr Vetterlein.

In cross-examination, Mr Lawson suggested to him that 'there was *no* London Advisory Committee of the Communist Party consisting of members of the ETU, but that individuals who were members of the Communist Party *and* the Union were from time to time invited to attend meetings to give their advisory assistance on problems relating to the electricity industry generally that might arise. Is that right?'

'No,' said Mr Vetterlein, 'it is not correct'. They were official and regular meetings. (But as the Judge was to point out when he delivered his judgment, only those bodies officially appointed by the Communist Party were properly called 'committees'. The 'advisories' were more like self-propagated gadflies.)

Mr Leslie Tuck, of the London, S.W. Branch, then gave rather similar evidence about the 'committees' and 'advisories', and in the course of it touched off a prolonged argument between Mr Gardiner and Mr Lawson. He alleged that when he was secretary of the Communist Party's 'South-West Advisory Committee', he had visited the house of Mr Pat Hamilton, secretary of LSE No. 12 Branch, and had there seen Mr Frazer (one of the Defendants) 'picking up spare ballot papers'; and that he had immediately protested, because he 'strongly objected to this particular practice'.

Mr Lawson strongly objected to the mere mention of this, because it wasn't 'in the pleadings'. Mr Gardiner implied that a great deal of the Plaintiffs' case would be established by no other means than by grasping opportunities as they came along, since the Defendants had been reluctant to supply full details of the picture. In the end, Mr Justice Winn said that the story about the ballot papers at Mr Hamilton's house was 'probative material', evidence of system in the rigging of elections.

'Out of charity, our *criminal* law doesn't use it. I did say earlier that I wasn't going to have it said: "He is a Communist, therefore he does these things." But that does not seem to me to be the same thing as the proposition: "He was not only a member of the Communist Party—he was partly, by reason of what he had learned as a Communist, one who held the belief that the end justifies the means, whatever the means might be." I would have thought that was relevant and proper material for the determination of that issue. That is the way I looked at it, Mr Lawson, and I think on that ground I must take the responsibility of saying that this is admissible evidence because it is relevant.'

To Mr Seymour Moss, of the LSE No. 23 Branch, who gave similar evidence about the formality and regularity of the Communist 'advisories', Mr Ralph Millner (for the Defendants) suggested that his story was 'utterly untrue'.

'You were never a member of *any* group which sent delegates or any other persons to any committee of the kind you have mentioned.'

'In other words,' said Mr Moss, 'you're saying I'm lying?' 'Yes.' 'Well, that's incorrect. I'm not lying.'

'I suggest that as regards ETU matters, the only discussions that have gone on will have been discussions between members of the Communist Party who are members of the ETU of a purely informal kind, getting together and exchanging their views as to what is best for the Union. Is that right?'—'Well, again you are wrong.'

And when Mr H. W. R. Townsend, of the Finchley Branch, had given similar evidence, the Judge asked him how he knew which way to vote, as his branch's representative but as one with no mandate, when matters of policy were put to the vote at these Communist Party 'advisories'.

'You would make up your mind as to what you would do in the way of voting—supporting or opposing anything on the basis of your own reasoning? Or how would you decide?'—'At that time, being a member of the Communist Party, I would probably support the Communist Party policy.'

'Really,' said the Judge thoughtfully, 'you went to this ETU policy conference merely to vote blind for whatever the Communist policy was?'

'It could be expressed that way,' said Mr Townsend—the first witness to make this admission in as many words.

3   Mr Chapple in the Witness-Box

It was now the turn of Mr Francis Joseph Chapple ('Frank Chapple' to the ETU) to forsake the role of assiduous listener and come into the witness-box as Plaintiff.

He joined the ETU twenty-one years ago, he told Mr Gardiner, and the Communist Party about five years later. Before he joined the Army in 1942 he was a full-time paid organiser for the Young Communist League. From about 1948 to 1956 he was a member both of the 'London Advisory Committee' and of the 'National Advisory Committee' of the Party. Meetings of both committees were 'summoned by written notice to those people who could be trusted to destroy the written notice after they had received it— and where they *couldn't* be trusted to do this they were told by word of mouth'. (At the end of the trial Mr Justice Winn said that this, in his opinion, 'had the appearance of picturesque embroidery'; which was a reference only to the torn-up copies.) The 'London Committee's' business was 'to control the conduct of elections and ballots within the London area of the Union', but every Communist meeting about anything opened with a long 'political statement', to which (Mr Chapple implied) good delegates had to listen and look as if they liked it.

'Were there occasions,' Mr Gardiner asked him, coming to the question of ballots and elections, 'on which there was discussion as to whether it would be wise to have a Communist candidate?'— 'Oh yes. Quite often the discussion would centre round, "Is it necessary to expose the Party to still further accusations that they control the ETU by having a Communist? Wouldn't it be better to have somebody who supports us but isn't a Party member?"'

Mr Gardiner wanted to find out who was on the 'National Advisory Committee'.

'It was composed,' said Mr Chapple, 'of Mr Haxell, Mr Frazer (he was the Secretary—Haxell usually acting as Chairman), Mr Foulkes occasionally, Mr Cosby, Mr Hendy, Mr Ward, Mr Gregory, Mr Benson, Mr Batchelor. I've seen at various times practically all the officials of the Union who were members of the Communist Party in the London area: Stride, Turner, Tilbury, Ward, Mr Vetterlein before he was an official.'

'Who was the Secretary?'

'At one time Jack Hendy. But he got a scholarship to the London School of Economics, and about that period he also complained in a letter to Harry Pollitt—' (no objection to all this came from Mr Lawson) '—about the fiddling of ballots at the Union elections; and at that same period he was removed from being secretary of the "National Advisory" and Mr Frazer took over.'

There was an assembly called the 'National Aggregate', which met about once a year before such big occasions as the election of a General President, and among its fifty or sixty members were all the Defendants. There was an annual 'Policy Conference', always preceded by a hush-hush meeting at which the faithful were told which of the resolutions the Executive Council of the Union were to support or oppose.

'Delegates,' said Mr Chapple, 'would say, "Well, my branch has got this resolution on the agenda", and Mr Frazer or Mr Hendy or one of these people would say, "Well, the Executive are opposing this one—you'd better agree to withdraw it". If the delegate was insistent that he couldn't withdraw it because of some special reason, perhaps because his branch had a bent and it would mean he would never attend a policy conference again if he had to withdraw it, they would say: "Fair enough; you go into the box and speak for it, but we'll be easy on you, we'll let you down fairly lightly." If a fellow was still insistent, as sometimes I was, they would say: "You'll have to go into the box and take the consequences—we'll give you a bashing if you attempt to bash us." '

There was also a Rules Revision Conference (a monument, you might say, to the British vice of constitution-mongering), which again was preceded by a pre-conference meeting to train the yes-men in their prescribed postures.

'You left the "London Advisory Committee", did you, in 1956?' asked Mr Gardiner.

'Well, my position on the "London Advisory" became difficult in 1956. After the Hungarian rising there were large numbers of disillusioned Communist Party members who were leaving the Communist Party. I associated myself with a couple of meetings to try and persuade these people that the correct course to take was to stay inside the Party, fight for their particular policy, try to democratise the Party and change the leadership. These two meetings were discovered through political spies; I was suspended for a brief period from the "London Advisory" and from my duties as Secretary of a divisional "Advisory". That lasted, I think, about nine months, during which time discussions went on at the District

Office of the Communist Party.' He resumed sitting on the London 'Advisory', but soon he was receiving no more notices of meetings.

On October 18, 1958, he wrote to Mr Haxell about the election for General President, as follows:

> I thought I should give you some advance notice of information I would like at the next meeting of the Executive Council. The following items are those on which I require information: (1) The total number of ballots sent to each branch under the branch serial number. (1a) Number of ballots returned unused by the branch. (2) Number of branches disqualified under Rule and the exact reason for each disqualification.

He never got that information. He persisted with his enquiries, with consequences that eventually formed the subject of a prolonged correspondence between the ETU and the General Council of the Trades Union Congress. This is printed on pages 512 to 523 of the 1959 Report of the TUC and was read out in full by Mr Gardiner. In summary it is as follows.

First, on December 17, 1958, the TUC asked the ETU for its comments on the growing publicity about Communist influence and rigged elections. Then on January 23, 1959, the ETU wrote to say that its affairs were controlled, *not* by the Communist Party but by its Annual Policy Conference and Rules Revision Conference, and put all the blame for the adverse publicity on the desire of the Press to discredit trade unionism. It added that the ETU was going to do all it could to 'nullify and minimise' the growing public criticisms. On February 25, 1959, the TUC asked what it was actually doing? On March 20 the ETU replied that it had been unable to get the editors of the *Daily Telegraph*, *Illustrated*, and the *New Statesman* (all of which had carried articles about the rigged elections) to publish a letter of the modest length of 1,500 words. Also it had been thinking about legal action against these papers but considered it too expensive and 'not in the best interests of the trade union movement'. And it had published two pamphlets replying to the Press onslaught, both of which were attacked by such newspapers as noticed them. On March 26 the TUC rejoined that this (in effect) was not nearly good enough, and that the ETU must hold an official enquiry and issue a statement. On April 16 the ETU wrote to say that it was asking its members for proof of the allegations some of them had made, and on April 22 the TUC replied that this did 'little or nothing' to remove the dissatisfaction with earlier replies. At last, on April 29, the ETU set up a committee of three to investigate charges of Communist interference made by Mr Cannon and Mr Young, two of the complaining members—who, incidentally, had themselves been 'charged' by the Union with 'divulging Union business outside the Union'. This ETU committee heard evidence from Brothers Haxell, Frazer, Vetterlein, and Hendy, and 'discovered no evidence whatever of Communist interference'.

This kind of correspondence drifted on until November 25, 1959, when at last the TUC wrote as follows (*and sent copies to all affiliated unions*):

> The General Council can do no other than take your letter of November 18 as further and indeed conclusive evidence that the majority of the present leadership of the ETU is more concerned to evade than to deal adequately with the questions put to your Union by the General Council, and to delay rather than to assist the General Council in bringing this matter to a conclusion. The General Council therefore asked me to inform your Executive Council that in view of the evasive nature of the replies sent by your Union's leadership in answer to the comparatively simple questions put to them, and their persistent habit of seeking to delay the General Council in reaching a conclusion, the General Council do not propose to engage in any further abortive discussions of this character with the present ETU leadership.

The ETU replied that perhaps they would take legal action against the accusing newspapers if the TUC would foot the bill—and sent copies of *this* letter to all the affiliated unions. This the TUC found less satisfactory than ever (though a temporary stop was then placed on the proceedings by the issue of the writs that led eventually to the present trial); and on seeing the correspondence circulated, Mr Chapple himself wrote to the ETU leadership:

> I am in receipt of your circular letter of November 27, 1959. I cannot allow to go unchallenged your statement that the Executive Council has repeatedly denied the existence of Communist Party organisation within the Union. You neglect to mention that I have never supported either yourself or the majority of the Executive Council in these lies. As you and I

well know, your assertion that 'Communist Party Advisory Committees do not and never have existed' is not correct. I must make clear that the reason I have refused to speak out before is that I believed some solution could be found within the constitution of the Union. For this reason I supported the proposal from my branch that a special conference of the Union be called to investigate the allegations, so that justice could be done to all concerned . . . It is my view [Mr Chapple's letter went on] that the responsibility for our Union being faced with this crisis rests squarely on your shoulders. I note, in this circular, your constant reference to the subject matters contained therein as having been dealt with by the Executive Council. The use of such terms as 'my Executive Council' and 'we had understood' is clearly intended to give the impression that the exchange of letters between yourself and the General Council of the TUC has had the consideration of the full Executive Council. I wish it to be made perfectly clear that these letters have never been before the Executive Council, and that I only learned of the substance of the exchange when the correspondence was made public in the General Council's report to Congress.

'Is that right?' asked Mr Gardiner at the end of this lengthy reading.

'That is correct,' said Mr Chapple. He had concluded the letter with a request for permission to send a copy of it to every branch of the ETU (and a statement that he had already sent one to Sir Vincent Tewson, General Secretary of the TUC).

At the ETU's Executive Council meeting on December 19, 1959, Mr Chapple's letter was read and 'considered'. The following notes from the minutes of that meeting (originally tape-recorded) were read to him in Court by Mr Gardiner:

Humphrey: I move that permission should not be given.
Foulkes: Moved that permission be not granted to circularise.
Cosby: I second that, Mr Chairman.
Walker: I move that permission *should* be granted in view of the procedure which is now adopted that minorities have the right of expression on this Executive Council.
Chapple: I'll second that.
Foulkes: That's a direct negative.
Goldberg: Well, I don't know what we're moving or seconding, because the damned circular is round the branches now, and in fact Brother Chapple's letter has a foreword to it saying 'We believe Brother Chapple's letter is so important that all branches

should see it'. Who's 'we'? I don't know. Some sort of special advisory committee, I suppose.

The minutes ended with a majority decision that Mr Chapple be charged with a breach of the Rules in making known to the Press and other persons the internal business of the Union.

And after much tape-recorded argument the Executive Council of the ETU decided by an eight-to-three majority that Mr Chapple be fined £5 and warned that if he did it again he would be expelled from the Union.

Mr Gardiner then came to the minutes of the meeting in February 1960 at which Mr Haxell was declared the elected General Secretary.

' "Ballots—December quarter 1959," ' Mr Gardiner read out; ' "Results—full-time General Secretary. We, the undersigned, have scrutinised the above-mentioned ballot and declare the result to be as follows: Byrne, J. T., 18,577; Haxell, F. L., 19,611. F. L. Haxell elected." Then Mr Frazer says: "Move." Up to that point, had he said any more?'—'I don't recall him saying any more,' said Mr Chapple.

'Did he say anything up to that point about anybody being disqualified?'—'No. That's the way the report is presented—the figures, and anything concerned with the scrutineers' report comes later.'

'Then Mr Foulkes says: "All those in favour? Against?" Then you said: "I'd like to ask some questions on this before you take such a motion. We're entitled to have a scrutineers' report, which includes—." Then Foulkes said: "Brother Chapple, Brother Walker, and Brother Hadley are against the motion." You said: "This is the second election that's been rushed through in this manner." What did you mean by that?'—'Mr Foulkes' election was similarly done ... Before I could get any words out of my mouth, the same situation had arisen—somebody said "I move", "I second", and we're going on with it.'

'Then you said: "I wish to ask, Mr Chairman, were any branches disqualified in this ballot?" Foulkes: "The answer is Yes." Then you asked: "Now can I know how many there were, and who they were?" Then Mr McLennan said: "Well, there was a whole number of branches disqualified, as there usually is . . .

Probably more so on this occasion, because all kinds of people seem to have been having circuses running round the country trying to find out faults in ballots." Then you ask for the names. Mr McLennan said: "Some branches are still being investigated, but in any case, I mean, whatever the results of those branches, it makes no difference to the final result. It doesn't alter the scrutineers' report or its acceptance." You said: "Now can I have them slowly, please, because I'd like to make a note of them, if you don't mind." Frank Foulkes said: "Just read them in the normal way. We're not giving Press publicity now." At what speed were the names in fact read?'—'Brother McLennan read them at the speed I presume he normally reads,' said Mr Chapple, 'but he had a slight accent, and it's difficult—at least for me—to get down what he says unless he reads slowly and deliberately. I think I got about twenty or so of the branches written down.'

'Then Mr Foulkes called on the next business—"Full-time Officials"—and you said: "Now, hold on. I'm still asking questions arising out of the scrutineers' report." Foulkes said, "No, you can't", and you said, "But that's only one question—I've got several more to ask. I want to know if any branches' ballots were sent to the Head Office on this occasion and were counted by the national scrutineers", and you asked for the names of those branches and Mr Foulkes said you couldn't have those because they weren't in the scrutineers' report.'

Mr Chapple assented to all this, and Mr Gardiner's reading from the minutes went on. It showed that Mr Foulkes had delivered a long homily on the inefficiency of branch secretaries, and their habit of carrying unposted letters in their pockets for ten days.

Under cross-examination by Mr Lawson, Mr Chapple was reminded of a passage in Mr Gerald Gardiner's opening speech, to the effect that by December 1959 'the anti-Communists had learned a thing or two', and accordingly put up only one candidate at each election. The implication seemed to be (and Mr Lawson was out to refute it) that they had lost previous elections to the Communists mainly by splitting the votes among anti-Communist candidates.

'Do you remember Mr Foulkes standing for re-election as General President in September 1959?'

Mr Chapple did.

'On that occasion there was only one anti-Communist candidate, was there not, in the person of Mr Blairford?'—'Yes, that's correct.'

'The anti-Communists had "learned a thing or two"?'—'I should imagine they had.'

'And were you one of those who supported Mr Blairford against Mr Foulkes?'—'I was.'

'It's true, isn't it, that in previous elections, going back I think over the last ten years or so, for the office of General Secretary there has been only one anti-Communist candidate?'—'I can't recall that, but I know there has been only one Communist candidate.'

'Do you not know that Mr Byrne has been the only anti-Communist candidate putting his name forward in elections over the last ten years?'

Mr Chapple, after some hesitation, agreed. And then—

'You know that there is an allegation made here of what one calls a "Communist conspiracy"?'—'Yes.'

'*Are you saying that you were a member of that conspiracy?*'— 'I am saying not only that I was a member of that conspiracy,' replied Mr Chapple in a very distinct voice, 'but that I am heartily ashamed of my part in it'.

'But do you not appreciate what your position is? What you are telling my Lord is this: "Here is a conspiracy of which I was a member, and I am asking the Court to give me relief from the consequences of this conspiracy".'

But to Mr Justice Winn, long accustomed to the stratagems of the criminal bar, this seemed a little naïve.

'It would really be for Mr Byrne also,' he said, 'to decide whether to sue Mr Chapple, wouldn't it?'—'Yes, my Lord,' said Mr Lawson.

'I mean, it's a little amusing?' And his Lordship adjourned the Court for lunch.

Resuming after lunch on this eighth day of the trial, the Court went into a prolonged discussion of the statistical documents which the Judge had asked for on April 24. The Defence, under Mr Lawson's instructions, were still working on these.

'Would it be a great burden,' asked the Judge with exemplary patience, 'and I think it would if it were not done by a computer, to set out against each branch the result of subtracting the loser's vote from the winner's vote? That of course is just a matter of the simplest subtraction, but it's got to be done about six hundred and fifty times.'

Mr Lawson undertook to have it done, but there was a difficulty about the disqualification of branches for breaches of the Rules—they were not always disqualified for *one* repetition of a breach, especially if it was a breach of the same Rule.

'I do feel that I am going to be in a difficulty in trying to assist your Lordship towards seeing that there was a firm practice covering all kinds of breaches at all times. I believe your Lordship will ultimately find that there was really nothing very firm about it. Your Lordship will remember Mr Fairlam, one of the Plaintiffs' witnesses, saying: "Oh well, there was a custom that if you were late once you were warned, and the second time you were rejected. And that, so to speak, was the broad line." '

But Mr Lawson now selected a case—that of the London Lift Engineers' Branch—in which there had been no disqualification when there could have been.

'On page eight of the statement of claim,' he reminded Mr Chapple, 'you are complaining that the Defendants, "as one of the means of faking the Cannon-Frazer election, accepted the votes of the London Lift Engineers' Branch although scrutineers had *not* been elected at the previous meeting . . ." That is a clear allegation that that was part of the faking of the result, is it not?'—'Not the acceptance of the vote so much as the acceptance of the fact that there had been a breach of the Rules, since the scrutineers were not elected correctly. I don't know what the votes were. I don't recall them, you see.'

'I'm going to put what the votes were to you in a moment, but it's quite clear that you are alleging that this was part of the fake—favouring a branch by not disqualifying it when it should have been disqualified?'—'That is correct.'

'Would you be surprised to know that the voting in the London Lift Engineers' Branch was fifty in favour of Cannon and six in favour of Frazer?'—'No,' said Mr Chapple stoutly, 'I'm not surprised'.

'Does that shake your view that that was part of the fake?'—
'No, it doesn't. If anything, it confirms my view that they accepted
one of the other side in order to make all their other fiddles look
legitimate.'

Mr Gerald Gardiner interrupted this colloquy to remind the
Court that, in his opening speech, he had omitted any reference to
the London Lift Engineers.

'Did you hear Mr Gerald Gardiner say just now that he had
not "opened" this particular matter?' Mr Lawson now asked
suggestively.

'If that's what he said,' replied Mr Chapple, who gave nothing
away, 'I accept that. He hasn't challenged it.'

Mr Lawson turned then to the London Technical and Supervisory Branch. 'My learned friend, Mr Gardiner, told my Lord
that that was "a well-known Communist branch". Is that your
view?'—'No, that's not my view.'

'That's nonsense, is it not?'—'I think he made a mistake.'

'This "notorious Communist branch" voted fifty-two in favour
of Byrne and fourteen in favour of Haxell, did they not?'—'I don't
recall the votes. I haven't got them in front of me. I can't recall
every vote of seven hundred branches.'

Then there was the Jarrow Branch election in 1958, when the
Executive Council had agreed that Jarrow must be disqualified
because the scrutineers had found that 'of sixty-three ballot papers
returned by post, sixty-one envelopes bore exactly the same type of
cancellation mark, namely an Empire Games 3d stamp cancelled
with the words *10 a.m., 22.9.58 Jarrow*. Asked whether, as a
member of the Council, he had agreed to this, Mr Chapple said:

'I don't know whether I voted in favour of that or not. I
wouldn't like to say.'

'There is no note,' said Mr Lawson, 'of your voting against it'.

'I wouldn't place too much importance,' Mr Chapple advised
him, 'on what's there'.

'Among the matters you complain of,' Mr Lawson went on, 'is
the suggestion that false and trumpery charges were made against
people who were anti-Communists? Is that right?'—'Yes.'

'Yet the only matters on which you are relying are the two
charges against *you*. That's right, is it not?'—'That's right.'

'This is right, is it not, that before the charges were made against you in December 1959, charges had been made against a number of people (whose names I will put to you in a moment) for what one might call activities in relation to giving improper publicity to the Union's affairs? That is right, is it not?'

This was too long for Mr Chapple. 'I don't know,' he said, looking round the Court. 'If you'd like to shorten the number of words, I might be able to answer your questions, Yes or No. You're making a statement and you're asking me to say Yes or No to it.'

Mr Justice Winn stepped in with a down-to-earth précis. 'You weren't the first one carpeted for talking to the Press?' he translated. But Mr Chapple's response to this was that he was not carpeted for talking to the Press 'on this occasion'.

'You understand perfectly well, Mr Chapple, the question I'm asking you, do you not?' said Mr Lawson acidly. Mr Chapple said he didn't, but he was able to confirm that similar charges had been brought against Mr Reno, Mr Collins, Mr Cannon, Mr Sullivan, and Mr Walker.

'These weren't false or trumpery charges, were they?'—'I now believe they were, yes.'

'How long have you believed that—since you left the Communist Party?'—'No. I've believed they were false and trumpery charges since charges have been laid against me for similar reasons. I've had a basin of it myself, you see.'

When Mr Lawson came to the question of the Communist Party 'advisories', he suggested to Mr Chapple that any such meetings were 'purely informal'.

'I went to informal meetings,' Mr Chapple replied, 'but the meetings referred to as "advisories" were *not* informal'.

'There was no such thing as a "National Advisory Committee" which dealt with ETU affairs?'—'You're wrong. There is, or was, a National Advisory Committee. Maybe there still is.'

'Did you know that there was a National Advisory Committee of the Communist Party which dealt with *electricity supply*?'

'There are advisory committees of the Party which deal with every facet of life in Britain, including all the trade unions, and all the things that are not industries, including the Law Courts.'

He added, in reply to the Judge, that there were committees on economics, on teaching and on history, and in those the people were 'very highly qualified', professional and graduate types of mind. He agreed that there was one on the building trade, 'but that is separate from the one which deals with the building trade unions'. And whom, the Judge asked him, did these advisory committees advise?

'Well, generally speaking,' said Mr Chapple, 'they advise the political committee or the Executive Committee of the Communist Party. They usually, perhaps yearly, produce reports, and these can be purchased from Communist Party bookshops.'

'In the nature of a special study group for the political Party cabinet?'—'That's right,' said Mr Chapple, and most people present in Court then knew for the first time what an 'advisory' was.

'I know it's irritating for you, Mr Lawson,' said the Judge, 'to be interrupted like that, but I wanted to try and clear it up for my own assistance'.

'If your Lordship pleases,' said Mr Lawson: but everyone was pleased.

At the end of Mr Chapple's evidence, which was also the end of the eighth day of the evidence, the Judge said he thought there was 'a great deal of fringe matter undergoing exploration by both parties for personal gratification and indulgence, such as quarrels between the parties'.

'Now,' his Lordship said, 'if ever I do feel really sure that that is what is being done, then I shall be disposed, I fear, to be rather strong and drastic about it. I have suspected it on several occasions, and I have had to give Counsel or witnesses the benefit of the doubt. But it would be really shocking if witnesses—I am sure Counsel would never do it—thought they could come here, at public expense, to indulge their own specific motives.'

4   More Disqualified Branches—'Working to Rule'

Mr Stanley Withecombe, Secretary of the Southampton Docks Branch, the first witness on the ninth day, said that in a 1957 ballot his branch nominated Mr Frazer, who was opposed by Mr

Cannon. It was a small branch—eighty or ninety members only—
and although it was then a rule of the ETU that branch scrutineers
be elected at the meeting *before* the quarterly meeting counting the
votes, this was impossible because most of the members were on
'shift work' and the elected scrutineers would quite possibly be
missing on the election night (they had tried it twice). So they
elected them on quarter night. At the September 1957 meeting one
of the scrutineers so elected was a Mr Gibbs, who happened to be
'a very strong supporter of the Communist Party' and made no
secret of it. He had never been a scrutineer before.

'And although your branch had nominated Frazer as the branch
preference,' asked Mr Jonathan Sofer, 'was the voting for Cannon
seventeen and for Frazer nine?'—'That's right.'

A few days later Mr Gibbs, the Communist, questioned the
validity of the ballot on the ground that his own election as scrutineer was irregular. So the witness, as Branch Secretary, had to
write to Head Office for a ruling.

'We had endeavoured to work to rule as far back as 1954,' Mr
Withecombe wrote,

> but the branch being almost entirely composed of members who
> are shift workers and maintenance men, it was found more
> advantageous to the efficient working of the branch to put the
> election of scrutineers the first item on the agenda for quarter
> night.
> It was also suggested that the reason for the election of scrutin-
> eers at the previous meeting was to allow large branches to
> commence the counting of the votes before the start of the
> meeting, to enable the result of the ballot to be announced before
> the close of the meeting. In our case this procedure is not neces-
> sary. With only a score or so of returns to cope with, two
> scrutineers can easily manage after the meeting has been declared
> open to complete the ballot returns in time for announcement.
> Although accepting these explanations as reasonable, our
> scrutineers still expressed the wish that we should have the ruling
> of the Executive Council on this matter.

The reply, said Mr Withecombe, was that the branch's vote was
rejected. Southampton Docks had never in the past been 'warned'
for a breach of any kind, and Mr Withecombe was instructed to
write a strong protest. In it he wanted to know what the position
was to be when properly elected scrutineers failed to turn up on

the night because they were on shift work (to this he never got an answer). He also pointed out that if Southampton Docks Branch was disqualified for the reason given, then so were many others—the procedure was widespread among 'shift-work' branches. He added that the Union officials attending the ETU Training College at Esher were always told that 'the Rule Book was in fact a guide, and it was realised that in some instances it was impossible to adhere strictly to the letter'.

All these entreaties were rejected.

'What is said about Southampton,' commented the Judge, 'is that Gibbs produced the result because he was a Communist, and wanted to upset those particular works, isn't it?'

'I feel that is the suggestion,' said Mr Lawson.

Mr R. J. L. Allum, Secretary of the Reading No. 1 Branch, gave the Court another glimpse of the strength of branch meeting attendances. The membership of his branch was 'between five hundred and seven hundred'. Normal attendances at meetings were from seven to thirty. At the meeting before the September 'quarterly', i.e., the meeting at which the scrutineers should have been elected, there were five or seven men. 'Towards the end of the meeting there were only two or three members left in the room.' So when the 'quarterly' came round there were no scrutineers, and to the general surprise *Mr Frazer, the Communist candidate, himself turned up*. He was present while the scrutineers were then chosen, at what purported to be an adjourned session of the previous meeting. He saw what was done, and then said that they ought to write to Head Office for a ruling on its legality. Mr Allum wrote. Head Office declared the election void. Its figures were: Cannon 51, Frazer 10.

Then the Court heard about votes that were never counted at the branches at all, but by some means arrived at Head Office and were counted by national scrutineers there—though the returns bore no branch signatures. This evidence came from Mr Ernest Hadley, of Sheffield, a non-Communist member of the Executive Council; at his first Council meeting in February 1960 he had listened to a long statement from Mr Foulkes, the President, the effect of which was that the Council was to do what Mr Foulkes told it, and say nothing to anyone outside the Council (even to anyone belonging to the Union). Mr Hadley asked to see a copy of the Standing Orders that made this kind of dictatorship possible. 'We will consider your request,' said Mr Foulkes. Mr Hadley asked that this be recorded in the minutes, and his request was refused. *Then the result of the Byrne-Haxell election was announced.*

After the meeting he wrote to Mr Haxell, the new Secretary, and told him that 'a number of members' ballot returns for the position of General Secretary were received, counted and included in the final ballot return by the national scrutineers . . . Would you inform me under which Rule the national scrutineers conducted this part of the ballot returns, also would you advise me how these individual members' returns will be shown in the printed analysis of the ballot returns from branches?'

He got no reply; but in April, at another Executive Council meeting, the General Secretary announced that the national scrutineers had 'some time back' been given authority to count ballot returns. Could Mr Hadley see the relevant minute? No, he couldn't. 'Also,' said the General Secretary, 'I'm not obliged to answer letters from Executive Councillors.' Mr Hadley promptly moved a resolution that no further ballots be counted by national scrutineers. It was seconded but defeated.

The Judge wanted to know (as did many people present in Court) why it was necessary or desirable for national scrutineers actually to *count* votes, which was the job of the branch scrutineers. So Mr Lawson asked the witness:

'Has it occurred to you that in some of the branches you may not have sufficient people at the branch quarterly meeting to produce branch scrutineers?'

'I can only reply to that,' said Mr Hadley, 'by giving the reason given to us by the General President why the national scrutineers *did* count any at all; and that was because, he said, certain branches had not held meetings'.

Another cat was out of the bag.

A larger one emerged when the trial went back for a few hours to the kind of evidence it had opened with—the envelope racket. One of the candidates in the Jarrow election was the Secretary of the branch, Mr Carr, a Communist (he had actually tried to get into Parliament as such). Usually about four members voted by post in a Jarrow ballot. This time there were sixty-three postal votes, all addressed to Mr Carr. Mr Fenwick was the branch scrutineer and Mr Carr handed the envelopes to him. He thought it was such an unusually high number that he examined them very closely. They were all postmarked and dated at the same time and place. And all the votes in them turned out to be in favour of Mr Carr, the Communist candidate.

The long and futile correspondence with Mr Haxell began. The Branch Committee decided to send all members a questionnaire —(1) Did you receive a ballot paper? (2) If not, have you changed your address? (3) Did you vote? (4) How—by shop steward or by post? (5) If you didn't vote, do you know what happened to the ballot paper? They thought they might thus get at the truth of the matter, and the Secretary sought permission from Head Office ('possibly,' said the Judge later, 'not wholly disingenuously') to incur the necessary expense. No, said Head Office.

There then ensued a prolonged game of Box and Cox (or its Communist equivalent) between Mr Haxell and Mr Carr which lasted until the following September. But at last a Head Office sub-committee did enquire into the affair, and the following paragraph from its report is worth quoting:

> The total number of ballot papers forwarded to members was 274, out of which 201 state that they did not vote. The maximum possible vote, therefore, was 73. The number of ballot papers received by the branch scrutineers was 137, that is, 64 more than the maximum possible vote.

The Jarrow case inspired an article in *The Times* of September 25, 1959, which (Mr Fenwick told the Court) was ninety-eight per cent true. This quoted some remarks of Mr Fenwick's to a *Times* reporter which Mr Haxell thought should be withdrawn. He therefore wrote a long letter telling Mr Fenwick how to do this. Mr Fenwick absolutely refused, and implied that if he *did* make any further communication to the Press, Mr Haxell would like that communication still less. (Mr Haxell cannot have liked, therefore, the Judge's remarks in his final judgment: 'The vote at this branch was undoubtedly rigged, fraudulently, with the motive of securing the choice of Mr Carr, who was then the Secretary of the Jarrow Branch.')

Jarrow's vote was declared void through 'breach of rule'.

'What was the alleged breach of rule?' asked the Judge.

'The alleged breach of rule, my Lord,' said Mr Lawson, 'I think is the report which was sent to Head Office, to which the witness has referred.'

'What does it mean?' persisted Mr Justice Winn.

'If your Lordship is asking me the question—' began Mr Lawson, rather with the air of a man setting out on a journey to which he can see no clear end.

'I'm merely trying to follow it. I'm not *complaining*,' said the Judge, 'that no one has yet told me what this is all about. The whole of this "area" business is something to do with someone's idea that some rule had been breached in some way. Well, having been listening to it for hours, what *is* it all about?'

'Well, I suppose there may be a number of breaches of rule committed,' boxed Mr Lawson.

'But why does a branch commit any breach of rule if bogus ballot papers turn up at the Secretary's address through the post, any more than a hen knows that the egg it has been sitting on is a duck egg?'

'There might be any number of breaches of rule, depending on the circumstances, my Lord.'

And so on for some little time. Mr Fenwick's cross-examination was at length resumed, but the Judge's question went unanswered.

Back now to Mr Chapple's story of the Executive Council meeting on February 6, 1960; the meeting at which he had tried to write down the names of the disqualified branches, reluctantly and rapidly read out by Mr McLennan, and at which Mr Hadley had unsuccessfully asked for a copy of 'Standing Orders'. Some more news about this meeting was given now by Mr Colin Walker, recently Secretary of the Greenock Branch—and 'Executive Councillor for Scotland'. Mr Walker, after thirty-one years' membership of the ETU, had now resigned from it and obtained employment outside the electrical industry. (There was some conflict of evidence as to his reasons for resigning. He told Mr Gardiner that 'the Party in power had decided I was going just as far as they intended to allow me'—presumably in trade union office. Later he agreed that, in his letter of resignation, he regretted leaving the Union, and that he left to change his field of employment.) His branch balloted on December 18, 1959, and the very same evening he had to leave Greenock for London to attend an Executive Council meeting. He got back to Scotland on Sunday the 20th, collected the scrutineers' ballot returns, and posted them to Head Office on Monday the 21st. It wasn't until he went down to London again for the Executive Council meeting on February 6, 1960, that he heard about the branch's disqualification for 'late posting'—and he heard it then because Greenock was one of the few names read out by Mr McLennan in response to the importunity of Mr Chapple. His branch disputed the late posting, but to no avail.

The Court then heard a succession of witnesses about alteration in the ETU Rules (the Registrar of Friendly Societies was involved here), and the delays to the Christmas mail (this from GPO witnesses, who had never heard of delays amounting to as much as two weeks, though Mr Lawson reminded them that letters sometimes got delivered after twenty years).

The Kirkcaldy Branch in 1959 had voted Haxell 113, Byrne 94; and, in spite of irregularities at its ballot, it had not been disqualified. Mr James Irving, Secretary of the Falkirk Branch (who was President of the local Labour Party) went to the Kirkcaldy quarterly meeting as a 'visitor', and noticed that unused ballot papers were lying about and that members were being allowed to deposit ballot papers on the Treasurer's table *before* the scrutineers were elected. There were other irregularities, too. He pointed them out to the Branch Secretary, Mr Bogie. A correspondence with Mr McLennan ensued, in which the Branch Secretary repudiated or explained away all the criticisms. He was never asked to attend any enquiry about the conduct of the ballot, and he was 'completely astounded' when Head Office told him, in effect, that it was no business of his.

'Then,' said Mr Sofer, 'Mr Henderson, please . . . My Lord, I'm afraid I am back to substituted envelopes again.' And from the story of Mr Frank Henderson, Secretary of the Bury Branch

(Byrne 31, Haxell 4), the Judge was to find that the substitution of envelopes was conclusively proved. Mr Henderson's envelope was postmarked January 2, 1960; and this, although he had posted it himself 'in the pillar-box opposite Bury General Hospital' at seven-thirty a.m. on December 24, would have meant that he allowed nine days to go by without posting it. He agreed with Mr Lawson that his branch had at least twice previously been warned for late posting—in 1953, when the vote was nevertheless allowed, and in 1958, when it was rejected. But he would have known it was too late to post on January 2.

'If you had yourself posted it then,' said the Judge, 'you could hardly have forgotten doing it, could you?'

'No, I could not,' answered Mr Henderson firmly.

Mr George Fazakerly, of the Widnes Branch (Byrne 100, Haxell 11), posted his ballot return at seven-fifty on the morning after the meeting—December 19. It was postmarked January 2, and the branch was invalidated for late posting (having, as it happened, been warned for late posting before). It was thus quite certain to be disqualified next time its returns purported to be late.

Mr Frank Toner, a Scot, was Secretary of the London Station Engineers No. 4 Branch (LSE 4). It had voted Byrne 45, Haxell 11. He posted his returns at twelve noon on December 20 in Tillers Lane, Willesden, the meeting having been held on the 18th. He went to Scotland for Christmas, and came back on the 30th. The envelope that purported to be his was postmarked December 31 ('an unlikely time,' observed the Judge later, 'for a Scotsman to have posted Union papers'). The vote was rejected by Head Office. The branch had previously been warned for late posting (March 1958) and this time it was disqualified.

Mr Clifford Brodie ('a solid, firm character of sixty,' said the Judge—'I believed him'), of the Twickenham Branch (Byrne 32, Haxell 5), had posted his returns on December 27 at the Twickenham GPO, the meeting having taken place on the 23rd. 'The reason for the delay was that the Christmas mail was heavy, and I decided to hold it back till the twenty-seventh.' The envelope in which it purported to have arrived at Head Office was postmarked 'January 1, Richmond and Twickenham'. The branch, which had had a previous warning (before Mr Brodie's time) was disqualified—and decided that it was not worth while to argue about it. But in cross-examination it emerged that Mr Brodie, who worked at London Airport, was weil informed about local postmarks.

'London Airport, of course,' said Mr Lawson, 'is in the Uxbridge postal area, is it not?'—'No, it's in the Hounslow postal area.'

'*Is* it?'—'Yes.'

The Judge cleared this up.

'It wouldn't produce a Richmond and Twickenham stamp in any case,' he observed. 'If you posted something at the Airport, you wouldn't get a Richmond and Twickenham stamp?'—'No,' said Mr Brodie. 'Far from it . . . You'd get a Hounslow registration on it.'

'So I should have thought.'

The next witness, announced Mr Sofer, was 'an arrival-before-departure one'. It was Mr Edgar Dew, of Hythe, Southampton (Byrne 18, Haxell 5); and Mr Gerald Gardiner, in his opening speech, had referred to the Woolston, Hythe and Southampton Central branches as instances of 'arrival before departure', or of votes coming in the post before the ballot papers had even gone out. Mr Dew told Mr Sofer that just before the December 1959 election (Byrne *v.* Haxell), i.e., on December 13, a Sunday, he and his wife addressed all the ballot paper envelopes for those members entitled to vote, and put them in a cupboard with the ballot papers —which had been received from the printers three or four weeks earlier, to the exact number ordered. The next day, Monday, December 14, he went to work at the Esso Petroleum Company. When he came home at lunch-time (twelve-fifteen p.m.) he had a shock.

'I put the key in the door,' he said, 'and on the mat facing me were six ballot papers returned through the post'.

They were sealed envelopes postmarked Southampton. He picked them up and put them in the cupboard 'with the rest of the envelopes that were there ready to send to members'. Then he rang up the Area Organiser, Mr Phillips.

'He refused to have anything to do with it and said: "You must get in touch with the Executive Council right away." '

The next day, Tuesday the 15th, he told his senior shop steward at Esso, who was also Treasurer of the branch; and a special branch committee meeting was arranged for that night. At the meeting, with only four members present, the ballot papers from Mr Dew's cupboard were checked with the list of qualified voters. *They were still intact.*

'Was anything done,' asked Mr Sofer, 'to find out for whom the votes in those envelopes' (i.e., the six envelopes that had come in too soon) 'had been cast?'—'Yes, we got them up against a very large electric lamp, about a hundred and fifty watts—it's quite easy to discern through that type of envelope.'

'And for whom had the votes been cast?'—'Mr Haxell.'

It was arranged that Mr Dew should send the six suspected envelopes to Head Office by 'express delivery'. There was an investigation, this time by Mr George Scott from Head Office. Mr Scott, exonerating Mr Dew from all suspicion, found that the branch committee held the view that 'actions by individuals of this nature were responsible for creating antagonism against the Executive Council'.

'That's not a correct statement about the branch committee,' said Mr Dew. 'I would say that was the opinion of *one* member of the branch committee.' But, he said, the committee *did* express the view that in the light of what had happened the whole ballot should 'be declared null and void'.

'At this meeting,' said Mr Sofer, 'was any suggestion made by Mr Scott as to whether he had any idea as to where these six ballot papers might have come from?'—'No,' said Mr Dew, 'I don't think he did comment.'

Finally the branch vote was disqualified for late posting.

'It was suggested,' said Mr Lawson in cross-examination, 'that some unknown person, who had an intimate knowledge of the branch ballot procedure and administration, was a possible source of responsibility?'—'Yes.'

'And the quarter to look to were people who were trying to create trouble against the Executive Council?'—'That,' said Mr Dew, 'was the expression of one individual'.

'Did you have knowledge of a group, comprising members of branches in Southampton, who were active in campaigning against the Executive Council?'—'No, sir, definitely not.'

There were many mentions, during the trial, of some such group or body, but all the witnesses denied knowledge of it (almost as though it would be a shameful thing to acknowledge). Such a body came into the open after the trial, and was countered by a 'Campaign for the Defence of the Policy of the Union' (which still, unabashed, supported the Communist leadership).

There then emerged the story of the Preston Branch election, in which the result Byrne 52, Haxell 101, mysteriously became Byrne 52, Haxell 191.

Mr Francis Clarkson, of the Preston Branch Committee, was Chairman of the Preston meeting on December 30, 1959, at which this result (52-101) was read out. He signed the minutes of the previous meeting, including those figures, as correct. Six months later, when the analysis of voting was published in the Executive Council's minutes, a member (Mr Tom Breakell) asked that the Head Office minutes be compared with what was read out at the December meeting. The branch Secretary, Mr Fraser, replied that the Executive Council's minute of the Preston result was 'F. L. Haxell 191, Mr Byrne 52'.

'This was immediately challenged by the branch Chairman, in a not very audible voice,' said Mr Clarkson, 'but he no doubt did challenge the figure, and I immediately challenged on top of that, saying, "That figure is incorrect". Mr Fraser said, "It can't be incorrect—it's here in writing. *It's also in the minute book as 191*".'

'Are you clear,' said Mr Gardiner, 'that it was 101 when you signed the minutes immediately after the quarterly meeting?'

But Mr Clarkson very honestly said that he had not *seen* the figure—he didn't actually read the minutes, though he remembered clearly enough what he had heard read out. A meeting of the branch committee discussed the discrepancy, decided that a mistake had been made, and wrote to Head Office saying that the correct vote was 101-52.

No one at the branch ever heard of a reply to that letter; and Mr Clarkson remembered no previous occasion on which a candidate had polled more than a hundred votes.

Nevertheless, said Mr Clarkson under cross-examination, the branch committee at the end of the meeting unanimously passed a vote of confidence in the Secretary—who at the time of the trial was still in office—though this may have been on the assumption that he had made a genuine mistake. The evidence of several further witnesses who had been present at the meeting reduced the likelihood that mistake was the explanation.

The story of disqualified branch votes was then continued by Mr John Will, of London Station Engineers No. 2 (LSE 2), who had voted Byrne 32, Haxell 7. Only five members of his branch had attended the meeting, only two of those being eligible to be scrutineers because the other three were all branch officials; so they were thus appointed, not 'elected'. There were 'visitors' at the meeting whom Mr Will obviously thought to be 'spies' from the Haxell faction on the look-out for irregularities. Sure enough, his branch was disqualified on 'a complaint relating to an alleged breach of rule . . . there was no election of scrutineers'.

'It is quite obvious where this complaint has come from,' wrote Mr Will to Head Office, 'but it has taken five weeks to work out how to do it. If ballot had gone the other way nothing would have been said.' He did not know (he told Mr Lawson) that to solve his problem about scrutineers he could have sent all the ballot papers to Head Office to be counted.

'One might piously pray for aid for these branch secretaries,' said Mr Justice Winn, 'who have to try to understand these Rules. The more complex they become, the less time these men can put into productive work, and the greater the probability that politicians rather than workmen will be running the branches of the unions. There are political animals and non-political animals. It is only the political animal by congenital predisposition who is likely to have the time, energy, or application to understand these Rules.'

Mr Lawson suggested that the solution to this was to do away with elections altogether, and appoint the 'permanent people'. To the witness he said:

'This is right, Mr Will, is it not, that you're in a pretty well continuous state of election?'—'Near enough, I should think,' said Mr Will.

'There are often several elections every quarter?'—'Either nominations or elections every quarter.'

Then the Southampton story was resumed, the 'arrival before departure' mystery. Mr Eric Storrer, Secretary of Southampton Central, received his branch's ballot papers about three weeks before the meeting, found that he had been sent the exact number he indented for, and posted them off to members at ten-thirty on the morning of Saturday, December 12, 1959. When he got home from work to have his dinner at twelve-ten on Monday the 14th, five ballot papers had already arrived by post—four of them post-marked 6.45 on the 13th, and one postmarked on the 12th. ('The boys are getting their envelopes in quick this time,' remarked his wife.) The story got into the national Press, and Mr George Scott was sent down from Head Office to investigate.

He asked at the post office and was told that it was impossible for any of his envelopes to have been *delivered* on Saturday, the 12th; the only delivery on Saturdays was before he did his posting. None of his envelopes would be *delivered* before Monday, the 14th. Mr Storrer didn't know on that Monday about the exactly similar mystery at Woolston and Hythe branches, but when he heard about them (on Wednesday the 16th) he seems to have been both excited and relieved: excited that something very unusual was afoot and relieved that he had not made some mistake himself.

He had a long telephone talk (tape-recorded without his know-ledge) with Mr Haxell, who told him it was very worrying, that he must carefully preserve the four envelopes and on no account speak to the Press (who were, said Mr Storrer, on his doorstep every day). Then Mr George Scott came from Head Office to in-vestigate. The result was complete exoneration of the Secretary and final admission of the branch votes as valid (Byrne 70, Haxell 24).

In the case of Belfast Central (Haxell 127, Byrne 41) Mr James Fulton, the branch Secretary, said that an unprecedentedly high postal vote—ninety, as compared with the normal five to twenty-five—made him suspicious, though the main ground of suspicion was that this heavy postal vote supported a candidate who had opposed the branch nomination. And he found that forty-eight of them bore an identical postmark and date-stamp. No one who had previously opposed Mr Byrne had ever got more than thirty-two votes. The evidence of the next nine witnesses followed the now familiar pattern of disqualification and futile protest: they represented Long Eaton (Byrne 49, Haxell 20), Salisbury (Byrne 41, Haxell 33), Yate, near Bristol (Byrne 47, Haxell 36), Liverpool East (Byrne 34, Haxell 17), Liverpool Instrument Makers (Byrne 48, Haxell 30), Birmingham Traction (Byrne 31, Haxell 2), Prescot

(Byrne 29, Haxell 18), Blackburn (Byrne 49, Haxell 7), and Luton (Byrne 103, Haxell 21).

And then came Mr Lewis Britz, a member of the Finchley Branch, who happened to have been present at the quarterly meeting of the Redcar Branch on December 18, 1959, when the Byrne-Haxell ballot was taking place (Haxell 228, Byrne 42). He found many irregularities in the procedure, and reported the fact to Head Office. All his allegations were declared unfounded, though he saw none of the correspondence or reports that followed his complaint. His cross-examination was interesting:

'This wasn't the only meeting you attended,' Mr Lawson suggested, 'at December quarter, 1959, which was not your own branch meeting, was it?'—'No,' said Mr Britz. 'There were several.'

'Were you going round with a Mr Young visiting other people's meetings?'—'I went to several meetings with Mr Young, yes.' (Mr Young was the Chairman of the Finchley Branch.)

'Was that a matter of pure curiosity or was it some kind of idea that you would—'

'You see,' interrupted the witness, 'we've had the Communist "circus" at our branch on quarter night on several occasions, and we were taking a leaf out of their book. It was their common practice to send groups round to check up on branches' procedure; and we thought that since *they* appeared to be able to do it under the Rules of the Union, there was no reason for other people not to do it also.'

Mr Edward Nash, another ETU member, told the Court that he was once a 'national scrutineer' and usefully described the Head Office procedure at an election. 'Could you tell me,' Mr Gardiner asked him, 'how many days it took you to open the ballot envelopes and count the votes?'—'That isn't the procedure,' replied Mr Nash, the scrutineer. 'It is, in fact, an accountancy procedure. One doesn't have envelopes—one doesn't see them. The scrutiny proper takes place at the branch. All that happens at Headquarters is just a collation of figures. You see nothing but the branch scrutineers' returns and the actual collated figures, which are handed to you in paper-backed covers. It's your duty to check those collations with the figures on the branch scrutineers' returns.'

'So *you* were not in a position' (since he saw no envelopes) 'to
check whether or not anybody had sent in their return too late?'

Mr Nash agreed.

5   Cobbett's 'Rural Rides' (The Postal Tour)

The thirteenth day's evidence was remarkable for the story told
by Mr William Cobbett, a private enquiry agent whose services had
been retained by Mr Hooberman, the Plaintiffs' solicitor. Mr Cobbett's contribution to the building-up of this monumental case had
been to go round England with an AA route map on a series of
long car journeys and put into practice a plausible theory about
the postmarks on the 'substituted envelopes'. The theory was that
he was thus doing what someone else had done at the time of the
December 1959 Byrne-Haxell election.

He started, he said, from Croydon (where he lived) on January
18, 1960, and drove first to Peterborough. He went straight to
Peterborough's GPO and studied the times of the postal collections
and deliveries. It was then two-fifteen p.m., he told Mr Sofer.

'I found that there was a collection at four p.m., and as I didn't
want a time-stamp until five-fifteen, I realised I would have to wait.
So I had lunch and a look round until four-five, when I posted No.
1.' (No. 1 was an envelope addressed to Mr Hooberman.)

'From where did you get your information as to what time-
stamp you were supposed to get?'—'Is that relevant?' interposed
the Judge. 'And if it is, it's surely hearsay.'

The witness said that on his list of towns to be visited the time
'four-five p.m.' was written against Peterborough, but nothing
came out in Court as to the origin of that instruction.

He then went to Boston, found the GPO and saw that he was
in time to post a letter for the five-thirty collection. He checked this
with the post office counter clerk, posted his envelope, and hurried
on to Spilsby, getting there at six-five p.m. There he posted an
envelope at six-forty to cover the seven o'clock collection—'having
verified with the counter clerk'.

'Well,' said Mr Lawson, getting up, 'I don't know about these
verifications with the counter clerks.' (No counter clerks were
being called as witnesses to say what they had said to Mr Cobbett,

the private enquiry agent. He was giving hearsay evidence about what they had told him.)

So Mr Sofer handed Mr Cobbett the bundle of envelopes, and from those he read out the times of posting. He then told how he had gone on from Spilsby to Brigg (seven forty-five post), and Doncaster (eight forty-five), where he stayed the night.

'I should think you were ready for some sleep,' said the Judge. 'You had already done some two hundred and thirty miles. Did you find it tiring?'—'No, my Lord.'

'What car were you driving?'—'A Ford Prefect on that day.'

The next morning he left at eight o'clock for Barnsley and caught the ten-fifteen post. Then to Huddersfield (10.45), Whitby (2.45), Billingham (3.30), Bishop Auckland (5 p.m.), Seaham Harbour (6.15), and Stanley (6.30)—and he stayed the night in Sunderland. Next morning, on to North Shields by eleven-thirty, and posted his envelope at twelve thirty-five for the three p.m. collection. On then to Galashiels, where he spent the night of the 20th, posting his letter at five-past nine the next morning for the ten-thirty collection on the 21st. Thence to Edinburgh (10.30 also), Cambuslang (1.30), and Ayr (2 p.m.)—and that was the end of his 'first tour'.

The second one started from Croydon again, on February 1, and the car this time was a Ford Consul. Armed again with a typed list of towns and the times of collections he was to catch, he went first to Reading (11.15 post), and thence to Eastleigh (1.30).

'Did anything untoward happen there?' Mr Sofer asked him.

'Yes, there was almost a cloudburst and it considerably slowed me up—my average speed went down to something around fifteen to twenty miles an hour.'

He went on to Yeovil (2.45), Bideford (7 p.m.), and Bristol (9.30), where he spent the night of February 1. On he went in the morning to Pontypool (1.45 p.m.), Rogerstone (5.15, postmarked Newport), and then spent the night at Newport. Next day, Abertillery (10 a.m.), Cwmbran (1.30), back to Swindon (2.45 or 2.15), and lastly Wallingford (4.15).

On his third journey, on March 17, he went from Croydon to Silloth, Cumberland, a drive of 345 miles, and posted an envelope at seven-fifteen that evening to catch the first post on the 18th. He got to Penrith at eight-thirty p.m., missed the last collection, but posted his letter and spent the night there. By ten the next morning (the 18th), he was in Kendal and caught the ten forty-five post, then Blackburn (1.15 p.m.).

'That's a remarkably good run, is it not?' said the Judge. 'You went in a maximum of seventy minutes fifty-two miles, and some of us know the country between Kendal and Blackburn.'—'I agree I had to move, in parts, my Lord.'

'I'm not sure that the whole enquiry was not contrary to public policy,' said the Judge. 'You covered a good deal of ground at high speed, didn't you?'—'I did, my lord.' He later admitted that he did the thirty-two miles from Widnes to Bury, passing through Bolton—'a whole maze of towns, built up the whole of the way'— in fifty-five minutes.

On the Saturday, Blackburn to Gilmos (Liverpool), where he could catch nothing earlier than the Sunday collection (March 19), 4.15 p.m. On to Widnes, 4.30 p.m., and then Bury, 4.30 again.

He was then cross-examined. Having asked him why he took certain indirect routes from one town to another, Mr Lawson said:

'What I am putting to you is this, that there were places which were very near your route, or towns through which you actually went, where there were very heavy votes in favour of Byrne against Haxell?'—'That I wouldn't know,' said Mr Cobbett.

'But you didn't have any instructions to post any envelopes there?'—'No.'

(The Plaintiffs' solicitors had in fact made a selection of the disqualified towns, rather than any attempt to include the whole of them in Mr Cobbett's rural rides.)

At the end of Mr Cobbett's story, Mr Gerald Gardiner called his ninety-second witness—Mr John Thomas Byrne, the principal Plaintiff in this action.

6   Mr Byrne in the Witness-Box

Mr John Byrne, of McGregor Street, Clydebank, became a member of the ETU in 1927 and by 1932 he was Secretary of the District Committee, which was composed of one representative from each of the branches on the Clyde; and the following year he Clydebank Branch. In 1935 his branch elected him to the Clyde became secretary of that. In 1941 and 1942 he was in the Ministry of Labour, helping with labour relations in the electrical industry, and then he was elected Area Official of the ETU for the West of Scotland—a whole-time paid job. In 1947 he stood for election as General Secretary of the ETU.

'Is this your election address?' asked Mr Gardiner, handing him a photostat copy of his 1947 appeal to the ETU electors.

Mr Lawson objected. This was something new, he said. 'I wonder whether it has any relevance to any issue?'

Mr Gardiner urged, successfully, that the witness was entitled to explain how he became known to the membership as a man who believed that the Communist influence in the Union was excessive and harmful. 'I think you were defeated in that election?' he asked Mr Byrne.

Mr Byrne said he was. He got about 11,000 votes out of 42,000. The following year he stood for Assistant General Secretary, against Mr Haxell and Mr J. Lowdon, of Belfast. Mr Byrne got 27,000 and Mr Haxell 25,000, but the third candidate got just enough to keep Mr Byrne out. In 1950 he stood for President against Mr Foulkes. In December 1959, as was now well known, he stood for General Secretary against Mr Haxell; and he sent out his election address to the electors in the usual way. Mr Gardiner asked him:

'Did you then receive this letter from Mr McLennan—'

Mr Lawson rose to object for the fifth time since Mr Byrne had gone into the witness-box. 'Is this directed to any particular pleaded issue, my Lord?'

'Mr Lawson,' said the Judge rather impatiently, 'you seem to object rather in advance. Do help me not to get cross . . . The whole of the case is really about this. Am I not entitled to follow what he was campaigning for and how he was presenting his candidature to the members?'

The evidence proceeded. 'This is Mr McLennan's letter to you dated October the 21st, 1959: "Your election address has received the attention of the election address sub-committee of the Executive Council, and they have decided that the following wording should be deleted as it does not comply with the provisions of Rule 21, Clause 30:

A perusal of the Executive Council minutes shows that the returns from ballot voting have fallen off, and that with almost all ballots there is a surfeit of complaints about the conduct of the ballot. This is not a happy state of affairs and I would advocate the scrapping of the present system, and its replacement by a postal ballot where each member entitled to vote would receive a stamped return-form which would be subject to scrutiny by independent scrutineers.

(Election to office in the ETU, therefore, was not like election to Parliament or the local council. You could only tell the electors what the present office-holders would allow you to tell them.)

Mr Byrne agreed that his own words were disallowed, his election address being more or less written for him (by those who didn't want him elected).

'Now, in December 1959, having stood for election as General Secretary, did you hear that Mr Haxell had been said to have been elected by about a thousand votes?' (i.e., a majority of a thousand).

'Yes,' said Mr Byrne.

'And that over a hundred branches had been disqualified?'—'I heard first that Haxell had been elected. I wasn't really very surprised, until I heard the later news that had come filtering through, and that was that a hundred branches had been disqualified. I certainly began to marvel *then*, and I've been marvelling ever since.'

'Did you see and hear Mr Foulkes in the television programme "Panorama" in February?'—'I did, to my deep disgust.'

This brought a rebuke from the Judge.

'Before you go on, Mr Byrne,' he said, 'you heard me say fairly sharply the other day that I wasn't going to allow witnesses to ventilate their own spite and indulge their own feelings of malice against any persons in this Court, and I will have you observe what I said then. If you do not pay attention to my ruling, then I shall take action about it. Do you understand?'

'I'm very clear on it, my Lord. I'm sorry.'

In the past two years, went on Mr Byrne, he had got to know two other opponents of Communist influence in the Union—Mr Chapple and Mr Cannon. In 1959 they introduced him to Mr Hooberman, of Messrs Lawford & Co, solicitors, and they decided to issue the writs that had led to this trial. The correspondence that led to this step merits one or two quotations.

Byrne to Haxell, March 25, 1960:

I write you concerning the result of the recent election, particularly in the light of the many statements that have appeared in the Press and in the various circulars being issued to branches by Head Office. I have attempted to obtain information through my branch in relation to the names of the branches disqualified, but the request of the branch to Head Office was rejected and we were advised to await the publication of the Executive Council minutes. I consider that as an interested party I should have access to that information, but while this is being denied me there is apparently no restriction on the presentation of one side of the case by means of Press articles and by circulars to branches. The latest circular (*The Poison Pen*) attempts to perpetrate the misrepresentation that the figure of a hundred disqualifications is not unduly high, and is intended to persuade the members of the Union that everything in the recent election was normal.

You make no reference to the alteration to Rules which took place in 1952, so that what is being concealed is that when the 1952 Rules came into operation, extending the time limit for receipt of ballot returns from seventy-two hours to 'the first post on the fifth day', a reform for which credit was allocated to 'the present leadership' in your article of February 24 in the *Daily Herald*, the immediate drop in the number of disqualifications was astounding.

Mr Byrne's letter ended with the threat that if the alleged misrepresentation were not withdrawn, he would feel free, notwithstanding the Rules, to write to the Press and to members of the ETU.

Mr Haxell's reply on April 13 was very long, and amounted to a total refutation of these complaints. The *Daily Herald* article, it said, was an interview—answers to questions—and the answers were designed to expose 'the lies of the Press, the "rebels", and the anonymous documents being circulated among members'. (Mr Byrne had admitted sending anonymous circulars and having talked to a representative of the *Daily Telegraph*.)

Your advice to me in the form of an ultimatum [Mr Haxell's letter went on] is at least a little premature, although I must point out that as a member of the Union you voluntarily accepted the restraint of the Rules, and you know that members cannot contract out of that obligation and still remain members.

The letter ended by reminding Mr Byrne that he had made 'certain statements' to the newspapers about the recent election. 'I had felt,' wrote Mr Haxell kindly, 'that in the particular circumstances you were no doubt under extreme pressure to make a statement . . . However, in view of the implication of your letter, I must advise you that any statements you make will receive consideration under the Rules of the Union.'

When these letters had been put to Mr Byrne, Mr Gardiner sat down and Mr Lawson rose to cross-examine. The first thing Mr Lawson wanted was a copy of a document compiled by Mr Byrne —a list of the ETU branches disqualified over the previous ten years. This showed that the quarterly disqualifications in 1950 were as high as 15, 67, 100 and 62, that in 1951 they were 84, 48, 74, and 14, and in 1952 they were 68, 67, 68 and 82. Then came the change of Rule, extending the time for posting results of ballots. In 1953 the figures were 1, 12, 9 and 5, in 1954 they were 8, 8, 7 and 7; and so it went on—in 1958 they were 9, 17 and 9.

'When did you actually do this little piece of work, Mr Byrne?' Mr Lawson asked him.—'In February and March 1960.'

Mr Lawson remarked that at each of the elections named in it the only anti-Communist candidate was Mr Byrne himself.

'I was the only one who would stand,' said Mr Byrne.

'You saw the various unofficial circulars which were going around, I take it, attacking the leadership?'—'Yes.'

'You probably agree with me that they did constitute very violent and vicious attacks?'—'Well, the leadership would certainly think that, yes.'

'You wouldn't suggest that the leadership were not justified in taking a very poor view of these circulars?'—'Let me put it to *you*,' said Mr Byrne, with slow Scottish emphasis. 'Criticism has been virtually stifled in the organisation since the time I spoke about it in 1946, and in these circumstances it isn't surprising that resort has got to be taken to unofficial methods. It's their own fault.'

'But this Union had an annual Policy Conference. That was a change, was it not, which had been introduced under the present leadership?'—'It was a change, but I hesitate to say it was a conference. It was a parade of Communist ideas, and the Communist attitude to, shall we say, political matters. I think that was more important than any of the industrial matters that were put on the agenda.'

'Nobody has suggested that in the negotiations which the General President, the General Secretary, and the Assistant General Secretary have undertaken with employers or Government Departments, they have not stood for the benefit of the membership?'—'I give credit where it is due. They've done certain things, they've negotiated freely in many cases. What I do object to is that they are not freely elected.'

The Judge asked a question about the effect on Mr Byrne's salary and pension of being elected General Secretary; and Mr Byrne's evidence, and with it the whole of the evidence for the Plaintiffs, was thus concluded. Mr Byrne went back to his seat behind Mr Gerald Gardiner and resumed his stoical contemplation of the proceedings.

III THE DEFENDANTS' ANSWER

1 Mr Lawson Opens the Defence

MR NEIL LAWSON, QC, in the speech with which he began the Defendants' answer to all these allegations, made it clear from the outset that there had been no kind of attack on any of them 'in respect of their work for the Union'. In particular, Mr Foulkes, Mr Haxell, and Mr McLennan had built up the ETU to a position of great influence in their trade.

'What your Lordship is concerned with is a struggle for power between conflicting groups, and whether unlawful methods have in fact been used. There is all the difference between misunderstandings of the Rules, muddle and inefficiency, lack of co-ordination in decisions, on the one hand, and fraudulent conspiracy on the other.' Mr Lawson saw the Plaintiffs' attack as coming under two heads—the alleged Communist conspiracy to control the ETU, and the faking of ballots.

There were no formal Communist Party 'committees' of the kind alleged. Only irregular meetings 'concerned with the general work of the Communist Party in the trade union movement'.

As to the allegedly fraudulent alteration of the Rules—'Your Lordship,' said Mr Lawson, 'sees the way in which it is put: "The Defendant Haxell falsely and fraudulently filed Rules purporting to show by Rule 39(6)(j) that the said right of appeal had been abrogated by the Rules Revision Conference"; and that then, having filed the Rules with the Registrar of Friendly Societies, he printed and published them containing this abrogation of branch rights, and used them to prevent appeals against the acceptance by the Executive Council of scrutineers' reports. But "if the Executive Council disqualified a branch under Rule 20 of the 1954 Rules, that would be recorded in the minutes" (and there could be an appeal against it); whereas "if it was a decision made in the control and conduct of an election, then that was not the subject of an appeal". That,' said Mr Lawson, 'was the view that was taken'.

The Judge interrupted him. 'I can understand almost any view being taken of these Rules,' he said.

'Yes, my Lord. This is an illustration of the clear and distinct line between things which are done fraudulently, and a mistaken view as to the construction of the Rules, which I think we are all agreed are of extraordinary complication.'

'Yes,' said his Lordship, and he seemed to be agreeing only about the complexity of the Rules.

And then, went on Mr Lawson, there was the allegation that the accepting of branch returns was done 'capriciously' (Mr Lawson's word and a neatly chosen one). 'The misfortune for certain of the Defendants is that it has received a very, very sinister interpretation.'

But on the subject of 'warnings' for errant branches, the Judge quoted from the documents before him that 'the practice is that any prior breach *exhausts* the right of a branch to be excused and warned'. His Lordship thought that the word 'exhausts' meant that such a branch was disqualified for ever.

'I respectfully agree, my Lord, as a mere matter of English. I feel that what it meant—'

'You can't *tell* me what it means,' the Judge reminded Mr Lawson.

Mr Lawson replied that there was no case in which a branch had been held to be disqualified without committing *some* breach in the election then current. He then dealt with individual instances of late posting, and of improperly constituted branch meetings; and came to the allegations of 'false or trumpery charges of breaches of rule against prominent non-Communist members of the Union' (e.g., Mr Chapple) 'in order to discredit them or prevent criticism'. He submitted that Mr Chapple's communication of ETU affairs to the Press was not a thing of a 'trumpery' character.

'I'm not sure whether it's "trumpery" or "trumped",' said the Judge—'a reference to the unexpected trump up the sleeve. You remember what Disraeli said to Gladstone about a trump up the sleeve. Perhaps you don't.'*

* Neither, really, did his Lordship. It was Henry Labouchère who said that he didn't object to Gladstone's always having the ace of trumps up his sleeve, but only to his pretence that Almighty God had put it there.

'It isn't said to be a trumped-up charge, but a trumpery charge.'

'Yes,' said the Judge, 'I suppose that's right'.

Mr Lawson then went on to concede that, for a variety of reasons, the Byrne-Haxell election of 1959 was not a valid election. But not all the blame for this lay on the Defendants. 'You are saying,' the Judge prompted him, ' "I concede that the votes for Haxell were not validly returned by the scrutineers, but I say that that equally applies against Byrne"?'

'Yes,' said Mr Lawson.

'So it is really a counter-claim to have the election declared void by the Court,' the Judge went on, adding later that the Plaintiffs wanted him, on the contrary, to make a declaration that Byrne was validly elected.

Among the specific branch elections to which Mr Lawson referred in his speech were the three at Southampton—Hythe, Woolston, and Southampton Central. 'Your Lordship has heard the three branch secretaries,' he said, 'and I feel that you will have no hesitation in taking the view that none of those gentlemen were implicated in any improper practices in relation to those ballot papers.'

'I can say at once,' his Lordship remarked, 'that it will take an enormous amount of evidence to convince me to the contrary. I think all three of them were entirely free from blame. I am glad to find that is common ground. Those three were very good types.'

Then Mr Lawson made it plain that his witnesses were going to attribute the high 'postal voting' at certain branches to the 'glare of publicity' and the public excitement about the ETU elections. He mentioned most of the criticised branches separately, particularly those that had received extra ballot papers; but he got in a rather telling dig about one that had not come in for any criticism. 'No complaint, oddly enough,' he said, 'is made in respect of Bolton Supervisory, who were issued almost forty-six additional ballot papers at about the same time. Perhaps the reason why no complaint is made of that is that the Bolton Branch concerned voted for Mr Byrne. But that is something which, in my respectful submission, is not in pattern with what is alleged as a conspiracy.'

The Judge showed himself to be very puzzled about the

'estimated numbers' of required ballot papers given to Mr Norman
Swift, the printer. Why did they have to be mere estimates? By
waiting a few days longer, Head Office (Mr Humphrey and Mr
Oliver, in particular) would have known *exactly* what numbers each
branch needed.

'But your Lordship will remember,' said Mr Lawson, 'that Mr
Swift wanted to get on with the job, and therefore the estimate idea
was hit upon . . . Here is the problem: these people are by trade
and vocation electricians. They have probably all of them served
apprenticeships and become qualified electricians. They really
know nothing at all about accountancy or office management, and
I hope I'm not being offensive, but your Lordship may think they
sort of try to muddle along. Obviously if one got an efficiency
expert examining the way in which this administration is conducted,
the results might be very startlingly different.'

'And save a lot of money.'

'Indeed, yes. Well, there it is, my Lord. Mr Oliver was sent up
to Manchester' (i.e., to the printers) 'to watch over the dispatch. He
stayed in Manchester for a fortnight, and watched over the
dispatch—'

'I don't want to appear critical,' Mr Justice Winn interposed,
'but all that expense could have been saved if the printer had had
the actual September membership returns and been told to send
them out in those numbers. It would have saved Mr Oliver's fare
to Manchester, the hotel expenses, and everything else.'

'I respectfully agree,' was all that Mr Lawson could possibly say
to that.

But finally, on the question of the 'itineraries', the three car
journeys described on page 94 as Cobbett's 'Rural Rides', Mr
Lawson may well have sowed a doubt in the Judge's mind; or if
the doubt was already there, he watered it. 'If one wanted to produce the result of favouring Haxell against Byrne,' he said, 'by
making such a journey and posting such envelopes, one could have
saved oneself an enormous amount of trouble by going to far
fewer places, and by choosing places where the differential was
very much greater. In other words, an intinerary which involved
somebody fooling around with envelopes which produced a differential of under twenty is rather a stupid sort of itinerary, when by

going to one place on the same route you could produce a differential of something like a hundred and fifty or two hundred. In
other words, it's a little too elaborate. It's rather like the thirteenth
stroke of the clock: that is to say, it casts a certain amount of
doubt on the validity of what has gone before. The itinerary is
such an elaborate and dangerous procedure that it is really incredible that any of the Defendants would have undertaken it . . .
I have indicated to your Lordship the lines upon which my
evidence will be directed, and with the assistance of my learned
friend I will now call the Defendants before you.'

Before beginning with the Defence, the Judge wanted to clear up
the possible liability of the ETU itself to pay damages. In the
struggle of the trade unions towards full legal existence, they had
unavoidably—and properly—acquired liabilities as well as rights.
In 1901, in the case of *Taff Vale Railway Company against the
Amalgamated Society of Railway Servants*, a trade union had for
the first time been held (by the House of Lords) liable to be 'sued
in tort'*; and the removal of that danger by the Trade Disputes
Act of 1906 was one of the fulfilled promises of the Liberal Government that had then swept the country at the polls.

'The last Defendant in this case,' said Mr Justice Winn to Mr
Lawson, 'is the Electrical Trades Union. Have you any observation to make about that? It must be manifest, mustn't it, that no
relief in the form of damages can be granted against the trade
unions?'

Mr Lawson agreed. 'My learned friend Mr Gardiner has said
nothing about it, and I'm not quite sure whether he is suggesting
that the Defendant union should pay Mr Byrne damages if he is
entitled to any.'

'I don't want to leave the matter tacitly aside for too long,' the
Judge explained. He thought that the Union must be a Defendant
because of the character of the 'relief' being sought by the Plaintiffs. 'If it were not,' he said, 'there might be some duty on the
Court to see that Union funds were not being expended
unnecessarily'.

---

* i.e., sued for damages in a civil court.

2   Mr Haxell in the Witness-Box

It was the fourteenth day of the evidence and the twenty-second of the trial. Mr Lawson began by having Mr Joseph Thomas re-called—the Secretary of Luton Supply Branch. On the seventh day (see page 66) Mr Thomas had left the witness-box with his tale not fully told: Mr Batchelor, who was said to have suggested to him that there might be some way of getting hold of extra ballot papers and a Luton Branch stamp, was at that time indisposed and unable to instruct the Defendants' lawyers about this unexpected turn of the story.

'Mr Thomas, you know, do you not, that the rubber stamps provided for the branch secretary to use are supplied by Head Office?'—'I assume that to be correct.'

'Mr Batchelor was at that time a national officer? There is no difficulty in anybody at Head Office getting hold of a branch stamp?'—'No, but each branch stamp is different.'

Mr Lawson observed that Mr Batchelor did not recollect having any private conversation with the witness—'except possibly in the way of chat'.

'He never made any suggestion at all about the branch stamp?'—'That is incorrect. Mr Batchelor suggested the question of the branch stamp, and I said to him, "It may be possible for me to get hold of a branch stamp"—because I wanted to see what he had to say on the matter. He then proceeded to tell me that it might be possible for him to supply me with fifty to a hundred ballot papers in the forthcoming elections.'

Mr Lawson then challenged all the witness's previous evidence about what had transpired at advisory committee meetings, suggested that he had been telling lies throughout, and was about to call his principal witness, Mr Haxell, when Mr Gerald Gardiner raised a point of great importance to the immediate affairs of the ETU.

'I have been accumulating evidence,' Mr Gardiner told the Judge, 'that since April the 17th, when Mr Lawson admitted on behalf of Mr Haxell that he was no longer the General Secretary of the defendant Union, he has still been *acting* as General Secretary. If it is so, it does in my submission give rise to a somewhat serious situation. In the first place I apprehend that his remuneration can't validly be paid by the Union; and he—'

'I have a number of problems present in my mind,' said Mr Justice Winn reasonably enough, 'but is this a matter that I either should or can deal with at this stage?'

'What is very much in my mind is that it would look as though this case might not finish this term, with the whole of the Executive Council nominations approaching in June. I am instructed that the Trades Union Congress might be prepared to recommend suitable persons, on whom the parties might agree, to perform the duties of General Secretary and Assistant General Secretary now that it is common ground that this Union has *no* General Secretary and no Assistant either. I am not asking that Mr Byrne should act as General Secretary meanwhile, because that would be prejudging one question which has to be decided.'

'Yes,' said the Judge. 'Well, if I may say so, Mr Gardiner, you have now said almost exactly what I thought—and partly expressed in the first full moon of the first day of this case' (see page 17). 'Until I finish with this case I cannot make any order about *any* issue which arises. I could do it only by consent of the parties . . . I don't think I can impose any such change upon this Union or upon Mr Haxell. But they have heard what you have said.'

'And of course,' concluded Mr Gardiner, rubbing it in, 'one doesn't know whether Mr Haxell wants to go on announcing in public that he is the General Secretary when he knows he is not'.

But Mr Haxell did. And it was now his turn to enter the witness-box—where he declined to take the oath, explaining that he had no religious belief.

He was forty-eight years old, he said, and had been in the ETU for thirty-two years. He joined the Communist Party in 1935. But Communist influence was not very apparent in the Union even four years after that, for in 1939 he was banned for five years from holding any office in the Union for supporting an unofficial electricians' strike at Chorley; but since his reinstatement in 1944 he had had various elective offices and was now (*pace* Mr Gardiner) General Secretary. He supplied the interesting information that the

Union's membership was increasing at the rate of about ten thousand a year and now had a total strength of 244,000.

Mr Haxell described the work of his departmental heads—Mr Burns, who looked after 'rules revision' and the policy conferences; Mr Oliver, who had been Office Manager and looked after the ballots; and Mr Humphrey (one of the Defendants), who took over from Mr Oliver in 1959; none of whom was a member of the Communist Party.

'You,' said Mr Lawson, 'are a member of the Executive Committee of the Communist Party?'

'That is so,' replied Mr Haxell.

'Now, as you know, Mr Haxell, it is alleged in this case that there were what are called committees of the Communist Party, consisting of members of the ETU, called the National Advisory Committee, the National Aggregate Conference, the London District Advisory Committee, and four London Advisory Committees. And it is alleged against you specifically that you were a member of the National Advisory Committee and attended the National Aggregate Conference from the year 1945 to date. First of all, has the Communist Party got advisory committees?'

'Yes, it has—in a similar way to other political parties.' Their function, said Mr Haxell, was to give advice and assist in the preparation of pamphlets on building and housing. It was not true that he was a member of any *national* advisory committee of the Communist Party 'consisting of Communist members of the ETU'. There wasn't such a committee. 'I have been on the National Building Advisory. So at one time was Mr Hendy and so was Mr Frazer,' he said. 'And from time to time we felt it necessary to call together active *members of the Union who were also members of the Communist Party* to give consideration to special and specific problems such as wages policy and payment by results.' He had attended about ten or twelve such meetings since 1945.

'Were those meetings concerned with who was to be nominated for office in representative positions, and how you were to get those people elected?'—'They were not concerned with those things at all. At the end of the meeting, obviously a discussion would take place if there was a particularly important election on—it would be untrue to say that didn't occur.'

Mr Lawson asked him whether he knew of the existence of 'London Advisory Committees'.

'I have no knowledge of them,' said Mr Haxell. He added that so far as the Communist Party was concerned (meaning as distinct from the ETU) 'the Communist Party at the district level will, I'm quite sure, have advisory committees, in the same way as the Executive of the Party does'.

'Has your own conduct as an official of the Electrical Trades Union ever come under discussion at these meetings?'—'You mean my job as an official?' said Mr Haxell incredulously. 'How I should do my job?'

'Yes.'—'No,' said Mr Haxell with emphasis.

Mr Lawson moved on to the question of the Byrne-Haxell election. The Head Office arrangements for this, said Mr Haxell, were in the hands of Mr Humphrey, Office Manager, and Mr McLennan, Assistant General Secretary.

'Did you have anything to do with the arrangements yourself?' —'Nothing to do with it at all.'

Nor did he know anything about the occasion when Mr Swift the printer dispatched all those extra ballot papers to St Pancras Station 'to await collection'.

'It is alleged that additional ballot papers were either sent to Communist branch secretaries or to Communist members of branches for the purpose of inflating the vote in your favour. Do you know anything about that?'—'Nothing at all,' said Mr Haxell steadily.

Nor did he know anything about the substitution of envelopes bearing false dates of posting for original envelopes bearing earlier dates of posting.

'I think forty secretaries have given evidence about that,' said Mr Lawson. Mr Haxell knew nothing of it.

As for the story about Woolston, Hythe, and Southampton Central, and the receipt by those branch secretaries of voting papers (all pro-Haxell) before they could possibly have got into the hands of the members—

'All I know about that,' Mr Haxell assured the Court, looking round rather truculently, 'is that I read it in one of the newspapers. I believe it was the *Daily Express*.' He thought it couldn't be true.

He called the three secretaries together, gathered from them that there was 'substance in the Press report', and sent Mr George Scott down to investigate (and, as it turned out, to exonerate).

Mr Haxell's examination-in-chief proceeded all that day and most of the next (May 9). He defended the way in which the Rules had been so changed as to remove the branches' right of appeal against Head Office decisions. (The Plaintiffs said that this was done, after a Rules Revision Conference in 1957 by a last-minute change when the printers' proofs of the new Rules were forwarded to the Registrar of Friendly Societies for his approval. The Judge later called this 'a wicked fraud upon the members of the ETU'.) He described the appointment and duties of national scrutineers, the method of warning branch secretaries about late returns and other irregularities, and how any such irregularities requiring an investigation were a matter for the Executive Council, while 'technical' (i.e., self-evident or obvious) breaches of Rule were dealt with by the General Secretary himself.

He said that when votes were counted by the national (as distinct from the branch) scrutineers, that was irregular, but sanctified by long usage. (There was nothing in the Rules about it.) Mr Lawson took him through many of the allegations that witnesses had been making and he denied them all. And finally—

'What I am anxious for you to tell my Lord is this,' said Mr Lawson. 'There are two things one could do. One could, perhaps, see that the affairs of the Union were so conducted that the lay members had little say in its affairs, or one could do it the other way round. What have you striven to do, so far as it lay within your power?'

No one could have said that Mr Haxell's response to this opening was not impressive. 'I personally have been responsible,' he said, 'for making a number of propositions from the time that I first went on to the Executive. Firstly, from the part-time District Committees to a form of election to Trade Committees. Then the breaking down of the areas into smaller units with a representative of every branch on the Area Committee. Then the expansion of the number of areas from ten to forty-six, and an increase of Area Offices from twelve to fifty-six. I played some considerable part in the research into the finances of the Union, which enabled us, by a method of budgeting, to introduce the Union's College' (at Esher) 'for the purpose of training the members, to take them for a week's course and reimburse them as much as we can for their loss of earnings. The introduction of a Convalescent Home. A fortnight's holiday for the older members. In general, I tried to improve the position of the Union. I always encouraged people to play a greater part in its affairs, and assisted in amending the Rules as far as I could in any way. But I couldn't be credited,' he concluded modestly, 'with the transference of the power for disqualification from the General Secretary to the national scrutineers. That was not my suggestion at all. I agree with it, but it certainly wasn't my suggestion.'

'Thank you,' said Mr Lawson, and sat down.

Mr Gerald Gardiner's first question in cross-examination was a body blow.

'Mr Haxell, are you the General Secretary of the Electrical Trades Union?'

'I think so,' said Mr Haxell with a greater show of confidence than the mere words imply.

'Your learned Counsel's statement when this case was opened, that his clients could no longer maintain that you were validly elected—that is nonsense, is it?'

'Well, I don't now whether *you* regard it as nonsense or not. As far as I am concerned, the Executive Council took a decision in connection with the ballot, and declared me General Secretary.'

After some further exchanges about this, the Judge saw that it could be shortened by confronting Mr Haxell with the transcript of what his Counsel had really said:

'On the defence as it stands, there is the assertion that the Defendant Haxell was duly elected, and in the circumstances that assertion cannot now be maintained by the Defendants.'

'I accept that, yes,' said Mr Haxell.

'You accept the fact, then, that you are not now General Secretary?' went on Mr Gardiner—'Yes, I suppose that is the position.'

'Would you look at Saturday's *Daily Worker*? Does that contain the usual May Day greetings from the ETU among others?'— 'Yes.'

'And do you there represent yourself to be the General Secretary of the Union?'—'Yes.'

'Why are you going on representing that which you know to be not true?'—'Because I am the person carrying out those responsibilities at the moment.'

This went on for quite a long time, the Judge and Mr Lawson joining in. The upshot was that Mr Haxell was General Secretary *de facto* and intended to go on like that until the Court stopped him.

'Do you think your election was rigged?' Mr Gardiner asked him.—'No.'

'Have you heard practically the whole of the evidence given in this case?'—'I have.'

'And you still don't think it was rigged?'—'No.'

Mr Gardiner took him through the figures showing the very small proportion of branches which, after the 1953 change of Rules gave extra time for posting results, were disqualified for lateness. In any year, there were never more than seventeen. Did he think it odd that in 1959 there should suddenly be a hundred and twelve? He did not. There had been a 'tremendous Press campaign', he said, and about eighty branches took part in the election which normally did not. He agreed, though, that this was all the more reason why they should be careful to get their returns off in time. And, under pressure, he *did* think it was odd that a hundred and nine out of a hundred and twelve should be anti-Communist branches. (To the observer, it seemed possible that Mr Haxell and Mr Gardiner were not giving the same meaning to 'odd'. Mr Gardiner meant sinister. Mr Haxell may have meant unusual.)

Mr Gardiner showed him a list of seventeen branches arranged in a line running northwards from London to Ayr, and times of posting (all between December 30 and January 1) running in strictly parallel chronological order. These times were taken from the envelopes *produced by the Defendants*. Was that odd, asked Mr Gardiner? 'No,' replied Mr Haxell steadily.

'You could produce a table like that,' Mr Haxell said, 'in almost any election.' (But throughout the trial, nothing like it was produced by the Defendants.)

'What this suggests, does it not, is that somebody, about a week after the elections were over, took a car and went north from London to Scotland, posting envelopes as he went?'—'I wouldn't *think* of such a thing. I wouldn't think *anybody* would be capable of anything like that.'

Mr Haxell had heard it alleged that all these envelopes were substituted envelopes, posted a week or more after the genuine ones had been sent off: and that someone had made a car journey to post them. The ETU, he agreed, had a fleet of about sixty cars. He used a Humber himself, and sometimes a Triumph.

'Where was Mr Gregory on the 1st and 2nd of January, 1960?' asked Mr Gardiner suddenly.

'Who? Mr Gregory?'—'Yes.'

'*I* don't know.'

'You do really take these charges seriously, do you?'—'Yes, I do take them seriously,' said Mr Haxell. And he did know it was being alleged that someone under him had taken a car or cars and gone and posted substituted envelopes, and that that would be a fraudulent thing to do.

'*Why* don't you know where Mr Gregory was on the 1st and 2nd of January?'—'Because I never asked where he was.'

'Didn't you think it was your business, in view of this allegation, to find out where your Head Office staff were?'

Mr Haxell said that was a matter for the defending solicitors. He had never enquired himself. 'Why should *I* want to know?'

Treating this as a rhetorical question, Mr Gardiner went on to the decision of the Executive Council in 1957 to begin issuing circulars to the branches refuting the Press allegations about the rigging of elections.

'In 1958, when it was suggested there was a large number of voting papers at Jarrow, that must have been a shock to you?'— 'As far as I remember it was asserted that there were sixty envelopes all posted at the same time bearing the same stamp. I wouldn't regard that as a shock.'

'You wouldn't?'—'No. I would say that on the face of it it would look unusual and should be investigated.'

'And you and Mr West and Mr Goldberg investigated it?'— 'That is correct.'

'And you found that no more than six of these envelopes had been posted by the members?'

Mr Haxell agreed, conceding also that 'the only person who stood to gain by that was the Communist branch secretary'.

'Do you remember saying yesterday that you knew nothing about there being any surplus voting papers at Head Office until January this year?'

Mr Haxell did, and added that it was correct. Yet he agreed, when asked, that in the previous June an injunction was granted against him in relation to the election of the Assistant General Secretary, and that the evidence then was that at Woolston and LSE 5 the branch secretaries had taken the precaution of stamping all the envelopes containing the voting papers, in spite of which Woolston got twenty back *without* the branch stamp on them, and LSE 5 got thirty-nine.

'Can you tell me this,' Mr Gardiner said: 'Are the Plaintiffs going to be told how many further ballot papers have been found over the weekend?'—'I should imagine that if we found any further ballot papers they would be told then and there.'

'Can *you* tell *me* how many have been found?'

Mr Haxell said he thought that the papers found related to about forty branches, but he didn't know which ones.

After the lunch adjournment that day—the fifteenth of the evidence—Mr Gardiner came to the BBC 'Panorama' programme in February 1960, in which Mr Foulkes had been pilloried by Mr John Freeman. In this television interview Mr Freeman had challenged him to sue the BBC and himself for libel if the assertions made against him and the ETU were false.

'As a result of that, there was considerable discussion everywhere about the results of this ballot, and exactly how many branches had been disqualified, and so on?'

'Yes,' said Mr Haxell. But until the day of the Executive Council meeting where the result of the 1959 election was declared (Haxell 19,611, Byrne 18,577) he didn't know, for example, that *any* branches had been disqualified. He only knew then from the newspapers.

'And you seriously say that Mr Foulkes never told you?'—'No.'

'Are you sure?'—'Yes. I *think* I'm sure. I don't think he did.'

'Mr Chapple says: "This is the second election that has been rushed through in this manner." Was that a fair statement—that Mr Foulkes' own election had been rushed through in just this very manner?'—'It wasn't a fair statement at all. As a matter of fact, when I first dealt with any scrutineers' report I would read out all the branches which were disqualified.'

'Then Mr McLennan was dealing with it in an unusual way, was he?'—'No,' said Mr Haxell. 'He dealt with it in the way *he* always did. And you have to remember the atmosphere of the meeting at the time, which was electric.'

'Then Mr Chapple has to enquire: "Were *any* branches disqualified in this ballot?" '—'That's right.'

'And then bit by bit it comes out, doesn't it?'—'I don't know about bit by bit. The point is there's an argument going on, and once the request was made the argument still went on.'

Mr Haxell agreed that a branch could not appeal against a decision of the Council until that decision had been recorded in the minutes, and Mr Gardiner wanted to show accordingly that a convenient way of stifling or indefinitely postponing appeals was simply to forget to put decisions in the minutes. The next meeting was on March 12, but Mr Haxell did not produce at that meeting any minutes of the February one. It was the same on April 3. So, said Mr Gardiner, 'While all the members of this Union were waiting to hear what had happened at the meeting in February, you didn't put the minutes before the Executive Council even on April the 3rd?'—'I *think* that's right,' said Mr Haxell imperturbably.

'And it wasn't until the meeting in May that you did so?'—'That's probably right.'

Mr Gardiner pursued this as far as the meeting in July, when Mr Haxell had made a speech beginning like this: 'On December the 17th my attention was drawn to a report in certain national newspapers alleging that completed ballot papers were being delivered to the secretaries of Hythe, Southampton Central, and Woolston branches at the same time as they were being delivered to the members' homes.'

'Then,' said Mr Gardiner, 'you said you had asked Mr Scott to report. Mr Goldberg said: "I think the ballots should stand." Mr

Foulkes said: "Sam moves that the ballots of the three branches should stand. Somebody second?" And *you* said: "Well, I think all you need do is to note the report, in which case it'll be included in the returns. You don't decide *not* to invalidate something." That appears to be what happened at that meeting, doesn't it?'—'Yes.'

But the *minutes* of that meeting were rather different. Mr Gardiner read this from them: 'The General Secretary advised that the national scrutineers had rejected the scrutineers' form from the branch, as it had not been received within the time limit laid down by the Rules.'

'That wasn't true, was it?' asked Mr Gardiner.

Mr Haxell said that it was.

'But you've got the transcript,' Mr Gardiner pressed him. 'Will you just find it in the transcript? We've read the whole of the transcript, haven't we?'—'Yes,' Mr Haxell agreed. And then, after a long pause: 'No, it's not in the transcript.'

And when this had been made abundantly clear, Mr Gardiner said:

'This statement which you later published in the minutes of this meeting, that you had advised the Executive Council that the national scrutineers had rejected the scrutineers' form from this branch, as it had not been received within the time limit laid down —that is untrue, is it not?'—'It's not strictly accurate.'

' "Untrue" is a very ordinary English word, Mr Haxell. It's untrue, is it not?'—'It's untrue, then. I'd prefer to say it is "not correct".'

'And the only scrutineers' report which had been published had *not* disqualified Woolston or Hythe on the ground that they were late, had it?'—'The minutes don't show it, but the transcript clearly shows that they were.'

'*What* transcript?'—'The transcript of the meeting.'

'Are you saying that the scrutineers' report which was published to the members in the minutes was a false document?'—'False document?' Mr Haxell seemed to play for time.

'Yes.'

'In the sense that it left out Woolston and Hythe,' said Mr Haxell, 'yes'.

The Judge turned to him. 'It's rather a pity, isn't it?' he observed.

'It would be a question of not wishing to confuse the membership, my Lord.'

'What they don't know, they don't bother or worry about?'

'No,' Mr Haxell told the Judge. 'It's not that at all. It would be reported to them at a later meeting.'

Mr Gardiner came to the 'later meeting'.

'At the meeting in July, the Council did *not* disqualify them?'—'Not according to the minute.'

'It's *your* minute, is it not?'—'Yes.'

'Isn't it right?'—'Yes, it is right, and accepted by the Executive as a true and correct record, too.'

'You just decided to add a bit to your majority?'—'I didn't decide anything. The Council dealt with it.'

Then the cross-examination moved on to the misfortunes of the Jersey Branch, which had been disqualified in 1957 for not electing its scrutineers properly (though it had never had a warning before). Mr Haxell had done this off his own bat, without reference to the Executive Council—this, he said, was quite a long tradition, although nothing in the Rules authorised it. Mr Gardiner pointed out that Jersey had voted for Mr Cannon and against the Communist candidate, Mr Frazer. The Reading Supply Branch, on the other hand, which had voted for Mr Frazer, had committed a similar breach of the ballot Rules, but was let off with a warning and its votes were counted.

'Jersey and Reading Supply are in the same position, are they not?' said Mr Gardiner. 'They had both infringed the Rule for the first time?'—'Yes.'

'One voted for Cannon and the other for Frazer?'—'Yes.'

'The one that votes for Cannon is disqualified: the one that votes for Frazer is not?'—'Yes, but it's got nothing to do with the votes at all, and if you want me to explain, I will.'

'Please,' said Mr Gardiner, and the Court settled down to listen.

'The position is,' Mr Haxell said, 'that the Executive has taken the view that the responsibility for failure to appoint the branch scrutineers is the responsibility of the whole of the branch. It is not a matter that is the responsibility of an officer; and the warnings were introduced where the breach or infringement was the responsibility of or caused by the officer. So therefore on this question, of whether a branch fails to appoint scrutineers, the question of warning is not taken into account. If the branch advises Head Office prior to the holding of its quarterly meeting that it has not been able (and gives the reasons for it) to elect the branch scrutineers, then the practice is that they will be given authority to elect them at the quarterly meeting. If they didn't advise the Executive before they held their quarterly meeting then they would be rejected.'

The question whether Reading had complied with this while Jersey had not complied remained unanswered—remained, indeed, unasked. But Mr Gardiner did ask where this decision of policy was recorded. Mr Haxell didn't think it was.

'But this is a matter which vitally affects the voting rights of the member, does it not?'—'Yes,' said Mr Haxell defiantly, 'and this is a matter which was dealt with long before I was General Secretary'.

'I suggest to you that no such decision was ever discussed or reached by the Executive.'—'Then you are completely wrong.' But he agreed later that since it had never been minuted, no branch could ever appeal against it.

Mr Haxell was thus taken through the disqualification story of a number of branches, with similar exchanges across the Court, in an atmosphere of mounting tension, and with a noticeable deterioration in Mr Haxell's self-confidence. Then Mr Gardiner asked him about his removal from the Executive Council in its less Communist period in 1939.

'In 1939 you were removed and prohibited from holding any office in the Union?'—'That is correct.'

'And that was because you had preferred the interests of the Communist Party to the interests of the Union?'—'That's completely untrue,' said Mr Haxell vehemently. 'The position is that I went with the General Secretary and President at that time—'

Here the Judge interposed. 'Would you answer the question first?' he said. 'Was that what was alleged against you?'—'A part of the charge was that I was a Communist, yes.'

'And had preferred the Communist Party interests to the Union's interests?'—'No, I don't recall that being part of the charge.'

'Then your answer is "No"? You will have an opportunity to explain later.'

Mr Gardiner went on: 'It was a case in which the Executive Council had decided not to support a strike at Chorley?'—'I'm not sure about whether the Council had come to such a decision. I think the matter had not in fact been before them when we went to Chorley.'

'Of course, all this is recorded, isn't it?'—'It's all recorded, yes.'

'I suggest that the Executive Council had decided not to support the strike, and that you, in disloyalty to your colleagues, then went off to foment the strike because that was the policy of the Communist Party at the time.'—'I never went off to foment any strike at all.'

The Judge asked Mr Haxell if he now wanted to give his own version of what happened. 'I promised I would give you a chance.'

'What really happened,' said Mr Haxell, 'was that, arising out of negotiations with the employers, the General Secretary and the President and myself were instructed to go to Chorley . . . I attended a meeting of the whole of the shop stewards, and convinced them that they should recommend to the members to return to work. They decided to do that and the strike terminated.'

'So you were a peace-maker, and not a strike-maker?'—'Yes, on that occasion, my Lord.'

'There was an enquiry, wasn't there,' asked Mr Gardiner, 'a fairly long enquiry?'—'Yes.'

'And they didn't believe you?'

Mr Haxell explained that a charge *was* made against him but withdrawn—what took its place was a decision that he had been 'disloyal to his colleagues' and should be banned from office.

Coming to the 'advisories' and their function, Mr Haxell agreed that there were in the Communist Party 'advisory committees of experts who advised the Executive Committee', but that there had never been such a committee of expert electricians; and he did *not* agree that there was a 'National Advisory Committee'. But whatever these meetings were called, they did discuss wages policy, payment by results, time-and-motion studies, and important elections.

They did *not* discuss whether it would suit the interests of the Communist Party if the boundaries of the voting areas were altered.

'Have you never heard that discussed?' asked Mr Gardiner incredulously.—'No.'

'Things like alterations of boundaries affect elections, don't they?'—'I can't quite see how they do.'

But Mr Haxell was known to be much more intelligent than this.

'Haven't you heard,' said the Judge, 'or don't you take an interest in Parliamentary affairs, the sort of fuss that is made if the boundary of a constituency is altered?'

Mr Haxell thought that was different, without being ready to explain why. He then went on to deny the existence of local advisory committees, and Mr Gardiner reminded him that he had often been seen at their meetings.

'You heard the evidence of Mr Blairford, Mr Reno, Mr Townsend, Mr Thomas, Mr Moss, Mr Chapple, and Mr Vetterlein, who appeared on subpoena, and whose livelihood depends on the Union? They all say they saw you at meetings of the advisory committees.'

'Well, they are wrong.'

An even longer string of witnesses had been wrong, said Mr Haxell, when they said on oath that they had written to Head Office asking for an enquiry into the conduct of the Union's affairs.

'I have put it to every witness who has been called, Mr Haxell, and they all say that until Mr Chapple asked whether you had had such a letter from any branch, you never told the Executive for nearly two years of branch after branch after branch wanting the Executive Committee to call a special delegates conference?'

'That is not true. In point of fact it couldn't possibly happen. Here we were in this position with the Press saying all sorts of things, and to suggest that members of the Executive would attend a meeting and not ask questions about it is absolutely ridiculous.'

'I suggest,' said Mr Gardiner patiently, 'that these letters were concealed from the Executive Council?'—'That is not true.'

But there was no minute about any of this. 'And that,' said Mr Gardiner, 'prevented any branch from appealing, did it not?'— 'Yes.'

Mr Gardiner took Newcastle as an example of the arbitrary exercise of authority in disqualifying a branch on a technicality— its secretary had forgotten to write 'Newcastle' on the voting return. The branch secretary wrote to Head Office and pleaded that 'apart from the Rules of the Union, every member was also entitled to what in legal circles was termed "natural justice" '.

'Do you agree with that, Mr Haxell?'—'Yes.'

'Do you think it is just and right if all the votes of a branch are disqualified because the branch secretary omits to put the name of the branch on the form, when those in control at Head Office *know* which branch it is?'—'They're given a warning. But after they are warned and told about it, then I think it's quite right.'

It was shortly after this that Mr Justice Winn said to the witness: 'I want to make it clear to you that I have begun to form my own assessment of your intelligence and ability, and that will be one of the factors when I come to weigh up the important question whether I believe that you did hold certain *bona fide* opinions about the meaning, effect, and scope of the Rules at different times. You understand?'

And Mr Haxell, who was thus being informed that he was no fool and could not successfully pretend to be one, said that he understood.

Ruislip Branch had been disqualified at the 1957 election and had wanted to appeal. There was what the Judge called 'a simple, straight answer to this request', namely: 'This is a function of the Executive Council, which cannot be challenged.' Yet in January 1959 Mr Haxell was still allowing the Council to discuss whether or not the appeal could take place, if the wording of it was changed.

'With such a busy Council as you have got,' said the Judge, 'and such a busy office as you yourself were holding at that time, do you often waste time discussing entirely academic questions about the wording of an appeal, where there is a short and simple answer—*that no appeal lies, under the Rules as you understand them*?'—'It does happen, my Lord.'

'Really you are just beating the air with idle nonsense?'—'I'm afraid so, my Lord. It very often happens, unfortunately.'

Mr Gardiner took up the question of appeals.

'It was while all this was going on, was it not,' he said, 'that it occurred to you it would be a brilliant plan if you could introduce into the newly changed rules an express provision clearly forbidding any right of appeal?'—'That is not so. There were a number of alterations to the Rules. Two of the most important cases didn't emanate from me at all.'

Mr Gardiner suggested that after the Rules Revision Conference in 1957, Mr Haxell had told the Registrar of Friendly Societies that there had been a mistake in the Rule about appeals.

'Mr Burns told me there had been this mistake,' said the witness, 'and I told him he had better ring up the Registrar and correct it.'

'Did you look up the transcript' (i.e., the report of the 1957 Rules Conference proceedings) 'to see?'—'No, I didn't. I accepted what Mr Burns had said and told him to get it corrected.'

In August 1960 Mr Haxell got a letter from the Registrar pointing out that the alteration registered in 1958 had been further altered in manuscript, in a way that had never been passed by the Conference, and asking for an explanation. 'If what *you* say is true, the answer was very simple?'—'Yes.'

'But if what the Plaintiffs say is right, this was a very awkward letter for you to answer, was it not?'—'If what *you're* suggesting is true, yes.'

The letter, at any rate, was not answered for two months. It was dealt with by Mr Tarlo, the Union's solicitor.

'And the answer which after two months was given was untrue, was it not?'—'Yes,' said Mr Haxell.

'I suggest this was a brilliant scheme on your part, so that in the future you could produce a rule which would completely squash any attempt to appeal against anything the Executive Council did in relation to elections at all.'—'It's another one of your suggestions that is just completely wrong.'

There was some mystery about the disqualification of branches on the ground that they had held their election meetings on the wrong night. 'Do you know, Mr Haxell, that fifty-six branches which voted for you met on the wrong meeting night and were *not* disqualified?'

'No,' Mr Haxell said, 'I don't know that'.

'Have you taken any trouble to find out what it is that accounts for the fact that the one hundred and nine branches which were disqualified had all voted for Mr Byrne?'—'I know that of the one hundred and nine branches the majority was for Mr Byrne, but I haven't gone into precise details in regard to it.'

'What is the Rule which says that if a branch holds its meeting on a different night of the week from the night on which it usually holds it, its members are all disfranchised? Where do you find that?'

The Rule Book was handed up to Mr Haxell, and he thumbed it through. Then he said:

'It's page thirty-four, isn't it, of the 1958 Rule Book? It says "Quarterly Meetings".'

'That says: "Each branch shall hold a quarterly meeting on the last ordinary meeting night on or immediately prior to the last Saturday in March, June, September and December of each year, or in special circumstances on such other dates as may be approved by the Executive Council."'

'So it says that they shall hold their meetings on that night,' said Mr Haxell, 'and if they don't they are obviously in breach of the Rule'.

'If the Rule bears that interpretation, do you say that Christmas Day has ever been regarded as an ordinary meeting night? It says "on the last ordinary meeting night".'—'Of course,' said Mr Haxell, as though a sudden thought had struck him, 'Christmas Day would mean nothing to our members in Scotland. It would mean nothing at all to them.'

'What about your members in England?'—'Well, it's a holiday for them.'

'But by at least your members in England Christmas Day has never been regarded as an ordinary meeting night?'—'If the ordinary meeting night is scheduled for the 25th,' said Mr Haxell, 'under the Rules that is their meeting night, but there is provision in the Rules for them to ask the Council to authorise them to hold it another night'.

But if they did ask, it was Mr Haxell who would deal with their request, and against his decision there could be no appeal. The *coda* to Mr Gardiner's cross-examination now held the attention of the Court, which on this last day of Mr Haxell's evidence was crowded to the doors with standing people.

'Do you know that there were four Liverpool branches, all of which met on December the 21st, all of which are marked as arriving on December the 28th? Two of them—Liverpool Central and Liverpool South—having voted for you, were *not* disqualified; and two of them—Liverpool East and Liverpool Instrument Makers—having voted for Mr Byrne, were?' (Mr Haxell was shaking his head.) 'You haven't been into any of these things yourself?'—'No.'

'The truth is, is it not, that as the returns came in and were opened by Mr Humphrey, he told you that it looked as if you had lost the election?'—'That is not true. Anybody who says that is telling a complete and absolute deliberate lie.'

'And that it was your idea' (Mr Gardiner was now 'coming down the straight') 'or at least you approved of the posting of substitute envelopes, either by reliable Communists in the branch, or, in some cases where there wasn't one, by sending an officer out from headquarters by car?'—'That is absolutely untrue.'

'There hasn't been any difficulty, has there, since May of last year, in your finding out where your Head Office staff were between December the 30th and January the 2nd?'—'No. I could have asked them.'

'Where were *you*?' asked Mr Gardiner, leaning forward.

'As every year on the Christmas Eve, I usually have a drink with one or two members of the staff. I then go off—I take a part of my holidays. I remain at home with my family, which is quite a fair size—not my personal family but my brothers and so forth. I would go into the office on New Year's Eve to have a drink with one or two there, and I would return to the office duties somewhere round about the 3rd or 4th. This is what happens every year so far as I'm concerned.'

'In effect,' said the Judge, 'you take a week away from the office from Christmas Eve to New Year's Eve?'—'Yes, unless I'm required for some urgent and important thing.'

A curious exhibition of shadow-boxing then entertained the Court. 'Where would you be on December the 30th, 1959?' asked Mr Gardiner.

'I'd be with my wife.'

'Where is that?'—'Where is my wife?'

'Where do you live?'—'I'm in the process of changing.'

'Where did you *then* live?'

'It's difficult for me, my Lord,' Mr Haxell explained to the Judge. 'I haven't really any permanent place at the moment.'

'Don't be hasty about it,' the Judge enjoined with a kind of ominous solicitude. 'Can you remember the end of 1959? That's not last Christmas but the one before.'

'I think on December the 30th I was staying at my sister-in-law's place. I'm almost sure that is so.'

'That's in what district?' asked the Judge.

'Finsbury Park.'

Mr Gardiner pressed on. 'And on the 31st?'—'I'd be there till the 31st. Then we would leave.'

'And January the 1st?'—'I would still be there.'

'Was anybody using the Triumph during those days?'—'*I* can't recall whether anyone was using the Triumph. I may have used it.'

'I am bound to suggest to you that the reason why you have made no enquiry,' said Mr Gardiner in a crammed and hushed Court, 'to see whether any member of your staff—from his returns and expense sheets, and so on—was going on those days from London to Scotland, is because you know quite well who it was.'—'I do *not* know.'

And Mr Gardiner sat down. After a few further questions from Mr Lawson to clear up what was understood to be 'appealable' and what was not, Mr Haxell then left the witness-box and returned, still rather jauntily, to his seat. A sorry figure, the Judge called him later: 'I noticed a nervous grin and shifts of stance—certainly he was ill at ease,' remarked the Judge.

3   Regrouping the Branches

Every boundary is a challenge to adventure—'we all love to overlook boundaries,' wrote Dr Johnson in *The Rambler*. Every boundary represents the decision of, at most, a handful of men arranging the geographical lives of a multitude. And the Reform Acts of the nineteenth century showed how, in a country with any pretensions to democracy, a balance of power can be tipped by redrawing lines on a map or by ordaining that town 'A' shall in future belong to group 2 instead of group 1.

Any branch of a trade union takes its geographical identity, as a rule, not from the place where its members work but from where they hold their meetings. The boundary line that encloses any group or area of branches can therefore be redrawn with the greatest ease, bringing in some branches, cutting out others, and presenting neighbouring groups or areas with new electoral colleagues.

Perhaps one trade union member in fifty—even perhaps in a thousand—would ever know that it had been done; and even that one would be unlikely to know why it was done. This was particularly true of the ETU.

Mr Percy Burns, of Keston, Kent, had for seventeen years been 'research officer' to the Electrical Trades Union. He told Mr Ralph Millner (for the Defence) that he organised the Union's various conferences—Policy, Youth, and Rules Revision. His work also included what Mr Millner called 'the question of the Divisions that the branches go into'. Mr Millner gave him an opportunity to explain, as an example, how it was that the London Station Engineers No. 11 Branch was moved from Division 10 into Division 9. The Judge decided to cut this short because the Court had heard it all before; and, as he said later, he thought Mr Burns in the witness-box was 'sullen and evasive'.

'A Mr Carnell wrote,' said the Judge, 'and said that his branch met in an hotel at South Kensington, and it had come to his notice that there was another branch which met at the same hotel, and why were they not in the same division. Is that right?'

'That is right, my Lord,' said Mr Millner.

Mr Burns then related how he had dealt with this on his own responsibility. 'Without mentioning it to anybody?' the Judge asked him.

'Yes, my Lord.'

There was also the case of London Telephone Engineers No. 1. In the 1954 edition of the Union's Rule Book this branch was in Division 8. In 1958 it was moved to another division. Mr Burns explained why.

'It was changed,' he said, 'because it was obvious that this branch had been wrong for almost thirteen or fourteen years, and so the whole of the branches were checked, and that one was put right. The branch had changed its meeting place.'

'Did you have consultations with anyone else, or directions from anyone else, about how to make the changes?' asked Mr Millner.

'No.'

The changes could not be made, he said, on a 'purely geographical basis'; and 'when it comes to the taking away of branches from one place to another, where they have been associated together, there are very often reasons why they don't like it'.

Mr Burns was examined at great length about the alteration in the Rules after the Rules Revision Conference of 1957—a tiny textual change that crept in 'by error' but nevertheless killed the right of all branches to appeal against decisions of the Executive Council. He told the Court that he was responsible for the alteration. He had noticed, in the course of a telephone talk with Mr Dunning, of the office of the Registrar of Friendly Societies, that the relevant Rule was wrongly printed; and he put it right.

'But as to the actual alteration,' said Mr Millner, 'do you know who *did* it or gave instructions for it?'—'I undoubtedly gave instructions to a typist to alter both copies of this report before it went to the binders.'

More still was to be heard about this pregnant alteration, of which the Executive Council knew nothing (at least as a body). But with Mr Burns' assurance that he himself belonged to the Labour Party and not to the Communist Party (he was not, by the way, a member of the ETU) his evidence-in-chief was over.

Mr Gerald Gardiner, cross-examining (with his mind no doubt on the events of Christmas 1959), elicited, first, that Head Office kept a record of all staff absences of more than half a day, and that the Assistant General Secretary would know about it; a preview of what Mr Foulkes was going to be asked in due course.

'It has always been the case, hasn't it, that under the Rules it was for the Executive Council to decide on the electoral divisions?' —'That's right,' said Mr Burns.

'What they might have done was to say: "Well, all the branches whose meeting places are in the South-West postal district are to be Division number so-and-so"?'—'That's right.'

'We know that they didn't do it, but if the Executive Council had drawn up a very short appendix saying: "Everybody in the South-West postal district of London is to be in Division No. 17," then any branch could, in effect, have chosen its own division by changing the place of its meetings?'

'That's right,' said Mr Burns again. He added that some branches had been in the wrong divisions for many years—'it was simply an error that was repeated all through the years and nobody ever drew attention to the thing'.

'I suppose there's nobody who knows the Rules better than you do?'—'That's right, as far as the routine part is concerned.'

Mr Gardiner read out Rule 10 (2) (M):

> The Executive Council shall have power to determine the boundaries of the eleven Electoral Divisions, for the purpose of elections of Divisional members of the Executive Council, by grouping the branches in geographical divisions covering the whole of the membership of the Union, and from time to time to vary such boundaries as they shall deem fit.

'Rightly or wrongly,' said Mr Gardiner, 'on purpose or by mistake, succeeding Executive Councils ever since 1946 had decided that LSE 11 was to be in Division No. 10, had they not?' —'It's gone by default all through the years. They hadn't "decided".'

'Did you take the view that you, Mr Burns, by a stroke of the pen, could do that which the Rules say can only be done by the Executive Council?'

'I have been altering that book for years,' said Mr Burns, 'and it had never occurred to me, until you put the point to me, that I am abrogating [sic] the powers of the Executive Council in relation to that matter.'

'It didn't occur to you, I suppose, that any decision made by the Executive Council had to be put in the minutes, and that any branch could then appeal against it?'—'I appreciate that, but I was dealing with a branch here. We get hundreds of things about branches every day, and I just put the thing through.'

'They had been quite happy in Division 10 for thirteen years,

had they not?'—'I don't know whether they were happy or un-
happy.'

Mr Thomas Vincent, of Port Talbot, said that he was an electrical engineer, a member of the ETU since 1916, a member of the
Labour Party (but never of the Communist Party), and for ten
years a member of the ETU Executive Council. He supported
Mr Burns' account of the alteration made in the Rules after the
1957 conference, and he explained the 'warning system' for
branches which broke the ballot rules.

'I am far from suggesting that it is not a desirable habit in an
Executive Councillor,' Mr Gardiner said to him, 'but you rarely
said anything, did you?'—'When I found it necessary,' replied Mr
Vincent.

'Which was pretty rare?'—'I wouldn't say that.'

'Because you were usually in agreement with Mr Haxell, were
you not?'—'I decided everything, when a decision was necessary
to be taken, on my own ability and my own conscience.'

He agreed that from 1948 onwards he had been trying to get
elected as a representative to the Trades Union Congress. Until
1955 he never got more than 5,000 votes.

'But in 1955 you suddenly got 18,000 votes, didn't you?'

He agreed.

'To anybody who knows anything about the ETU, that meant,
did it not, that in 1955 and thereafter you received the support of
the Communist Party?'—'I wouldn't know that.'

'Were you appointed one of the Committee of Enquiry to go
into the question of whether the elections in this Union had been
rigged?'—'I was.'

'You, and Mr Scott, and Mr West?'—'That is so.'

'Were Mr Cannon and Mr Young ordered to appear before
you?'—'They did.'

'And did they both refuse to produce any evidence on the ground
that the Committee of Enquiry were themselves not impartial?'—
'That is so.'

'And Mr Cannon said at one point: "If I'm making an allegation against you, Brother Vincent, somebody else should decide
whether it is true or not; not you"?'—'That is so.'

'And did you say, as an example of your impartiality: "You make the allegation and I will decide what I will do with you"?'— 'That meant,' said Mr Vincent improbably, 'that if Mr Cannon had any wish to charge me under the Rules, I would submit my case to the Union according to the Rules'.

On the question of Mr Chapple's misconduct in exposing Union affairs, Mr Vincent agreed that the real charge against Mr Chapple was sending his letter to Sir Vincent Tewson, and that the letter got into the Press because Sir Vincent released it. He also agreed that officials of the Union (e.g., Mr Byrne) were not now allowed to speak at a Policy Conference, and that any candidate who wanted to express his opinions had to confine his remarks in his election address to his own industrial record—the address being censored by a sub-committee which included Mr Foulkes, Mr McLennan, sometimes Mr Haxell, and himself. And he thought Mr Haxell was entitled to write letters in the newspapers saying 'My Executive Council thinks this or that', although the Executive Council had never discussed the matter.

The Judge said later that Mr Vincent was an accurate witness, but a man incapable of a judicial attitude and subject to muddled thought processes.

Mild surprise and a stir of interest greeted the appearance in the witness-box of Mrs Lilian Higgs, of Bromley, Kent, who had been a clerk in the ETU Head Office for five years and had just left to go to another job with 'a well-known charitable organisation'. It soon became apparent that Mrs Higgs had never, at the material times, had any inkling that there might be something wrong with the ETU and its elections.

'Are you a member of any political party?' Mr Lawson asked her.
'I am—the Conservative Party.'

And she had belonged to the Conservative Party for thirteen years. She had never been a member of the Labour or the Communist Party—'or,' said Mr Lawson sweepingly, 'any party of that kind'.

She had helped Mr Oliver, the then Office Manager, with the ETU elections at the end of each quarter, and early in 1958 Mr Oliver retired, to be succeeded (after a kind of tapering-off period) by Mr Humphrey.

Mr Lawson showed her the Head Office 'black book', a loose-leaf folder in which were recorded the branches that had been 'warned' for infringements of the Rules.

It started at the March quarter of 1953, because it was only then that warnings for infringement began to be given. 'Before then,' said Mrs Higgs, 'I understood they had always been rejected without warning.' At the end of 1958 the 'black book' was succeeded by a card-index system, and it was Mrs Higgs' job to keep this up to date, with details of the branches' membership, qualified voters, warnings, and rejections. She produced it in Court and explained how it worked.

The normal practice, she said, was that when a branch *first* infringed it got a warning. If it committed the same type of infringement again (e.g., wrong meeting night, late returns, etc.), and it still had the same secretary, it was rejected. If the secretary was new, it would get another warning.

'Was that practice carried out right through the time when you were helping with this?' Mr Lawson asked her.

'It changed,' said Mrs Higgs, 'in the December quarter, 1959'.

The Judge observed that he supposed Mrs Higgs might not know what difference it made in the end—'but why,' he asked, 'was there all this severity about the wrong meeting night? Do you know?'—'I don't know, my Lord,' said Mrs Higgs. As for lateness in sending in the ballot returns, 'if the branch return came in on a Monday, it was date-stamped on the Monday, and that was the date we took it as being received'.

'You simply compared the date of the branch meeting with the date stamp on the envelope?'—'Yes.'

'And checked one with the other to see if it was more than five days?'—'Yes.'

'You took no notice of whether it covered a Saturday or Sunday, or Christmas Day or Good Friday or a bank holiday?'—'No.'

It was she and Mr Oliver who together did all the sorting, separating the sheep from the goats before the national scrutineers ever came on the scene.

When she was cross-examined, Mr Gerald Gardiner asked her about the strange story of the four Liverpool branches, all of which were allegedly late, though it was only the two which had voted for Mr Byrne that were disqualified.

'Will you please understand,' he said, 'that in the questions I am about to ask you I am in no way attacking your honesty. There you have got what purport to be the envelopes of Liverpool Central, Liverpool South, Liverpool East, and Liverpool Instrument Makers. Will you assume that they all four met on their correct meeting night, which was Monday, December the 21st?'— 'Yes,' replied Mrs Higgs.

'Did they all arrive on the 28th?'—'Yes. I would like to point out one thing here, that before the December 1959 election Mr Oliver used to take note of the postmark, and if they were posted on the fourth day and should have arrived on the fifth day he used to accept that. I probably ought not to have put that in at this point,' added Mrs Higgs a little uncertainly.

'It's very interesting *indeed*,' the Judge reassured her.

But she had absolutely no idea how it could have happened in the 1959 election that two of the Liverpool branches were disqualified and two not, though all four were equally culpable.

Mr Gardiner asked her to look at the card-index records of about thirty different branches, all of which were disqualified for lateness in the 1959 election. Not one of them had been so noted by Mrs Higgs and placed in the 'infringement' file.

'Mrs Higgs,' he said, 'don't think I am suggesting for a moment that this is anything like a complete list of the branches which were late but were not disqualified, it is just those which have been seen. But can you help us at all as to how that came about in this rather important election?'—'I'm awfully sorry, I just can throw no light on that at all. It's a thing we were always very careful about.'

'We can all make mistakes. We all do. But are you satisfied that you could not by accident, or by about thirty different accidents, have failed to notice that those were late?'—'I shouldn't imagine so.'

Mrs Higgs was questioned closely, both by Mr Gardiner and by the Judge, about the lapse of time—sometimes a couple of weeks —between her knowing the correct number of ballot papers required by a branch for a forthcoming election and her giving the printers the necessary order to print. 'It's odd, isn't it,' said the

Judge, 'that the correct figures were not used when they were available?'

'It doesn't seem odd to me, my Lord,' Mrs Higgs assured him. 'I've tried to explain that my volume of work was such that I could not get down to it. That would just go on the pile with the rest of the branch membership returns.'

'I suppose from your point of view it only seemed like a few extra wasted bits of paper?'—'I wouldn't say that.'

'Did you realise that loose ballot papers were dangerous things?' —'It had never occurred to me, my Lord, so far as ballot papers were concerned.'

And the assurance carried conviction—Mrs Higgs, it seemed to those listening, would see no more danger in an unattended ballot paper than in an umbrella left in the corner or a pair of outdoor shoes in the office cupboard. 'You didn't think of anybody using ballot papers?' the Judge suggested to her.—'No,' she said.

'I am *quite* prepared to believe that, Mrs Higgs.'—'Thank you, my Lord.'

It was late on Friday afternoon and the Judge glanced at the clock as Mrs Higgs was about to leave the witness-box. 'Any employer who has the advantage of your services,' he told her, 'ought to regard himself as very fortunate'.—Thank you, my Lord.'

'Gradually,' said his Lordship, adjourning the Court until Monday May 15 at ten-thirty a.m., 'I am beginning to get a glimmer of light here and there, and some grip on this case. But not much.'

4 Mr James Humphrey's Evidence

A member of the ETU since 1930 and of the Communist Party since 1950, Mr James Humphrey said that he was now Office Manager of the Union. He had been Branch Secretary, Executive Council member for five consecutive two-year terms, and a representative of the ETU on various industrial councils and negotiating committees. Part of his current duties was the opening of the envelopes arriving from the branches after the holding of elections, though he did not check their contents for 'infringements'.

'It is said against you,' said Mr Lawson, 'that you were a

member of the "National Advisory Committee" from the year 1948 to date. Will you tell my Lord about that?'—'That is not true.'

'Do you know of any committee which had that name?'—'No.'

But he did go, about twice a year, to meetings at King Street and elsewhere at which those present were members both of the Communist Party and of the ETU, and at which the main topic of discussion was usually the building industry.

In September 1959 he took part in a discussion with Mr Swift, of the Express Printing Company, the purpose of which was to 'speed up the operation of the ballot procedure', especially the dispatch of envelopes to the branches. There had been complaints about late delivery from the printers. Mr Swift had said that he got his instructions too late, and proposed the resumption of a custom that had for some years been discontinued—the *estimating* of required quantities in bulk. It was arranged to do this, and also to have a Head Office ETU official at the printing works in Manchester to superintend the printing and dispatch of the ballot papers—some of which were thought to have gone astray (Jarrow was an example).

'How did you arrive at your estimate,' Mr Lawson asked him, 'from the material which you had?'—'As the basis I took the March and June number of members entitled to vote; I took the highest number. I also had regard to the highest number of members in the branch, and then tried to make an allowance in order that it would not be necessary, once we had the numbers printed, that we should have to go back to the printers again to have more printed.'

Mr Justice Winn leaned towards him. 'Did you use logarithms for this?' he asked.

'No, my Lord,' said Mr Humphrey seriously.

'Or a divining bowl, or what?'—'No, my Lord. As I say, apart from the basis of the March and June figures, it was largely a matter of guesswork.'

'You applied the annual uplift of 5·8 per cent and divided by four, or something like that, and added the number you first thought of?'—'No, my Lord.'

'It must have been a very difficult and long task?'—'It took a long time because I couldn't spend time continuously on it.'

Then Mr Lawson came to the fascinating incident of the surplus ballot papers sent by the printers to St Pancras Station 'to await collection'. Mr Swift, the printer, had been only too glad to get rid of them. Ever since the preparations for this action had started, many months before, the Plaintiffs had been trying to find out what had happened to them, and no help was to be had from the Defendants. It was now known, from Mr Swift's evidence (see page 40), that they had been sent to St Pancras. What happened to them then?

'Mr Humphrey,' said Mr Lawson, 'Mr Swift says he sent twenty-seven parcels to St Pancras for the Head Office, containing ballot papers. Can you help about that? What do *you* know about the parcels at St Pancras?'—'I can recollect having a telephone call from the Express Printing to say that they had started dispatching the excess ballot papers—they were sending them to St Pancras. I went myself and started picking them up.'

'Did you do it on one day or several days?'—'Over several days.'

The parcels were addressed to him. He used one of the ETU cars, took them to Head Office himself, and put them in a disused office on the ground floor, which contained only some bookcases and racks piled with contribution-ledger sheets from branches. Originally this room had three doors. One was boarded up and the other two led. respectively to a corridor and to the library. He locked these doors, and the key to the corridor he later that day handed to the caretaker 'in case there was a fire or anything like that'. The library door key he kept himself.

The parcels were made up according to 'Areas', or groups of branches. Twenty-six branches had complained that the printer had sent them no ballot forms. So Mr Humphrey himself opened the appropriate parcels and took out the ballot papers needed. He didn't know what date this was, but it was after the last day when they could have been of any possible use, for they did not arrive at St Pancras until November 20 at the earliest, and, as the Judge pointed out—

'Returns of the membership entitled to vote as at September

1959 were required by the Rules to be in within fourteen days at the latest after the last Saturday of September.'

'Yes,' agreed Mr Lawson.

'One of the many reasons,' said his Lordship, 'why this election was a complete nullity, this December 1959 election'.

Having taken out the ballot papers for the twenty-six overlooked branches, Mr Humphrey retied the parcels and (towards the end of November) told the Head Office handyman to destroy them in the brick-built incinerator in the grounds at Head Office. This burning operation took nine or ten days, and from time to time Mr Humphrey 'went round there to make sure it was being done properly'. No one else had had access to any of the parcels, concluded Mr Humphrey.

He was cross-examined first about the 'National Advisory Committee', of which all the Defendants were denying any knowledge.

'I suggest to you,' began Mr Gardiner, 'that all this about the building industry is nonsense, and that in fact the Communist Party do have advisory committees for the members of every trade union?'—'The suggestion is incorrect.'

'And that for every trade union there is a national advisory committee, as well as a local advisory committee consisting of those members of the union who are also members of the Communist Party?'—'That is not within my knowledge.'

'And so if Mr Blairford and Mr Vetterlein say that they saw you at meeting of the *national* advisory committee, that is quite wrong, is it?'—'That is wrong.'

'You see, Mr Townsend told us that he saw you at such a meeting.'—'That is not true,' said Mr Humphrey, and the Judge interposed:

'*Why* not go to such a meeting? Do you mean you don't know that they took place, or that you preferred not to go to them?'— 'I didn't know they took place, if they took place.'

'Would it seem natural to you,' the Judge went on, 'that there should be such meetings of the Communists interested in the affairs of the ETU?'—'I suppose it would be natural, my Lord, yes.'

'Well, it's missing a great opportunity, so far as the Communist Party is concerned, to refrain from telling members of the ETU what to do at their policy conference, is it not?'—'Well, as far as

I'm aware, the Communist Party *never* told members of the ETU what to do at a policy conference.'

'It seems a bit backward of them, doesn't it?'—'I don't think so, my Lord.'

'Well, what's the object of being a Communist except to do everything you can to forward the policies of the Communist Party?'—'You do that normally, my Lord, in normal contact with people. Not by calling special meetings.'

'Nor by taking special steps in policy conferences?'—'No: I *will* say they may be discussed by Communists during the conference, in the evening at the hotel, my Lord.'

'Yes,' said the Judge. 'Thank you.'

'In 1955,' Mr Gardiner resumed, 'there were rumours, were there not, in the Union that the fact that the Communists always seemed to get elected didn't mean that they had been genuinely elected but that the elections were being rigged?'—'I'm not sure about the date, but there certainly had been rumours, yes.'

'And in January 1956 the *Daily Telegraph* raised this question?' —'I believe so, yes.'

'The matter came to a head after the Cannon-Frazer election in September 1957?'—'It reached a sort of new intensity, yes.'

'Did you regard these as serious allegations?'—'Yes.'

'And by December 1957 the Union was issuing circulars to all branches, and to the Press, saying that all this was quite untrue?' —'Yes.'

'And Mr Foulkes was appearing on television about it?'—'I believe he did, yes,' said Mr Humphrey.

He believed also that the Union had published a pamphlet called *The Facts about the Press Campaign*, but could not remember what it had said.

When the Jarrow election of September 1958 was being enquired into by Mr Haxell, Mr McLennan, Mr Goldberg, and Mr West, none of those gentlemen asked *him*, as Office Manager, whether voting papers went to Jarrow direct from the printers or came to Head Office. He remembered the first intervention by the TUC, the reply from his office saying that the TUC's concern about the prestige of the trade union movement was shared by the ETU, and the ETU's rejection of the story that the elections were rigged.

'Did you make careful enquiry,' Mr Gardiner asked him, 'as to what steps were required to ensure that the Rules were being properly carried out in the September 1959 election?'—'No, I can't say that I did. I relied on the honesty of Mr Oliver and Mrs Higgs.'

'It isn't a question of honesty. There were Rules, were there not, which it was alleged had not been followed?'—'I don't know what Rules you mean.'

'Rules as to the conduct of elections. You had a detailed knowledge of the Rules?'—'Yes.'

'Are you telling my Lord that you didn't take steps in September 1959—the first election for which you were formally responsible—to consider the Rules yourself and see how they ought to be applied, and discuss that with Mr Oliver?'—'I considered that my responsibility was to see that the envelopes were passed to Mrs Higgs, and after that the responsibility was the national scrutineers'.'

It was he who gave the instructions, Mr Humphrey said, for the grouping of branch returns according to lateness, previous infringements, etc., and all the letters in the first place came to him unopened.

'So that if any envelopes had been substituted by the time they reached Mr Oliver or Mrs Higgs, you must have been a party to its being done?'—'If they *had* been. But they weren't.'

When Mr Humphrey said that the national scrutineers 'sometimes' made allowances for late posting, Mr Gardiner showed him a list of branches which had met on December 14 and 15, 1959, whose envelopes all bore a receipt stamp of the 21st, and which were therefore 'too late'. 'Can you give my Lord any explanation which is consistent with honesty,' said Mr Gardiner, 'of the fact that all the branches which voted in favour of Mr Haxell were passed, and that all those who voted in favour of Mr Byrne were disqualified?'—'I can't give an explanation for it, no.'

It was the same with a further list—the branches which had met on December 16, 17 and 18, their returns arriving on the 22nd, 23rd and 24th. 'I have no explanation other than the one which I have already given.'

'Which is . . .?' prompted the Judge.

'Which is that I understood the national scrutineers sometimes made allowances for late posting.'

After other similar instances had been put to him, Mr Gardiner said this:

'It was pretty obvious to you, was it not, by the day before Christmas, or at latest when you looked at the returns on the twenty-eighth, that Mr Haxell had lost the election?'—'*I* didn't know what the progress of the election was.'

'Come, Mr Humphrey!'—'I did *not*.'

'General Secretary is the most important position in the Union, is it not—that and General President?' Mr Humphrey agreed.

'Mr Haxell was on the Executive Committee of the Communist Party?'—'Yes.'

'And your and Mr McLennan's names would have been pretty good mud if Mr Haxell hadn't been elected, would they not?'— 'I don't think so.'

'Are you telling my Lord that, although you were the only person to open the envelopes, you didn't know how the election was going?'—'I did *not*, no.'

'Do you seriously say that you didn't keep a running poll of how it was going?'—'I did not, no.'

The Judge later observed that Mr Humphrey gave this evidence in an unconvincing way and 'his voice and face betrayed tension'. But at this stage his Lordship merely remarked that it was one thing to attribute these ballot results to the 'discretion' of the scrutineers, but what about the results that had been put in the 'Apparently All Right' file?

'I thought they examined all of them, my Lord,' said Mr Humphrey.

'I didn't ask you that. I asked to what extent you now suppose the scrutineers paid any attention to the returns in the file containing only branches which were in order?'—'It would be an extremely difficult job to do.'

'And most unlikely that they would tackle it, is it not?'—'Yes.'

'That means that you, Oliver, and Mrs Higgs could stop any effective scrutiny, for the default of any particular branch, by putting it into the "All Right" file?'—'Could have done, my Lord, yes.'

'I don't say that is what happened, but that is what could have happened?'—'It *could* happen, my Lord.'

'And of you three,' resumed Mr Gardiner, 'you were the man who had an interest in doing that, had you not? They hadn't?'—'*I* had no interest in doing that.'

'You're not suggesting you didn't want Mr Haxell to win, are you?'—'I certainly wanted him to win, yes.'

'If you went and took from the "Infringement File" the returns of a number of branches where the majority had voted for Mr Haxell, and put them into the "All Clear" file, that would very easily account for what happened, would it not?'—'It would account for what happened, yes.'

'Isn't that what you did?'—'No.'

'In this election, of the branches which voted,' Mr Gardiner next suggested, 'four hundred and eighteen wanted Mr Byrne, did they not, and only two hundred and ten wanted Mr Haxell?'—'I accept that, if that's an analysis. I haven't made one myself.'

'It's the very high postal vote in a few of the Communist branches which does the trick, isn't it?'—'I couldn't tell without looking through all the figures. I don't know.'

Neither did he know why it was, in 'estimating' the numbers of ballot forms to be ordered from the printers, that he ordered quantities like 628 for Belfast S.E. Branch and 691 for Belfast Municipal (both pro-Haxell branches). It wasn't, he told Mr Gardiner, to 'make it look as if it was an exact figure'. The printer, he said, 'knew it was an estimate'.

'Are you really telling me,' asked the Judge, 'that you calculated these figures to one and eight of the final digit?'—'No, my Lord. The last figure was just an amount that I added on to cover the possibility of not having to have the printer print again.'

'Do listen to what I said. You don't mean to tell me you added one to six hundred and ninety in order to cover the possibility of having to print again?'—'No, my Lord.'

'What *does* the "one" represent in six hundred and ninety-one? Is it the answer to a calculation?'—'I can only say, my Lord, that I must have said: "We'll allow about six hundred and fifty and add forty-one," or something like that.'

'Just for fun? Or how? How do you ever get to a figure like six hundred and ninety-one, unless in some way it's the result of a calculation?'—'I can't explain how I got to those figures, my Lord.'

'I can understand your adding fifty or a hundred or seventy-five, but not forty-one.'—'Yes, I know it seems strange, but that's the way I did it, my Lord.'

'How long did it take you to do it for six hundred and fifty branches?'—'Altogether it took me about three weeks.'

'Three weeks? Instead of going to a set of papers where the whole answer was set out?'—'But those papers weren't in any sort of order.'

'All you had to do was to sort them.'—'That was a terrific job in itself.'

'Sorting them? Just taking the files and putting them like that, in order?' (His Lordship shuffled a few files on his desk.) 'That's all you have to do?'—'Yes.'

'You did three weeks on this type of calculation? You want me to believe that?'—'Yes, my Lord.'

And the cross-examination proceeded with many further examples of this accurately clairvoyant arithmetic.

'You say you had in mind, during the election, the allegations made in the Press and elsewhere?'—'I'd had that in mind for a long time, yes.'

'And in spite of that you went on allowing branch secretaries favouring Mr Haxell to get these extra voting papers more or less as they wanted them?'—'It wasn't a question of branch secretaries who favoured Mr Haxell; it was a question of branch secretaries who wanted more.'

'If you do this on the telephone with the printers do you always write confirming it?'—'No.'

'Does that enable any good Communist on the staff to ring them up and say, "This is the ETU—we want fifty extra to be sent to so-and-so"?'—'I don't know. I wouldn't know. I shouldn't think so.'

'Has it never occurred to you that it would be desirable to confirm it in writing?'—'Yes, it would be. It has occurred to me now.'

Mr Gardiner came back to the 26,000 spare ballot papers sent to St Pancras Station 'to be called for'.

'It would have been much cheaper and simpler,' he suggested, 'rather than sending them to St Pancras and having them hanging about, and then brought to Head Office only to be destroyed, to have had them destroyed at the printers', wouldn't it?'—'Yes, it would be,' said Mr Humphrey. 'But Mr Swift felt it would be better to take them off his premises.'

Mr Justice Winn wanted to know who the suspects at Head Office were—who were the people who had to be frustrated by the use of the parcels office at St Pancras.

'Against whom were you taking precautions at Head Office?' he said. 'Against whom were you seeking to protect the ballot papers whilst they still existed, and to make sure they were duly incinerated?'—'Against the possibility of anybody on the Express Printing Company's staff doing anything with them, my Lord.'

'I'm sorry, let me make myself clear to you. *After the ballot papers had reached Head Office*, against whom were you seeking to protect them?'—'Against anybody who may have had some interest in them, my Lord.'

'Who would that be, Communists anxious to increase the vote of any candidate favouring Communist policies? Tories or other reactionaries infiltrating into the Union in order to vote for the anti-Communist policy? Or similar reactionaries acting as spies or *agents provocateurs* to cast bogus pro-Communist votes and then reveal what was happening? Does that exhaust the categories of malicious and evil-minded persons against whom the ballot papers had to be protected, or is there anyone else that you had in mind?' —'I think that is all, my Lord, that there would possibly have been,' said Mr Humphrey gratefully.

'Whom are you *really* afraid of, the Tory reactionaries, the newspapers, or other Fascist or capitalist spies or provocative agents?' —'I don't think I classified them in any way like that, my Lord.'

But he had thought it 'was more discreet' to have them sent to St Pancras than sent straight to Head Office by carrier. 'I thought it was a matter of security to try and keep it limited to as few people as possible.'

'Because they were going to be used for a wrong purpose?' said Mr Gardiner.

'No.'

'Could anybody walk into the parcels office and say, "I'm from the ETU. Have you got a parcel for them"?'—'I presume they could have done, yes.'

'That wasn't very secure, was it?' interposed the Judge mildly.

'No, my Lord.'

'You didn't tip off any of your friends,' Mr Gardiner asked, 'to do that with an odd parcel?'—'No.'

While the 26,000 ballot papers were in Mr Humphrey's custody, an enquiry was going on into the strange arrival of spare ballot papers at the three Southampton branches. Mr George Scott was busy conducting it. But Mr Scott didn't ask Mr Humphrey what surplus voting papers had all the time been available at Head Office.

'Were you going to keep jolly quiet about them?' asked Mr Gardiner.

'Had I been asked I would have told whoever asked me.' In fact, when the Press had come out with the Southampton story, Mr McLennan *did* ask him 'what the position was about the Hythe and Woolston ballot papers', and he told him that only the correct amount had been sent to those branches from the printers.

'Yes, and what else?' said the Judge.

'That's what I told him, my Lord.'

'Why did you stop there?'—'I think because he only asked me the way in which the ballot papers had been sent to Hythe and Woolston.'

'Did you tell him you had some at Head Office?' Mr Gardiner asked him.

'No, I didn't.'

'Why not?'—'I don't know,' said the trapped Mr Humphrey.

'Because he knew it?'—'He *didn't* know it, as far as I'm aware.'

But Mr Humphrey, after all, was a Defendant in this case. The law sometimes leans over backwards to be fair to Defendants.

'I think perhaps you are tired, Mr Humphrey,' said the Judge. 'I don't really think those last few answers can do you justice. Perhaps you would like to think it over—why you didn't tell Mr McLennan all you then knew about those ballot papers. I will rise now until ten-thirty tomorrow.'

But the next morning Mr Humphrey was able only to repeat that it had not occurred to him to tell Mr McLennan about the extra ballot papers at Head Office. He was able to say, though, that the 'national officers' (i.e., elected and salaried full-time officials employed at Head Office as assistants to the General Secretary) all had cars and kept records of their use, but that only the national officers themselves would know where they had been during those vital days surrounding Christmas 1959 when the substitute envelopes had been posted. And he steadily and finally refuted Mr Gardiner's closing suggestions that when he saw that Haxell was losing the election, he (a) changed the Head Office procedure so that Haxell branches could not be penalised for infringement, (b) transferred a lot of dubiously qualified Haxell branches to the 'All Clear' file, and (c) was a party to the posting of substituted envelopes. What Mr Gardiner did *not* put to him in this final show-down, but what the Judge later decided was a large factor in his guilt, was that he had 'deliberately ordered substantial excess quantities of ballots for branches where he expected that fraudulent votes could be registered, if need be, for Mr Haxell'.

There followed a succession of witnesses about the administrative procedure at Head Office—Mr Derek Warlow, a member of the Communist Party (but not of the ETU), who had dealt with 'branch membership work' and ballot returns. Mr George Acton, an ex-sailor who worked at Head Office as caretaker and 'odd job man'—he identified the locked room containing the surplus ballot papers because it was the one in which the staff 'kept the old wallop for Christmas', but then the Judge had identified him as an old sailor as soon as he appeared; Mr Ronald Sidey, who was in charge of the Dispatch Department and knew about the posting and receipt of ballot papers; and Mr Robert Oliver, former Office Manager (now retired), who substantially corroborated the evidence of Mrs Higgs and the less puzzling parts of the evidence given by Mr Humphrey, and described the procedure followed by the national scrutineers, with illuminating glimpses of what had happened to 'infringing' branches in a large number of elections. Mr Oliver, an elderly man, was not in good health at the time of the trial, but one passage from his evidence under cross-examination may perhaps be selected as typical:

'Did it strike you at all that it was a bit odd that a rather small branch like Rosyth, before the actual election, and apart from any additional ones they had later, should want fifty additional sets in December 1958; then in March 1959, seventy-five; and then in June, a hundred?'—'Additional ones?'

'Well, writing in to say they hadn't had them?'—'It *would* seem peculiar to me.'

'But did it seem peculiar to you at the time, do you remember, with regard to Rosyth?'—'I didn't have anything to do with it, did I?'

'You dealt with Rosyth, I think, at some point?'—'If Rosyth was the occasion when I was in the office and I left a memo on Mrs Higgs' desk to say "so many had gone to Rosyth", it would be on the instructions of Mr Humphrey.'

'And you never noticed yourself that it seemed odd that they were increasing at each election?'—'No, no,' said Mr Oliver; but it did seem, from his manner, that this was because it happened with so many branches that you got quite used to it.

Mr Alfred McBrowse was one of the national scrutineers. He had a long record of service to the ETU and to the trade union movement. One passage in his evidence-in-chief gave the Court a glimpse of the Head Office staff of the ETU living a life overshadowed by the famous Rules, whose complexity was felt to necessitate the maintenance of a Research Department.

'On one occasion,' he said, 'we were going through the branch returns. These had been accepted by Mr Oliver as being in order, but we found that one of them had not been signed by the branch president. We queried with Mr Oliver why this branch hadn't a branch president's signature, and asked him why he hadn't specifically brought that to our attention. And he said that in the case of branches with under thirty members, according to Rule, it wasn't necessary to have a branch president in attendance. And my colleague Mr Rowles' (this was the other national scrutineer) 'was quite confident that somewhere in the Rule Book—and so was I—there was a Rule saying that they had to have branch presidents. We went through to the Research Department and asked them to

look through the Rule Book for the Rule dealing with this situation. I think it appears in the Sixth Appendix that even in branches
with a membership under thirty it is not permissible for the branch
secretary to act as the branch president. We therefore said to Mr
Oliver that we insisted that the warning be sent. And it was sent.'

Mr McBrowse's story also made apparent the vast quantity of
documentary evidence that burdened the Court in this trial. Again
and again Mr Gardiner had called for documents which were not
available. 'I am afraid,' said Mr Lawson at one point, 'that a
number of these original documents have got mislaid'.

'Fate has been unkind,' said the Judge indulgently, 'in that
generally speaking the lightning has struck upon the more valuable
trees. A large proportion of the missing documents happen to be a
little more important than the others.'

'Well, the explanation may be, my Lord,' said Mr Lawson, 'that
these are the documents which have been handled most; and the
more they are handled and moved around, the more likely they
are to be lost.'

'I don't know,' Mr Gardiner said, 'whether it would be possible,
if this action has to go on much longer, to have the documents
somewhere rather more readily available?'

'It is extremely inconvenient,' the Judge agreed. 'On the other
hand, I suppose it's very difficult to have more than is physically
present already?'

'My Lord,' said Mr Lawson, 'here are these in Court, and there
are a lot in a consultation room, but altogether there are hundred-
weights of documents'.

'I think, Mr Gardiner,' the Judge said, 'this is one of those cases
where the mass of paper clogs the machine—it's a sort of Parkin-
son's Law in application.'

But the absence of the original documents to 'put in' as evidence
meant that there was a good deal of reading aloud from copies,
and Mr Lawson wasn't always able to stop this. He tried to stop
Mr Gardiner doing it in the case of the LSE No. 14 Branch. Mr
Gardiner was reading to Mr McBrowse a letter written on November 7, 1957, by the secretary of that disgruntled branch to Mr
Haxell, complaining that the national scrutineers had so dawdled
over their work that the entire ballot was defeated by the time limit:

It is the considered opinion of the members of this branch that the General Secretary has been guilty of a breach of Rule 10, Clause 2(f). We desire to seek the interpretation of the Rules, and in order to do this we seek the permission of the Executive Council to write to the Registrar General [this probably meant the Registrar of Friendly Societies, who would hardly have felt, however, that he could act as interpreter] for his advice. We would also draw your attention to the statement of Brother Bolt, of Peckham Branch, before the meeting commenced, which you no doubt read in our minutes, and in which he admitted having said that as far as this branch ballot was concerned we had 'had it'; and that the General Secretary would rule it out of order when he (Brother Bolt) sent in his report. This we take to be an instruction to the member to report any little thing he could and leave the rest to the General Secretary, who would rule it out of order on some pretext or other. Further, it is felt that the intimidation of some Executive Council members . . .

'I hesitate to interrupt,' said Mr Lawson, interrupting, 'but is my learned friend cross-examining the witness as to credit' (i.e., as to whether you could believe him or not) 'or as to some issue which is not pleaded at all?'

'But it is,' the Judge told him. 'It's pleaded that there was no return made' (by the scrutineers) 'within fourteen days.'

'I respectfully agree on that matter, but he is now cross-examining (or seems to be) as to what was being said as between LSE 14 and the Head Office. My Lord, *that* is not relevant to any pleaded issue.'

'Isn't he right to ask the witness whether the statements in these letters are accurate to his knowledge?'—'I respectfully agree so far as date of meeting and not finalising the report is concerned.'

'Yes—you take no exception to that?'—'I take no exception. Indeed I would be prepared to concede that there was *no* final report signed by scrutineers on October the 17th.'

'Very well. That point is established. What is it you are objecting to? As you unfortunately haven't the documents here to put before me, Mr Gardiner is reading aloud that which I should otherwise inevitably be reading with my eyes.'—'The letter he is now reading goes beyond the question of the date of the scrutineers' meeting or the date of their report.'

'Because it's someone complaining, and saying "you've had it", and so forth, you are worried lest I am being affected by it?'—'No, my Lord. I am concerned that your Lordship is not burdened with issues which are not "pleaded" issues.'

But the Judge let the reading go on.

Then came another of the Defendants, Mr John Rengert, of the Eltham Branch, who had once belonged to the Communist Party but transferred himself to the Labour Party in 1946 and was now chairman of a ward. He was elected a national scrutineer for the year 1959 and 'attended all the scrutinies' for that year. He described how the 'infringements' were detected and classified (too late, wrong meeting night, incomplete, unsigned, etc.), and said that at the 1959 Byrne-Haxell election it was he and his co-scrutineer—Mr Charles Shipman, another Defendant—who 'actually made the decision as to whether a return was to be rejected or not rejected'. And he said that 'there were a number of branches where complaints had been laid by members and visitors in attendance at those meetings'. Information about these came to him by way of letters that had passed between the persons complaining (e.g., the 'spies') and the indignant branch secretaries.

'Were they read out or summarised to you?' Mr Lawson asked him.

'I should say the letters themselves were read out to us.'

'By whom?'—'By Mr Foulkes.'

And thereupon they made their decision—accept or reject.

When Mr Rengert was cross-examined, this process came a little further into the light. Mr Gardiner took up the case of the complaint made by Mr Britz, of the Finchley Branch, about breaches of the Rules at the election (see page 93).

'Now the Branch Secretary entirely denied that, didn't he? There's a long letter from the branch saying it's all wrong. Now Mr Britz, who made the complaint, has told my Lord that everything he said was true. How do you decide that Mr Britz isn't telling the truth without hearing him?'—'We accepted the Branch Secretary's explanation.'

'Why? You didn't, of course, read the letters: Mr Foulkes summarised them, did he?'—'I wouldn't say Mr Foulkes summarised them. I should say Mr Foulkes *read* the letters.'

'Well, wasn't it plain to you when Mr Foulkes read the letters that there was a strong conflict as to what the truth was and what had happened?'—'No. I say that, rightly or wrongly, we did accept the Branch Secretary's comments and therefore accepted the vote.'

'But how did you come to the conclusion that Mr Britz was not telling the truth without hearing him?'—'Well, the branch itself had accepted the report,' replied Mr Rengert. But it turned out that the Judge had not.

'Just tell me,' said Mr Justice Winn, 'whether you consider that you investigated the matter'.

'We investigated the matter as far as we could.'—'Do you call that an investigation?'

'No, no, my Lord. We formed our opinion on the correspondence in front of us.'

'Yes. It's not an investigation, is it?'—'No, my Lord.'

'Would you be rather surprised to know,' went on the Judge, just as though he were once more Treasury Counsel at the Old Bailey, 'that McLennan wrote to the Branch Secretary of Finchley on November the 9th saying the complaint had been investigated? "The allegations made have been denied"—denied by letters only?' —'Yes.'

'It's putting it a bit high, isn't it?'—'Yes, my Lord.'

'You agree?'—'Yes, my Lord, there's no actual investigation.' The Judge rather approved of Mr Rengert.

Other breaches of the Rules, of course, had been condoned. 'Rules are made for the organisation and not the organisation for the Rules. We should surely endeavour where we can not to throw out the votes of the members, being lay members. We know how the branches proceed,' said Mr Rengert, 'in particular in December, with the rush of Christmas and all like that—with the branch secretaries and everybody possibly wishing him all the best for the year, and all like that'.

Oddly enough, this was one of the most effective little speeches in the whole of the trial. It had a simple warmth, a flavour of Christmas, and such an overtone of humanity as to make it seem that the real villain of the piece was the Rule Book. A few minutes later Mr Gerald Gardiner was saying this:

'My Lord, I have heard this witness's evidence, and Mr Oliver's and Mrs Higgs' and Mr Humphrey's, and I think it right, on behalf of my clients, to withdraw any allegation of fraud against the two national scrutineers. But I shall of course continue to maintain that the whole thing was quite wrong and was not in accordance with Rule, and so forth.'

'I'm glad to hear you say that, Mr Gardiner, because on this witness's evidence I was going to raise that very matter with you.'

'My Lord, I thought it right to do it at once.'

'Yes, very right, so far as Mr Rengert is concerned. And you extend that to Mr Shipman as well?'

(Mr Charles Shipman was the other national scrutineer, who had not yet given evidence in his own defence.)

'Yes, my Lord,' said Mr Gardiner.

'You understand, Mr Rengert, that all charges of improper conduct have now been unreservedly withdrawn, as a result of this investigation? May I say that is a very proper course, and from what I have heard of you I think it is incredible that you would have lent yourself to any dishonesty of any kind at all.'

And to Mr Charles Shipman, the other national scrutineer for the 1959 election, the Judge said: 'May I just tell you that the Court wholly accepts the fact that you have done nothing improper at any time in regard to this matter, and the matter is now over so far as you are concerned.'

Mr Rengert and Mr Shipman were not deceivers, Mr Gardiner said. They were themselves deceived.

Then came Mr Samuel Goldberg, another of the Defendants, who had been a branch president, an Executive Councillor, a member of Birmingham City Council, and since 1946 a member of the Labour Party and the ETU. Although the Judge disbelieved a good deal of his evidence, Mr Goldberg made an impression on his Lordship of 'possessing greater capacity to construe the Rules and noticeably more anxiety to conform with them than to override or ignore for practical convenience any obstacle they presented'.

Mr Goldberg described his participation in the Leicester and Loughborough enquiry in 1957, and how he had urged that at the forthcoming Rules Revision Conference the Rules should be so changed as to prevent branches from appealing against Executive

Council decisions in the way that Leicester had done. He thought, too, that even the national scrutineers' decisions should be above appeal. And he gave his version of the 'disciplining' of Mr Chapple for sending circular letters to the TUC and to the Union's membership making 'grave accusations' against the ETU leaders.

'Is it a fact,' Mr Gardiner asked him, 'that the Executive Council have agreed they will pay the costs of all the Defendants?'—'I beg your pardon?'

'Didn't you hear what I said?'—'I'm sorry?'

Mr Gardiner repeated the question.

'I believe that is a fact,' Mr Goldberg then admitted.

'Are you still a member of the Executive Council?'—'I am, yes.'

'Then you must *know* that it's a fact?'—'It *is* a fact.'

This was an inauspicious beginning; but it is charitable to remember that the great majority of answers given under cross-examination are given reluctantly, because the questions are coming from the 'other side' and are likely to be loaded. Nevertheless:

'Are you of the opinion,' went on Mr Gardiner, 'that if as a result of this action it is proved that the elections of the Union have been affected by the fraud of some of the Defendants, the costs of those Defendants should be borne by the Union?'

'That wasn't my opinion in joining with the other Defendants in agreeing that the Union should pay the costs of the action. I don't believe now and I didn't believe then that my colleagues were responsible for the charges which have been made against them, and—'

'Don't make a speech,' suggested the Judge. 'Just answer the question.'

'I'm sorry.'

'You've just told my Lord that you act in what you think are the best interests of the Union,' Mr Gardiner went on. 'This was an example, was it not, of your not acting in the interests of the Union?'

'I can't anticipate the findings of this Court,' said Mr Goldberg astutely. 'I merely say that I took a decision at that time which I believed to be right.'

(It turned out to be wrong.)

Mr Goldberg, now a Labour man himself, answered many questions about Communist Party influence. He appeared to agree that he was once 'associated with' something called the Trotskyite Revolutionary Communist Party—Mr Gardiner had suggested he was once 'a member of it', but he had already told Mr Lawson he belonged to the Labour Party. He couldn't get on to the Labour Party's 'A' list of candidates—

'You're rather too much to the left for them?'—'I think that's a fair comment.'

Mr Gardiner was establishing him as being something in the nature of a crypto-Communist, in order to suggest, for example, that when he and another 'non-Communist' were appointed on a committee to enquire into the ballot rigging at Jarrow, Head Office wanted to be able to say: 'Well, you see, it's non-Communists who are carrying out the investigation.'

'I don't think that was behind it at all,' said Mr Goldberg.

On the point whether the extra ballot papers in the Jarrow election could have come from Head Office, the General Secretary (said Mr Goldberg) had denied that there *were* any ballot papers at Head Office. 'They had all come from the printers.' But Mr Goldberg and his two fellow committee-men (Mr Haxell and Mr West) had never made any enquiry about this at the printers.

'As a member of this committee,' said Mr Gardiner, 'didn't you think it right to make further enquiries as to whether what Mr Haxell said was right?'—'No, frankly, I didn't.'

'Did you know that a few months before, Mr Haxell had given instructions to the printers that all surplus ballot papers were to be sent to Head Office?'

'I didn't know that,' said Mr Goldberg. He agreed that he might have taken 'a very different view' of the Jarrow affair if he *had* known. He seemed to be not only a man in the dark but a man unaccustomed to it.

Mr Goldberg wrote a letter to *Tribune*, in January 1958, replying to 'some of the allegations being made' about ETU elections, and ridiculing the suggestion that the Cannon election was void because of delay by the scrutineers.

Another member of the ETU wrote a reply to it, attacking both Mr Goldberg and the Council. This member was then 'charged' by the Executive Council with a breach of the Rules and 'censured' for writing a letter to the Press about ETU affairs without permission. But was Mr Goldberg's letter written *with* permission? Was that permission in the minutes, asked Mr Gardiner?

'It is not.'

'Because it had not been given?'—'No, that's not true. To the best of my recollection it *was* given.'

'*After* you had sent the letter?'—'Oh, no.'

'When Mr Chapple, as a member of the Executive, has had things said about him by Mr Haxell, if he writes to the persons to whom the statements have been made, like Sir Vincent Tewson, that is a breach of rule?'—'I don't think so, if he'd asked permission in the first place. But he didn't seek permission.'

'Do you think he would have got it?'—'Well, I don't think so, in view of what he said in his letter.'

'Do you know anybody who has ever got permission to make statements critical of the Executive Council?'—'No, I don't remember any of those.'

'I suggest to you,' Mr Gardiner said in concluding a very long cross-examination, 'that you knew at this time that the elections were being rigged by the Communists?'—'That is not true.'

'I suggest that all through 1959 you joined in their plans by voting with Mr Haxell?'—'*That's* not true.'

'Is there any case in which you did *not* vote for Mr Haxell?'—'I can't remember.'

'Is it true that at the Council meeting on February the 6th and 7th, 1960, Mr Chapple had to drag the contents of the scrutineers' report out of an obviously reluctant Mr Foulkes?'—'I didn't understand it in that way. It's true that there was some hesitation and altercation about this matter, but nevertheless it was read out.'

'I suggest that you knew that some one hundred and twelve branches had been disqualified, and you realised that the Communists had rigged the decision?'

'*That's* not true.'

Nothing alleged against him was true.

What was certainly not true, it transpired the next day, was that to have been a member of the 'Trotskyite Communist Party' meant that a man was on good terms with modern Communists. When he re-examined the witness, Mr Lawson referred back to the Trotskyite organisation, and the Judge remarked that he had never heard of it.

'Well, have *you* heard of it, Mr Goldberg?' asked his Counsel.

'Yes,' Mr Goldberg said, 'there *was* an organisation like that. It became defunct in 1947, I believe, but I had left it some time previously.'

'So far as "Trotskyites" are concerned are they *persona grata* with the Communist Party?'—'On the contrary, I would say there has been, and still does exist, a strong measure of disagreement, to put it no higher than that, between the two.'

'What it has to do with this case,' said the Judge rather testily, 'I really don't know.' But there was present to some minds the likelihood that a former Trotskyite might not, after all, nestle too cosily among the Communist leaders of the ETU.

Mr Harry West, of the Stratford Branch, was another of the Defendants in the case and a member of the ETU Executive Council. He now belonged, he said, to the Labour Party, though he had taken no prominent part in its policies. He gave a much shorter version of the evidence just given by Mr Goldberg, but was more specific about the committee of enquiry set up in 1959 to 'investigate' the growing scandals. Mr Gardiner suggested to him that, to his own knowledge, 'the sole object of this so-called committee of enquiry was to be able to tell the Trades Union Congress that such a committee had been set up'.

'I do not think that is so,' was Mr West's mild response.

'And that you were put on it because the Communists who control the Executive Council tend to put you on things where they want to be able to say that it is a member of the Labour Party who has done it?'

Mr West said that 'the only people really who *could* hold an enquiry would be members not affected by the allegations made'. But turning to the Jarrow affair, Mr Gardiner drew his attention to the fact that, out of a committee comprising Mr Foulkes, Mr Haxell, Mr McLennan (all Communists), Mr Goldberg (Labour), and himself, only he and Mr Goldberg appeared as having signed the 'whitewashing' report.

'To be perfectly honest with you,' said Mr West, 'it's only just recently I've noticed that only myself and Mr Goldberg *had* signed it'.

The Judge wanted to know how Mr West had privately felt about all this. 'Will you tell me whether you personally ever worried about the democratic nature of the voting in these elections?'

'I was very worried. I was always worried about the affairs of this Union. I was worried about the Press campaign.'

'Did it occur to you that if about a hundred and twelve branches had their votes disqualified, for any reason at all, in any one election, that meant that quite a considerable percentage of the total vote was not having any effect at all?'—'That is correct.'

'How comes it that you didn't say there and then, "Look, we'd better be a bit careful about this", or something to that effect, "because here we are, six hundred and fifty branches altogether, and a hundred and twelve of them are not going to count in this election. Are the disqualifications being imposed on too strict a footing"?'—'I had no reason to suspect the scrutineers. I had always trusted them and accepted their returns in the past.' Mr Justice Winn looked at him fixedly for a few moments. Then—

'It may be it's not the scrutineers. You were accepting responsibility for the report that had come to your Council from the two scrutineers, were you not?'—'That is correct.'

Mr Christopher Carnell, of Greenford, Middlesex, had been Secretary of the London Station Engineers No 11 Branch (LSE 11) since 1944, and an ETU member for thirty-five years. He was, he said, a member of the Labour Party and had formerly belonged to the Communist Party; and the scrupulously non-political Mr Justice Winn at long last gave vent to something that had been in his mind for about five weeks.

'I don't know whether it matters,' he said, 'but I haven't the slightest idea what is meant by being "in the Labour Party" or being "in the Communist Party". Does it mean voting that way at an election? I don't know?'

'By being "in it",' said Mr Ralph Millner, who was examining the witness, 'I mean being a member'.

'How does one become a member of the Party—by deciding that they are right, or by paying dues, or taking an oath, or what is it? I don't think it matters in the least, but *if* it matters I want to know what it means.'

His Lordship must have been genuinely seeking knowledge: he had no jury to worry about.

'I would humbly submit,' Mr Millner said, 'that it had very little relevance, but it is alleged against him, or in relation to him, that things have been done because he is a Communist'.

'I only say this,' said the Judge, 'that attending active groups, let alone committees, is one thing; being a member, or voting for or paying dues to a particular party, is something quite different, it seems to me. If you ask me what party I'm a member of, the answer would be none in any sense in which I understand the word, and yet I vote occasionally.'

Mr Millner asked the witness to explain.

'I joined the Labour Party and hold a Labour Party card, and contribute to Labour Party funds, the same as I'm in a trade union and hold a trade union card,' said Mr Carnell.

The Judge nodded and (it seemed) slightly shrugged. Then Mr Carnell said that his branch had about a thousand members, but that he would not be able to say that any one of them was a Communist. 'I can't say,' he explained. 'He's never shown me and I've never asked him. So I would be surmising.'

'About how many would you surmise *might* be members of the Communist Party in your branch?'—'I would surmise possibly two.'

The Judge's interest was rekindled. 'How many Conservatives would you surmise?' he asked.

'I can surmise a great number of Conservatives.'

'You mean you can detect them in some way, can you?'—'I know *definitely* that they are,' said Mr Carnell. When it came to Tories, surmising was out.

He had 'indented' for 743 ballot papers in the September 1959 election (for General President of the Union). They arrived from the printers two hundred short. He wrote to Head Office and said so, and received a telegram asking him to return the label that was on the parcel. He did this, and a few days later received two hundred more ballot papers, but *he didn't know where they came from*—'which,' he said helpfully, 'I presume you're trying to find out. I couldn't say.'

In the Byrne-Haxell election of 1959, his branch voted Haxell 405, Byrne 95. About four hundred members voted by post.

'What happened to the letter and telegram you've been telling us about?' asked Mr Gardiner in cross-examination.

'Well, I probably didn't keep them,' said Mr Carnell predictably. 'Anything appertaining to ballots I returned, as requested by my General Secretary, to the General Office of the Union.'

'I quite appreciate that,' Mr Gardiner assured him. 'When you wrote the letter to Head Office, did you keep a copy of that?'

He did, he said. He also put the telegram in a correspondence file and kept a copy of the letter by which he acknowledged it. He had since sent all these to Head Office as ordered.

'I call for the letters and telegrams,' said Mr Gardiner, more or less rhetorically.

Mr Lawson looked up. 'We have searched for those and cannot find them,' he said.

Mr Carnell then agreed that the usual vote at his branch totalled something like eighty or a hundred. It had recently been as low as sixty and fifty-seven.

'You see,' Mr Gardiner said, 'I suggest that when you have a vote, as you did here, of five hundred in Mr Haxell's election, that doesn't happen unless additional ballot papers have been introduced?'—'I can't agree with that. The election of Mr Haxell and Mr Foulkes is very important to my membership. My branch think a lot of the negotiating abilities of Mr Frank Foulkes. I should be very disappointed if I didn't get a good return for those officers' elections.'

'In the December election the members entitled to vote were seven hundred and sixteen were they not?'—'Yes.'

'Did you know that the Union had had printed for your branch one thousand and sixty-two ballot papers?'—'No, I didn't know.'

'Does that surprise you?'—'It *does* surprise me,' said Mr Carnell.

Mr Kenneth Scott and Mr Francis Rice, both of LSE 11 Branch, then briefly corroborated Mr Carnell's story about the deficit of two hundred ballot papers when they helped him count them at his house.

'Was the parcel open when you and Mr Scott got there?' asked Mr Gardiner. He had to repeat the question and then Mr Rice said that it was.

'You know, I suppose, that something less than twenty per cent of the members of this Union ordinarily vote, even in important elections?'

'I'm not aware of that,' Mr Rice said.

'Did it ever strike you as very extraordinary that at the December election in 1959, out of a total membership entitled to vote of seven hundred and sixteen, five hundred were said to have voted, mostly by post?'—'It never occurred to me.'

'There were a thousand members entitled to attend the branch, were there not?'—'Yes.'

'How many came—twenty?'—'Round about twenty-seven, I think.'

These, if anything, were 'jury points'; and there was no jury, only an extremely astute Judge. But they are points worth recording in the interests of trade union history.

There were some more witnesses about shortages in the ballot-paper parcels, and about the ease with which the shortages could be made up; but it began to seem stranger and stranger that they were being called for the Defence and not for the Plaintiffs. They were a gift to Mr Gardiner. Mr James Smith, for example, Secretary of the Hayes (Middlesex) Branch, a member of the Communist Party, said his parcel was fifty short for the September 1959 election (for General President). He wrote to Head Office and got the fifty ballot forms at once.

But Mr James Smith had been called to Head Office quite recently—within the previous six months, and long after the writs in this action were issued—to produce his branch's contribution ledgers and work out, under supervision, just how many Hayes members were really entitled to vote. The figure he had been returning was 422. The proper figure turned out to be 310. (Mr Smith never really admitted this in the witness-box, but he did agree that he had been making a quarterly 'mistake' of about a hundred.)

'Did it ever occur to you that it was a good way of getting additional ballot papers, to write and say you were short?'—'I would never dream of such a thing.'

'Have you heard that Communist branch secretaries who wanted some additional voting papers would get them if they wrote in and said they were so many short?'—'I have never heard such a story.'

And Mr Albert Aitkenhead, Secretary of London Station Engineers No 1 Branch, thirty-two years an ETU man, and a member of the Communist Party, had a similar tale to tell. He had requisitioned for 443 ballot papers, and the parcel he received was forty-three short. He telephoned to Head Office, spoke to 'a woman first and then a man', and received the 'missing' forms within three days by express post.

'Of course,' said Mr Gardiner, 'this is Mr Humphrey's branch, isn't it?'—'If you mean that he's a member of our branch, yes.'

'Don't you know Mr Humphrey?'—'Yes, of course I do.'

'When you rang up did you ask to speak to him?'—'No.'

'Had it ever been suggested to you,' asked Mr Gardiner (and he had to ask it twice), 'that a good way of getting additional ballot papers was to write and say you were short?'—'No, it has never been suggested to me.'

'You just asked for these on the telephone and then you got them?'—'Well, I reported a loss. I've never had such a thing happen before.'

'You reported on the telephone?'—'Yes.'

'To somebody you didn't know? Is that right?'—'Yes.'

Mr Gardiner reminded him that the number of members entitled to vote was 408 and the number who actually voted 198—practically half. 'Does that strike you as an unusually high vote?'—'No. As a matter of fact, I had been sending out a small circular, drawing attention to the privilege of balloting.'

'A lot of branch secretaries do that, don't they?'—'Well, I don't know.'

'Did you know that for your four hundred and eight members entitled to vote, the printers had been ordered to print five hundred and twenty-two?'—'No. How should I know that?'

Mr George Anderson, of the Park Royal Branch, was another Communist branch secretary to whose mind it had never occurred that you could rig a branch election by ringing up Head Office and getting more ballot papers—although once in his experience the original lot of ballot papers had never turned up at all and he had to obtain duplicates. In the 1959 election his parcel was fifty-one short, and he got the number made up by telephoning to Head Office and speaking to a girl. And so it went on. The Uxbridge Branch was twenty-seven short, and got them by writing a letter to Head Office. Gosport had once received too many, and sent the surplus back to Head Office; but it was twenty-five short in the December 1959 election for General President, and got those made good by writing to Head Office. Gosport's former secretary (Mr Albert Cook) admitted in cross-examination that for the Cannon-Frazer election in September 1957 he stated its voting membership as 723, whereas it should have been 522—'a big difference,' remarked the Judge. Its present secretary (Mr Frederick Tompkins) corroborated all this.

Then, as the Court prepared to adjourn for the Whitsuntide recess, the Judge asked Mr Lawson how many more witnesses he wanted to call. About thirty, said Mr Lawson, some of them very short ones. It might take about seven or eight days, he said. 'And a week for speeches, and a couple of months for me to consider my judgment,' said Mr Justice Winn wickedly. 'But jesting apart, it is obvious, you know, that being human I shan't be able to take my mind altogether away from this matter during what is going to be for some people maybe ten days' holiday. I had hoped that I should be in a position to think constructively about this case at this stage. I can't ask you, because it wouldn't be fair, to indicate the general character of what I am to expect. There will of course be denials of conspiracy.'

Mr Lawson said there would be some more evidence from the branches, and then the Defendants—against some of whom, at least (Mr Sell, Mr Davies, Mr Feathers) 'there is really nothing specific alleged'. And Mr Justice Winn concluded the pre-Whitsun stage of the trial with these words:

'I am not indicating a final view, but when one is dealing with fraud one does not want interminable investigations of what you, Mr Lawson, have been frank enough to admit are thoroughly unsatisfactory methods of conduct from the point of view of incompetence or lack of foresight. It's a very different thing from fraud—and this is not an action for negligence.'

The Court was then adjourned for ten days—until Tuesday, May 30.

The twenty-fourth day's evidence opened with Mr Francis Fraser, Communist Secretary of the Preston Branch, the branch where the ninety-one votes cast for Mr Haxell had mysteriously become a hundred and ninety-one when they were entered in the Executive Council's minutes. It may be remembered (see page 90) that a Mr Breakell had asked that the Byrne-Haxell voting results of certain branches be read out at a meeting. When the Secretary read out 'Haxell 191, Byrne 52', Mr Breakell challenged it. He thought the correct figure for Haxell was 101.

'After quite a discussion,' said Mr Fraser, 'they decided that no action be taken, and a vote of confidence was placed on myself as not being responsible for any alterations.'

But some action *was* taken. The branch minute books relevant to this occasion were forwarded to Head Office and they disappeared into the blue.

'Why didn't you take a receipt?' asked the Judge, referring to the dispatch of the minute books from Preston GPO.

'A receipt, my Lord?'

'A receipt for the parcel. You can get a parcel receipt from the post office, you know. You know that, as a branch secretary, don't you?'—'I send them ordinary parcel post, my Lord.'

'Why didn't you get a receipt for this parcel?'—'I've never had a receipt for a parcel in my life, my Lord, other than a registered letter.'

His Lordship may have started a new and salutary custom in trade union practice.

There seemed to be no other trace of the recorded voting figure —even the original piece of paper, the 'check sheet', had been destroyed.

'Who destroyed it?' asked Mr Gardiner in cross-examination.

'I would,' Mr Fraser answered, 'with a lot of papers'.

The branch meeting where Mr Breakell had put his inconvenient question had gone into a long discussion of 'how such a thing could possibly have occurred'.

'Did the meeting conclude,' asked Mr Gardiner, 'by instructing the branch secretary to write to Head Office informing them that the correct vote was 101, 52?'

'That didn't occur at all. The meeting closed, after passing a vote of confidence in myself; and Mr Breakell stood up and said to me that in view of the Court case he thought that Head Office ought to be informed.'

'You said you *would* inform Head Office?' asked the Judge.

'Yes, I did.'

'But you never did?'—'No. In view of the Court case coming on I thought there would be no useful purpose in doing that, because the minutes had been printed.'

'Is it the fact that you didn't write because you knew that the figure in the minute book was false?'—'No, certainly not. I didn't write to Head Office because the figures were then in the minutes.'

'Are there other figures in that minute book that you wouldn't want members to see?'—'Not at all.'

Mr Gardiner seemed not to believe that the branch minute books had ever been sent off to Head Office. 'Are you sure that you sent them by post?'—'I'm quite sure I did.'

'Have you in your possession any piece of paper to show that you made any enquiry at the post office, at any time?'—'Yes, I have it at home. I can send for it from home.' (He lived at Preston.)

This offer was not taken up. But, as so often in this trial, some supplementary questions from the Judge turned up some surprising information.

'What is the total of a hundred and ninety-one and fifty-two, which are the votes recorded on the scrutineers' form?'

Mr Fraser added them up. 'Two hundred and forty-three,' he said.

'And the number of members in attendance at the branch was eighty-six?'—'Yes.'

'If they had all voted (which of course would be unlikely) the difference between two hundred and forty-three and eighty-six is how much?'—'A hundred and fifty-seven, my Lord.'

'Is it a coincidence that as returned in the declaration form' (this goes to Head Office *before* the election) 'as the figures stand in it now they total a hundred and fifty-seven?'—'No, I don't know that it is, my Lord, because when the branch meeting starts you could have thirty or forty ballot papers at the branch before I get there.'

'And where are *they* recorded in the returns?'—'In the scrutineers' return.'

'As what?'—'As ballot papers returned.'

'Returned by whom?'—'Members attending the branch.'

'Which line on the declaration form shows the number of ballot papers left lying on the table while the meeting was in progress?' —'There isn't a line for that, my Lord.'

'Then where do they appear in the return?'—'They are shown in the two hundred and fifty odd.'

'Do listen to my question, *please*. Are they shown as votes brought in by a steward, or are they simply included in the difference between the total of a hundred and fifty-seven on the declaration and the total votes of two hundred and forty-three?'— 'They're left on the table and they are counted in the normal way.'

'All these loose ballot papers lying on the table, having been delivered before the meeting has begun, are counted in as ballots brought in by members delivered *during* the meeting?'—'Yes, my Lord.'

'Well, it doesn't surprise me, but *you* might be surprised to know that several branches were disqualified in December 1959 for accepting ballot papers which were left lying on the table in that way.'

'Well, I'm not aware of it, my Lord, because that is the general practice.'

'What on earth is the point of having *any* rules in this Union,' the Judge exclaimed later on, 'I don't know.'

There followed, in similar vein, Mr Horace Parker, of Hendon (35 lost ballot papers); Mr Alan Hoy, of Manchester Station Engineers (50); Mr William Christie, of Dundee (53); Mr John Maling, of London Electronic Engineers No. 2 (107)—from Mr Maling the Court learned for the first time that shop stewards and 'money stewards' at works and factories, having collected from Union members the contributions that qualified them as voters, then in theory (but not in practice at Mr Maling's branch) disenfranchised them by hanging on to the money for inordinate lengths of time. Mr Justice Winn, in return, gave *him* a piece of information:

'You wouldn't know this, but it is right that you should be told. Not only did the Head Office order one thousand and sixty ballot papers when only nine hundred and ninety-four were required (which is sixty-six to spare), but having those sixty-six to spare when you asked for this additional hundred and seven, the printers printed a hundred and seven *extra*, and not merely forty-one extra. Do you follow?'—'Yes, my Lord. I wasn't aware of that.' (It came out in cross-examination that the actual number of votes was about 650.)

Then came another Communist branch secretary, Mr Frank Monti, of London North-West Branch, to say that out of 282 members qualified to vote in the Byrne-Haxell election, 154 voted by post. He didn't consider this a high postal vote, he told Mr Millner—'not in relation to the work involved in sending these things out' (which was not perhaps the comparison expected of him).

'I suppose you appreciate the suggestion is that there was an abnormal postal vote in your branch, and that that was in some way a manifestation of faking on the part of somebody?'

'I can only say I think it's a lot of poppycock, myself,' said Mr Monti.

'Was the voting in that election a high vote because of any particular reason? Was there much interest taken in that election?' —'Yes, there was a lot of interest in the election. Even in the shop where I worked there was a lot of interest, and, believe me,' said Mr Monti confidentially, 'it takes a lot to interest *them*'.

'How do the members of your branch work?' asked Mr Millner.

'The majority of them are contracting members' (i.e., electricians working for contractors, and therefore at times away from their home areas).

'Does that fact have any bearing on the way they vote?'—'Yes. I should say the majority of them use the postal rule.'

When Mr Monti was cross-examined by Mr Jonathan Sofer about the high postal vote he agreed that forty per cent of the London North-West membership had actually voted in one way or another, but this didn't seem to him a very high poll.

'Let me put the national figure to you,' said Mr Sofer. 'Out of about two hundred and forty thousand members in the whole Union, including disqualified branches, forty-five thousand voted. That's a total poll of twenty per cent of the total membership?'—'Yes.'

'Can you explain to my Lord why your branch has a voting figure of forty per cent, twice as high as the national average?'—'I can't explain it to you.'

'This heightened interest in the election, I suppose, applies to the whole Union, does it not, and not merely London North-West?'—'Well, I consider that people in London are more conscious of what is going on around them than people in the Isle of Skye.'

'This heightened interest doesn't just apply to branches in which Communists are secretaries, does it?'—'I don't see why it should. It's the members who vote, not the secretary.'

'This is not the first time, is it, that there has been a suggestion made against your branch of fiddling votes by using false postal votes?'—'I object to "fiddling", my Lord,' said Mr Monti.

Then Mr Denis Wright, of LSE No 5, gave similar evidence about his branch; and Mr Thomas Longstaffe, of the London Jointers Branch, said that his postal vote (70 per cent) was higher because of the 'Press campaign' and because he himself had been urging members to use their vote—he got more ballot papers from Head Office because he was under-supplied, but had no idea that the printers had already provided seventy more than he originally wanted.

Mrs Kathleen Barker, the wife of Mr Albert Barker, Secretary of the Gray's Inn Branch, said that a parcel of 289 ballot forms arrived from the printers and her husband had sent for only 245. She posted back thirty-four on his behalf, but she had no idea what had happened to the other ten; and on this point Mr John O'Brien, President of the same branch, could only say that there had been a mistake, though he ackowleged that the branch had a postal vote of about 85 per cent and, he said, was 'very pleased to hear it'. Mr Frederick O'Connor, Communist Secretary of the LSE No. 9 Branch, was asked what he thought about the suggestion that a postal vote of 126 out of 203 qualified members showed that there had been 'faking' by someone.

'Shocking,' he replied tersely. 'No truth in it whatsoever.' But he remembered that Brother Collins had accused him in a 'Panorama' programme of rigging his branch ballot, and that he then charged Brother Collins with 'bringing him into disrepute' and got him suspended from office for five years.

And it was during Mr O'Connor's answers to Mr Sofer that the Communist control became particularly clear.

'Is your branch, LSE No. 9, a branch that has for the ten years that you have been Secretary always voted for the Communist candidate?'—'Yes. Even prior to my ten years.'

'And has consistently supported Communist candidates as delegates to the TUC?'—'Yes. It supports Labour Party members as well.'

'Would you agree with me that among the branches which we have charged here with having an unduly high postal vote, with the exception of LSE No. 5 all have on many occasions followed the Party line?'—'I wouldn't know about that.'

'Do you know Mr Blairford, from Edinburgh Central?'—'Yes.'

'Had your branch, from 1952 until 1958, year after year, supported the nomination of Mr Blairford for the TUC?'—'Yes.'

'When he left the Communist Party, your branch ceased to support his candidature, didn't it?'—'I wouldn't know when he left the Communist Party. We haven't put him forward since 1958, no.'

'And there are eleven branches, who all voted Communist, who all voted for Mr Haxell, who also suddenly came to the same decision in 1959? Does that strike you as being something odd?'— 'I wouldn't know about that.' (Later he said that probably Mr Blairford 'wasn't so active' as formerly.)

'May I put this to you, that what has been happening here is that the branches with Communist secretaries have been getting their directive as to how to vote, and for whom to vote, from Communist advisory committees, of which you well know?'—'It's new to me,' said Mr O'Connor.

And his branch's postal vote of over 90 per cent did *not* seem 'extraordinarily high'. He was supported in all this by Mr Walter Brown, his branch chairman (a Communist), who said that if he thought there was any fiddling or faking, or anything underhand going on in the branch, he would resign—from the chairmanship of the branch, at any rate, and probably, he thought (after some very close questioning by Mr Sofer) from the Communist Party too. He added that when Mr Cannon was barred from further office on leaving the Communist Party, it was because he had been appointed to the stewardship of the ETU College at Esher and was not entitled to run for office. 'And it appears,' concluded Mr Brown, 'that after he lost his position at the College the disruption began. That is my personal opinion.'

Mr Horace Eavery, the Treasurer of East Ham Branch, which had a thousand members (of whom 749 were qualified to vote) said that in 1959 they voted 'Haxell 114, Byrne 58', although a mere thirty-two members went to the meeting on ballot night. But the postal vote was not unusual and 'there was no fiddling'. Then Mr Sofer asked him why he, as Treasurer, was called to give evidence and not Mr Lazell, the Secretary. Was the Secretary ill? No. Was he a Communist? Mr Eavery didn't know.

'Have you heard Mr Lazell, though he's a member of the Communist Party, saying to several people that he believed the postal vote at this election had been rigged in his branch against him? Do you remember him saying that?' Mr Eavery did not.

Then came another Defendant, Mr Ronald Sell, an electrician employed by a national daily newspaper and a member of the ETU's Eltham Branch Committee. From 1945 to 1951 he belonged to a different union—the Clerical and Administrative Workers; for his job during that time was 'full-time South-East Midlands organiser for the Communist Party'. He was now a member of the ETU Executive Council, but had not begun his two-year period of office until January 1, 1960. So when Mr Lawson reminded him that he was alleged to have 'conspired with the other Defendants to rig elections and particularly to rig the election of December 1959', he was able to reply:

'First of all, I'm in no position to say one thing or the other. I don't know anything about it. I was in no position to rig any election, or to do anything about it.'

And although he attended Communist Party committees, he never took part there in any discussions relating to the rigging of elections.

Under cross-examination he denied all knowledge of the Communist Party 'National Aggregate Conferences', but seemed to know about the National *Advisory* Committee (whose existence had been denied by other Defendants). He told the Judge, however, that it would be 'quite out of order' for there to be meetings of ETU members who were Communists, discussing with Mr Kerrigan (the Communist Party's industrial organiser) how to deal with anti-Communist branches in the Union. 'Mr Kerrigan,' he explained, 'is not a member of the Electrical Trades Union'.

'So what it comes to,' said the Judge, 'is that Mr Chapple and all the other witnesses who speak of this structure with regular meetings, national advisory committees and district advisory committees, must be inventing something?'—'It's not within my knowledge, certainly.'

He had succeeded Mr Humphrey when the latter vacated his seat on the Executive Council and took the job of Office Manager. He became very worried about the 'smear campaign' in the Press (not in the *Daily Express*—'I never read the *Express*,' he said primly).

'When your mind was exercised by these Press reports,' said Mr Sofer, 'of ballot-rigging by Communists in the ETU, did it ever occur to you to speak to Mr Humphrey and exchange your worries about this smear campaign with him?'—'No,' said Mr Sell.

Mr Sofer asked him about his first day at an Executive Council meeting—'the new boy,' as the Judge called him.

'There you were, the first time on the committee, with a lot of worrying things having been said about rigging this election, and the first thing that happens is the announcement of the result: "Haxell elected." *Frazer*: "Move." *Mr Foulkes*: "Brother Frazer and Brother Sell. All those in favour?" You had seconded the acceptance of the scrutineers' report without seeing it?'—'The scrutineers' report isn't presented to each of us. The Assistant General Secretary reads it out. Having read it out—'

'Just wait for a moment. All that had happened was that there had been read out: "Byrne 18,577, Haxell 19,611. Haxell elected." *Frazer*: "Move." *Mr Foulkes*: "Brother Frazer and Brother Sell. All those in favour? Against?" You seconded it as your first activity on the committee, the first meeting at which you had appeared.'

'But not the first word I said on the committee,' said Mr Sell. He added that one of the scrutineers, Mr Rengert, was his branch chairman and 'a man in whose honesty I've got absolute and complete faith. He presented that report, and to me that goes a very long way'.

'The scrutineers disqualified a hundred branches,' Mr Sofer reminded him. 'They *investigated* about twenty. Did you ask for how long these two scrutineers were scrutinising?'—'No.'

'You've seen the statement of claim in this action, have you not?'—'Yes.'

'Even by the time of the statement of claim in June of last year, one did not then know which branches had been disqualified? I must put it to you, the speed at which the names were read out' (in reluctant response to Mr Chapple's insistence at the meeting) 'made it impossible for anybody to take down more than one in two names?'—'That's quite possible—I don't know.'

'Were there Press reports practically every day saying that "About a hundred branches have been disqualified, but only the names of about forty are known"?'—'I can't remember that particular phrase, no.'

'Your sole contribution to this discussion was to second the acceptance of the scrutineers' report at the beginning?'

But the Judge answered for him. 'No,' said his Lordship. 'His contribution was to explode and make a long speech. That's what he did.' He turned to Mr Sell and asked:

'Did you know, when you went to this Executive Council meeting for the first time, that it was part of the function of the scrutineers to disqualify branches?'—'Yes,' said Mr Sell, 'I knew that'.

'When McLennan read out nothing more than two sets of figures' (i.e., Byrne 18,577, Haxell 19,611) 'did you assume that no branches had been disqualified?'—'No, I didn't assume that.'

'If you thought there probably had been some branches disqualified,' the Judge went on, 'you knew the report was not complete when you seconded its adoption?'—'I didn't know that because I had no previous knowledge as to what constituted a complete scrutineers' report.'

'You just jumped in, in complete ignorance of the proper procedure, and then when Chapple made a fuss about it you blew your top, and made a two-page speech complaining of Chapple having asked for the information? It all arose through your own ignorance, is that right, of the proper procedure?' Mr Justice Winn had not, at any previous moment in the trial, sounded quite so withering.

'I don't accept your description of what happened,' said Mr Sell.

'You give *your* explanation,' the Judge suggested, sitting back to listen.

'What is true is that after a number of interjections by Brother Chapple—'

'You, as the junior member of the Council, saw fit to rebuke him?'

'*One* of the junior members, my Lord, and also not just because he was asking for the information, but on every previous item on the agenda Brother Chapple had adopted the same attitude. In my statement I *said* I was a new member of the committee, who had wasted so far an hour of my time in listening to Brother Chapple do nothing else but ask questions.'

The Judge sat back again.

'Isn't the truth of the matter this,' Mr Sofer resumed, 'that you knew the election had been rigged, and it had been arranged for you to second the acceptance of the scrutineers' report and try to rush the matter through?'—'It hadn't been arranged with *me*.'

'Then if that is the position, did you say at any time while Chapple, Walker and Hadley were protesting and asking and protesting again, and being sat on by everybody else: "Now just a moment—what *about* Woolston, and Hythe and Southampton Central"?'—'No, I didn't say that.'

'It never occurred to you?'—'No.'

'Having exploded about the matter' (of Mr Chapple's interruptions), 'after this meeting was over did you discuss the happenings at this Executive Council meeting with your fellow Communist members?'—'No.'

'Had you any anxiety about the fact that about a hundred branches had been disqualified?'—'Of course, yes.'

'Did you try to find out how many of your constituents had been disqualified?'—'No.'

'It didn't interest you in any way?'—'Of course it interested me. It's very difficult for me as a working electrician. You know, of course, that the Executive Council are not full time. We work on the job.'

'Let's not speak like this,' said Mr Sofer deprecatingly. 'Mr Walker, Mr Hadley and Mr Chapple were all working electricians at the time, were they not?'—'Yes.'

'They were looking after the interests of their members, trying to find out which had been disenfranchised and why?'—'Yes.'

'Between February and May there had been a spate of further Press publicity saying that the ballot had been rigged? Papers from *The Times* (among the more heavy papers) to the *Daily Mirror*, all saying "about a hundred branches have been disenfranchised—one doesn't know who they are, but there is something wrong here. Communists are being accused of having rigged the ballot"?'—'Yes.'

'Do you remember also there were interviews with various branch secretaries, who said: "I wasn't late—I've been told I was late, but I wasn't"?'—'Yes.' Mr Sell said that his first chance of discussing all this with his fellow councillors was at the meeting of the Executive Council, where he did not raise the matter.

In February 1960, Mr Sofer reminded him, there were two interviews on BBC 'Panorama'; one in which Mr Collins, of London Lift and Crane Branch, accused LSE 9 of ballot-rigging, and one in which Mr Satchwill, of Eastbourne, complained that his ballot returns were said to have arrived late and it was not true.

'I didn't see that,' said Mr Sell.

'Did you see Mr Foulkes on television replying to it?'—'I did.'

'He said that a lot of these people carried things around in their pockets, and that that was the reason why so many of them had been late.'

'Yes,' said Mr Sell, and he had discussed this with Mr Foulkes, Mr Haxell, and Mr Humphrey, but 'purely in passing'.

Lastly, there was an interlude in which Mr Sell, asked by the Judge about the various 'advisory committees' of Communist ETU men, explained when a committee is not a committee.

'There is a comrade responsible for each of them?' his Lordship asked.

Mr Sell agreed.

'Does it mean that the named comrade is to keep in existence committees who can provide information and advice?'—'In the South-East Midlands area of the Communist Party we certainly had no such regular kept-in-being committees.'

'Would you have a committee which kept you informed on anything that was thought to be of some interest?'—'No. I'd have a number of people to whom I could go, or call together, for the purpose of gathering such information as I might require.'

'But you wouldn't call them a committee?'—'It would be a committee in that sense, my Lord, but not in the sense of being kept together between meetings. There was no organisation in that sense.'

Sometimes, he said, the group were called to London; sometimes somebody from London came down to see them; but they were not a committee. The Judge looked at him fixedly for a time, and then sat back.

5 *Mr George Scott's Evidence*

Mr George Scott, an ETU national officer, another of the Defendants, said that he had been a member of the ETU since 1940, holding various offices, that he belonged to the Labour Party and had twice contested Parliamentary elections, and that he had been a Fife County Councillor. He described his investigations, on behalf of the Executive Council, into the Southampton, the LSE No. 2, and the Kirkcaldy ballot-rigging allegations; and he accounted for his whereabouts during Christmas and the New Year 1959-60, when the bogus envelopes were said to have been posted—adding that he knew absolutely nothing about that operation himself.

'Have you ever been a party,' Mr Lawson asked him, 'to some agreement or understanding with the other Defendants or anyone else to use fraudulent or unlawful practices in relation to elections in the Union?'

'Never,' said Mr Scott, 'at any time'. And Mr Sofer thereupon began one of the longest cross-examinations of the trial. He spent some time establishing Mr Scott's position on the extreme left wing of the Labour Party, and found significance in the fact that Fife, a large mining community, had for so many years elected Mr Gallacher ('Oh ay, Willie Gallacher,' said Mr Scott) as its Communist MP. He wanted also to establish that Mr Scott's election as national officer, heavily supported as it was by Communists and fellow-travellers, had the hidden purpose of putting a 'Labour' man among the five national officers (the other four were all Communists) so that he could go to Labour Party Conferences as ETU representative.

When an hour of this had elapsed Mr Justice Winn said suddenly: 'We've had all this. I really wonder, after an hour, whether much more time ought to be given up to what really is in the nature of a political novel. You have had an hour,' he said to Mr Sofer, 'to develop what is sometimes called the pre-cordium'.

Mr Sofer moved on.

'When the Cannon election created all this hullabaloo,' he said, 'were you asked by Mr Haxell to write an article for the *Daily Worker* of December the 14th dealing with the accusations in the Haxell election?'—'It's not true that Mr Haxell asked me to write it. I went to him and said that I would like to put my point of view, because I wasn't a member of the Communist Party and I regretted the attacks on my Union.'

Mr Sofer quoted this from the article in the *Daily Worker*, a copy of which had been handed to Mr Scott:

If a complaint is sent to the General Secretary that any branch has violated the correct procedure, then the General Secretary must, in accordance with the Rules, conduct an investigation. If the investigation proves that the complaint is justified and a serious breach of the Rules has occurred, the votes of that branch must naturally be invalidated. This, in fact, was the situation which the Press has inflated and exploited so viciously. The decision to declare invalid the votes of branches referred to by the Press was taken before these voting figures were known.

The fact which blows the Press fantasy to smithereens is that, even if these votes had been included, the result would have been the same.

'Do you see that passage?' asked Mr Sofer. 'It's on that that I am proposing to cross-examine you. Before you wrote this article, had you satisfied yourself that if all the branches' votes had been counted the result would have been the same?'—'Yes.'

Mr Sofer handed him the correct voting figures and asked him to look at them.

'When you wrote this article, accusing the opposition of distorting, and seeking to persuade everybody that the hullabaloo was a complete waste of time and just mud-slinging, the truth of the matter was that if those branches had been included Cannon would have been elected by a majority of thirty-four?'

'Yes,' said Mr George Scott. 'Well, this is the first time I've seen this. And I don't know if these are all the branches that were involved.'

'You told my Lord that when you wrote this article Mr Haxell had shown you the figures. You had them before you. And you then said the result would have been the same.'

'I thought it genuinely *would* have been the same. Your figures here would appear to show that Mr Cannon would have had thirty-four votes more than Mr Frazer—out of a total of about four thousand five hundred.'

'Please face the point,' interjected the Judge sharply. 'Do you agree that what you wrote was inaccurate? Never mind how you came to do it.'—'If these figures are correct, I would accept that.'

But this was not nearly good enough for his Lordship. 'I will stop everything,' he said, 'for the moment, and hear if any error can be pointed out for your assistance here and now'.

Mr Scott made the strange observation that 'if these are all the branches involved, then I haven't counted up the figures, but I would accept that the sums are the same'.

'You would accept,' said the Judge, still hoping for clarity, 'that if that be so you were inaccurate?'—'Yes. Not so inaccurate,' said Mr Scott incautiously, 'as the national Press'.

'Don't argue, *please*. What steps did you take to ensure that you were accurate before you wrote it? That's the point.'—'On the branches that I had assessed, on the votes, I thought that Mr Frazer was elected. The Press had run a campaign saying that Mr Cannon had been elected by over three hundred votes, which was subsequently altered to thirty odd votes.'

'Do you wish to answer the question?' The Judge repeated it.

'I understood, on the votes of the almost seven hundred branches, that I was correct in saying that.'

'What do you mean by "understood"?'—'From my examination.'

'What did you examine?'—'Returns of branches made to the Executive Council.'

(The reference to 'almost seven hundred branches' had been unfortunate. Mr Sofer had been checking up.)

'It is sixty-one branches who voted in the Cannon-Frazer election? It was an election in the division only?'—'I'm sorry, yes,' said Mr Scott. 'I misled my Lord.'

'What I'm afraid I have now got to put to you is this. Do you see the heading of this article: "The Press and the ETU: What are the Facts?"' (There followed an impressive little biography of Mr George Scott—for which, turn back to pages 173–4.) 'You were being put forward there as an honest and upright Labour Party supporter telling the facts in connection with this smear campaign against the Communists?'—'I asked to do that, yes.'

'And the facts you gave were quite untrue?'—'It would appear that I was wrong by thirty-four votes.'

'If this is your answer, do you think that when you got the ballot returns of the sixty-one branches from Mr Haxell, possibly one or two of them had been omitted so as to mislead you? There *are* only these two possibilities: either you deliberately misled the readership of the *Daily Worker*; or Mr Haxell, who gave you the facts, deliberately withheld one or two of these branch returns so as to lead you into error?'—'I don't believe that Mr Haxell would deliberately and dishonestly mislead me or any other member of the Union.'

Mr Scott then offered a third possible explanation: *he* could have made an error. He would like to have a look at the papers.

'It won't take you more than ten minutes,' said the Judge. 'I will rise for ten minutes. It's only right that Mr Scott should satisfy himself.'

'Have you had enough time to clear that up?' his Lordship asked when he came back.

Mr Lawson spoke up for him. 'Will your Lordship allow me to say this, as I am Counsel for Mr Scott, that I agree that these are the correct figures in relation to the branches which are named there.'

'The point which has really interested me since I sat this morning,' the Judge said, 'is what enquiries he made before he went on record as making this categorical statement'.

'Precisely,' said Mr Lawson; which, in the circumstances, was unexpected.

It was another half an hour before the Court had heard the end of the *Daily Worker* affair, and it was a period that brought no further comfort to Mr Scott.

Mr Sofer then took him through some of the 'investigations' he had made into branch irregularities, most of which had concluded in a manner favourable to the Communist leadership. In some of them, finding there was no substance in the original complaint, he took the opportunity to report irregularities not complained about; and came in for much criticism for doing so. In others (according to Mr Sofer, but not according to him) he had hushed things up. 'I'm not a trained investigator,' he explained at one point.

'In justification of your harsh treatment or harsh application of what you understood the Rules to mean,' said Mr Sofer, 'you were saying this: "We are being attacked in the Press for major ballot-fiddling. Therefore we must sit on every small branch that commits a minor infringement." Is that what you're saying?'

Mr Scott refuted it. Throughout a very long day he was refuting similar suggestions, and at intervals the Judge interposed to say that the process of putting the witness to that necessity was not impressing him. 'There is no jury,' he said more than once. A typical exchange between his Lordship and Mr Sofer took place over the printing of extra ballot papers.

'You understood at the beginning of this year,' Mr Sofer asked the witness, 'that there had been some change before the Haxell-Byrne election, as a result of which the printers had been asked to print more than the branches had asked for, and to send the surplus to Hayes Court. You were told that at the beginning of this year?'—'This year.'

'Were you shocked when you were told that? Were you astonished when told that?'—'I think it's fair to say that. I was very surprised.'

'And shocked?'—'It was rather a shock to me.'

'Did you also discover at that time that this system was stopped after the election between McLennan and Mr Chapple?'

Mr Justice Winn had had enough.

'Can we pause there a moment?' he said. 'Tell me what difference it makes to me whether he answers "Yes" or "No". Take either hypothesis and tell me how much it helps me.'

Mr Sofer 'left it'. He then gave Mr Scott the opportunity, customary at the close of a cross-examination, to refute all the allegations made against him, and finished specifically with a question about the posting of the bogus envelopes from branches.

'You went every New Year to Scotland?'—'Yes.'

'You say you didn't post these envelopes?'—'Definitely not.'

'I am not in a position to suggest that you did.'

'No,' said Mr Scott. 'I would say this, that if I was a party to a conspiracy, or my colleagues either, we would be rather more intelligent conspirators than we are being made out to be.'

'That,' remarked Mr Justice Winn, 'makes certain assumptions, which may be due to your not having heard the whole of the evidence, that comment of yours'.

And the next morning, in the last few minutes of his evidence, Mr Scott withdrew his comment, which he said had not been intended to give any offence. The Judge assured him that it gave none.

After Mr William Brand, Secretary of the Walthamstow Branch, had given evidence that in the December 1960 election he had to send back forty-two unwanted ballot papers (which showed that wrong quantities were still being dispatched, even after the events that led to the trial), the Defence recalled to the witness-box Mr Norman Swift, managing director of the Express Printing Company in Manchester. He was originally subpoenaed by the Plaintiffs, but this time he was there for the Defendants, to give evidence about the comparative ease with which ballot papers could be stolen at the printing works by e.g., 'casual workers in the pay of some person hostile to the ETU'. His evidence filled in a picture of printing works routine that was a 'documentary' in itself, but its relevance here may be stated in the confined sense mentioned above.

Mr William Tattersall, Secretary of the Bolton Supervisory Branch, had an unusual tale to tell. He had 'indented' for forty-nine ballot papers for the 1959 Byrne-Haxell election. The printers sent him forty-six, and (he thought) they never arrived. So he wrote to Head Office and got forty-six more, used them in the election—and then found the original batch in his own house. Worse, he had forgotten to send them back, despite a reminder from Head Office.

'Where are they now?' asked Mr Millner. 'Do you know?'

'At home,' said Mr Tattersall.

Yet it transpired that his branch had consistently favoured Mr Byrne and Mr Blairford, as against Mr Haxell and Mr Foulkes.

Then came Mr Patrick O'Neill, Secretary of the London South-West Branch, to say that an 80 per cent membership poll at his branch was not surprising, even though nearly the whole of that 80 per cent was by postal voting—not a single shop steward came from the factories and works to hand in votes on the night. Mr O'Neill was a Communist.

'The man you took over from was not a member of the Communist Party, was he?' said Mr Sofer.

'I couldn't say.'

'Since you took over as Branch Secretary the vote has shot up, hasn't it, from an average of seventy or eighty-five in 1956 to its present figure of three hundred odd?'—'Yes; and as I say, it's as a result of our activity and persuasion.'

'You see,' Mr Sofer said later, 'what is rather odd about this is that Mr Byrne's figure from 1948 to 1959 remains pretty low throughout—23, 11, 10, 11, 21. When there is a Communist Branch Secretary, Mr Haxell's figures are, from 1948 to 1959, 393 and 459; when the honest man is in charge 35 and 74; and when you come in again, 292?'—'I regard myself as an honest man.'

'I put it to you that you are a fraudulent fiddler of your branch ballot.'—'Your suggestion is absolutely ridiculous,' said Mr O'Neill angrily.

'Before we go on and get any more heated,' the Judge interposed, 'where are the envelopes in which these postal votes came?' —'I would say they are no longer in existence. We keep all the gear in a ballot-box. We meet in a pub, and as the box gets full up, we empty all the gear out that isn't necessary, and I should say the envelopes are no longer in existence.'

He didn't realise that the Rules required him to keep the envelopes for twelve months, he said.

Twenty-six men went to the meeting of the Peckham Branch on the night of the Byrne-Haxell ballot in December 1959. (The normal attendance was twenty-five.) Their Secretary, Mr Walter Bolt (a Communist), told the Court that the voting was Byrne 10, Haxell 169. Even of that twenty-six, some had already sent their votes by post. Yet the postal vote was 179.

Mr Bolt explained that the majority of the members worked for contractors 'all over the place'. And they were 'disgusted', he said, that, at the previous quarter night election, 'our General President, whom we hold in high esteem in our branch, did not do as well as we thought he should have done'. The branch officials had therefore paid personal visits to many of the members, urging them to use their ballot papers. (Mr Bolt said he thus visited at least a hundred, though Mr Sofer seemed not to believe him, and no addresses were forthcoming.) And great interest had been aroused by the Press allegations. So the high postal vote (over 85 per cent) was not at all unexpected.

Mr Bolt was an unusual branch secretary in at any rate one

respect: he had kept the envelopes in which the postal votes came —at least he had handed them now to the Union's solicitors. Mr Millner promised an immediately interested Judge that he would produce these later.

Otherwise true to form (except that he rather lost his temper), Mr Bolt assured Mr Sofer in cross-examination that he didn't know what an advisory committee was. Certainly no committee had ordered his branch to support Mr George Scott in the 1955 election for national officer, when they suddenly gave him 266 votes as against none at all in the previous year and two votes in 1951.

'Did you know that there had been printed for your branch, with your branch's code number, four hundred and fifty-four ballot papers, although you required only three hundred and thirty-six?' —'I didn't know that then. I know it now because you've just told me, and I understand the list you have in your hand is correct.'

'I put it to you that those extra ballot papers, some of which were used by you to post to yourself, were intended to support the figure that you declared to be the result in your branch ballot?' —'I refute your suggestion.'

Mr Bolt refuted also the suggestion that he had gone down to the LSE 14 Branch in 1957, as a 'visitor' (visitors are normally welcome from other branches), for the purpose of finding fault with its ballot in the Cannon-Frazer election—it was known to be pro-Cannon and anti-Communist—and getting it disqualified. He gave quite a vivid account of what happened.

'I was sitting on a seat outside the building—it was the Labour Party rooms, and a gentleman came along I didn't know from Adam, but I knew he was the Branch Treasurer because he had a branch treasurer's case in his hand. He opened the door with a key, and just as he was about to go in somebody came up to him; and they went in together, and I followed them. The chap who went in with him went behind the door of the Labour room, picked up a green-painted box, and on it was written LSE 14. They took that up into the branch room and I went with them. I was never challenged; I am entitled to be there and attend the meeting. The chairman then took a key out of his pocket and opened this box and took out of it a whole pile of ballot papers. Then he and the other chap—I found out later he was a Brother Green, an elected scrutineer—started tearing them open and putting them in piles on the table. And I did note that all of them that were in that box didn't have a stamp on, so they had not been through the post.'

Mr Sofer offered an explanation of this: 'What had happened there was that the members of the branch had put the ballot papers through the letter-box instead of posting them to the secretary.'

'Well,' said Mr Bolt, 'that's what Mr Gittins says' (Mr Gittins being an LSE 14 man who had written to Mr Haxell and complained that Mr Bolt was a nuisance).

Mr John Hendy, who had belonged to the ETU since 1936, had been a member of the Executive Council since 1957 and of the Communist Party since 1939. (He had served on a number of that Party's 'advisory committees', whose work he described, though he called them 'groups' and said that he himself had convened them.) From 1946 he spent four years as a student at the London School of Economics, and took the degree of B.Sc. (Econ.). He was also a Fellow of the Royal Economic Society.

'It is alleged against you,' said Mr Lawson, 'that you conspired with the other Defendants "by unlawful and fraudulent practices and devices to prevent non-Communist members of the Union, who were critics of the leaders thereof, being elected or appointed to offices in the Union, and to procure the election and appointment of Communist members or other candidates favoured by them". You know that allegation is made against you? The sting of it is "unlawful and fraudulent practices and devices".'

'Those are the only words you don't agree with, aren't they?' said the Judge. 'Take them out and the rest of it is a mere description of what you were trying to do?'

Mr Hendy agreed. 'There would be no point in having a belief,' he said, 'unless one endeavoured to promote it and to get other people to accept it'. But he thought it would be improper for Communists to monopolise all the jobs in the Union, though 'as between two men of equal merit he would support the Communist'. And he strongly denied taking part in any election-rigging.

'Do you remember a meeting,' Mr Gardiner asked him, 'and

don't bother about whether it was a committee or congress, addressed by Mr Allison, when he said that the Communists in the branches ought to fix in each branch a Communist vote to be obtained, *"and they ought to obtain it by hook or by crook"*?'

'No,' said Mr Hendy, 'I don't remember Mr Allison ever saying anything as—' he meditated, and concluded 'anything like that'.

'That is to your credit, Mr Hendy,' remarked Mr Gardiner, as though the witness had indeed said 'anything as wicked'. 'I suggest that you disagreed with that and wrote to Mr Pollitt about it.'

'I think,' Mr Hendy said, 'one ought to be clear on an issue of that kind. Mr Allison took a somewhat dim view of the complexity of union rules, and in my judgment, rightly or wrongly, he seemed to imply that there was a great deal of nonsense in many rule books, and that the thing was to get the votes of as many people as could be got without undue regard for their jots and tittles.'

' "By hook or by crook" is what he said, isn't it?'—'I wouldn't say by hook or by crook. That implies a somewhat different thing. Anyway, I took objection to this suggestion.'

'In consequence of your objection to the elections being rigged, you were known somewhat sarcastically as "Honest John"? Is that right?'—'No, the phrase "Honest John" was the invention of Mr W. C. Stevens' (a former General Secretary of the ETU) 'because of my unfortunate habit of saying what I really thought when most people showed him great deference.'

But later the Judge could not believe that Mr Hendy was 'saying what he thought' about a letter he had written to Mr Cannon on November 23, 1951, describing a meeting of the National Advisory Committee of the Communist Party at King Street, Covent Garden. Mr Hendy actually went so far as to say (Mr Gardiner politely dissenting) that some of the sentiments in this letter 'did him little credit'. It referred, at one point, to 'the need to ensure that future correspondence is less obvious and more personal'. Mr Hendy was closely questioned about the meaning of the phrase 'less obvious'; and after a time he said he thought the word 'obvious' was 'clearly erroneous'.

'Erroneous?' exclaimed the Judge. 'It's plain that it means that letters must be covered up as though they were personal letters, and not make it obvious that they are official Communist Party communications. That's what it means, doesn't it? Don't let us waste time.'

Mr Hendy denied this. The Judge made him read the passage twice aloud, and Mr Hendy stuck to it that it merely meant that Party letters should go to local Communist Party organisers. He was then subjected to a prolonged questioning about the domination of the ETU, 240,000 strong, by about five or six hundred Communists. He was at great pains to refute a suggestion of Mr Gardiner's that the Communist 'machine' by which the Union was controlled was in fact a 'well-oiled' machine. Mr Gardiner elicited from him that he himself, Mr Haxell, Mr Foulkes, Mr McLennan, and (name by name) about twenty other full-time officials, in addition to the majority of the Executive Council, and four out of five of the national officers were all members of the Communist Party.

'Bearing in mind the membership of the Union,' Mr Gardiner went on, 'the strength of the Communist Party in the Union, and the facts to which you have just agreed, do you still suggest that the Communist machine is not a well-oiled machine?'

'Well, it's certainly not the kind of machine which has been alleged,' Mr Hendy said. 'I may possibly be thought naïve, but it's my belief that Communists who hold office in the Union do so because of the record of their services to the Union.'

And after further questions about the fraudulent disfranchisement of branches for which he was responsible as an Executive Councillor, Mr Hendy faced this final one from the Judge:

'Didn't you feel any curiosity about this sort of matter during the time you have been facing trial as a Defendant in this conspiracy charge?'—'No, my Lord. I'm naturally concerned at being a Defendant on a conspiracy charge, but I have never been offered or even asked for any explanation as to the votes of any branches which were disallowed. I wouldn't normally doubt the integrity of my colleagues.'

'You are not normally sued for fraudulent conspiracy?' asked the Judge.

'No.'

'I suggest,' Mr Gardiner ended, 'that you have known for years that the elections in this Union have been rigged, and that although originally you were opposed to it you later adopted the Party line?'—'I can only say that I think that is a most unfair aspersion.'

The Defence then called Mr Leonard Gray, a Communist member of the Branch Committee of LSE No. 5, to say that the postal vote at his branch was high but not 'suspicious'. It seemed that the Defence chose not to call either the Secretary (Mr Smith) or the Treasurer (Mr Bennett), both opponents of the Haxell-Foulkes régime, because those two gentlemen had spotted the trickery in the 1959 Byrne-Haxell ballot at their branch and would probably have said so. More, they would have had a remarkable story to tell about the way in which they had frustrated an attempt to rig the June 1960 election in the same way. As it was, Mr Sofer got this story in by an adroit violation of the rule about hearsay evidence: he extracted it from the reluctant Mr Leonard Gray. Mr Gray was almost a burnt offering to the Plaintiffs.

'I put it to you,' Mr Sofer said to him, 'that after the December 1959 election they had decided that fraudulent postal votes had been posted in to their branch? You know that, don't you?'—'No, I don't, because they hadn't "decided" anything.'

'I want you to be very careful in your answer Mr Gray, because it's recorded in your branch minute book.'—'When?'

'In June and July 1960. When the Treasurer and the Secretary of your branch (who are against the Union leadership) became suspicious that they had received a high illicit postal vote, did they mark the insides of the flaps of the ballot papers, *in June 1960*, with the branch stamp, to enable them to identify whether there would be a repetition of false ballot posting in the Chapple-McLennan election? Do you know that?'—'I don't know that at all.'

Nor did he remember that Messrs Smith and Bennett then announced in the branch that they had received a considerable number of ballot papers which did *not* bear the branch stamp that they had secretly put under the flaps of the envelopes. And, according to Mr Gray, the branch members were given no reason for this extraordinary precaution. This was all going very nicely, with no objection from Mr Lawson that the witness was being used as a means of putting in what other people had *said*, when the Judge intervened.

'I may say,' his Lordship said, 'that I attach no importance at all to the hearsay evidence I have just been invited to listen to. There have been occasions in this case when objection has been taken to some evidence tendered, and I have allowed the objection though not thinking it well founded.' (His Lordship had in fact been very lenient, even implying at one point [see page 45] that the hearsay rule ought to be scrapped.) 'The whole of that last passage is nothing but plain hearsay.'

Mr Sofer admitted it; but the story was in.

Then came Mr Robert McLennan, another of the Defendants; a member of the Communist Party since 1926, and Assistant General Secretary of the ETU, of which he had been a member since 1924. He corroborated, in much greater detail, Mr Rengert's account of the December 1959 'scrutiny' at Head Office (see page 149), and the Defendants' general versions of the meeting at which Mr Chapple had vainly tried to get the names of the disqualified branches, and of the method of ordering and dispatching ballot papers to the branches. He accounted for his movements at Christmas, 1959, in a way that would have made it impossible for him to go round the country posting the fraudulent ballot papers of which so much had been heard; and he knew nothing about national aggregate conferences or advisory committees. The whole of the Plaintiffs' story was, in fact, 'utterly untrue'.

He had known Mr Haxell for twenty-five years, he told Mr Gardiner in cross-examination, and had complete trust in him. He agreed that although, in the Byrne-Haxell election of 1959, he, Mr McLennan, was in final charge of the election arrangements—because Mr Haxell was a candidate—Mr Haxell prepared the circulars to branches and similar documents.

'Did that seem all right to you?' the Judge asked him; and he said it did.

Mr Gardiner reminded him of the evidence of the many witnesses about irregularities on ballot nights, and of the fact, disclosed only during the trial, that the 26,000 extra ballot papers were printed and taken eventually to Head Office. The Executive Council had passed a resolution leaving the whole conduct of the Defence in the present trial to Foulkes, Haxell, and himself; so that he would have been under some obligation to follow the evidence closely. Yet the Defendants had not disclosed that the 26,000 voting papers had ever been in their possession? He didn't remember.

'Do you still think, now, that this election was not rigged?'— 'Yes, I still think that.'

'You really do?'—'Yes, of course I do.'

'Although an injunction has been granted by the Court,' said Mr Gardiner later, 'you are still acting as Assistant General Secretary, aren't you?'—'That is correct.'

'And it follows that whatever happens in this action, you and Mr Haxell will still be in a position to rig any election if you want to?'—'We shan't be in a position to rig any election.'

'Why not?'—'Because we don't rig elections.'

'Would you answer the question, Mr McLennan?' said the Judge wearily.

'If we want to, we shall be free to do anything.'

'The idea of collecting all branch documents occurred to you, did it, about a month or two before the trial of this action?'—'It might be so.'

'That's not a thing which has ever been done before?'—'No.'

As to the advisory committees of the Communist Party, he knew nothing of them. Mr Gardiner reminded him of Mr Hendy's letter to Mr Cannon, which had been read and discussed in Court for so long on the previous day, but Mr McLennan remembered nothing of the meeting which it described, nor, accordingly, whether he was there at the time.

'But you were a member of that committee, weren't you?'— 'There was no such committee, to my knowledge.'

'Mr Hendy called it a committee, didn't he?'—'Mr Hendy may have called it a committee.'

And unlike Mr Hendy, he could not be prevailed upon to offer even the vaguest estimate of the number of Communists in the ETU. The five hundred, he said, *might* be right, but he 'couldn't even make a guess'.

He knew nothing about the 26,000 extra ballot papers, and they were never even mentioned between himself and Mr Haxell. Once the Judge patiently wore him down, from having conceded that a lie is 'dishonest if wilfully done', to agreeing that a letter from Head Office 'might have been a lie, yes'.

In relation to the Kirkcaldy affair (Haxell 113, Byrne 94), Mr Gardiner recalled that the Defence had put in an answer saying that 'the return was accepted by the national scrutineers after an alleged breach of the Rules had been investigated by the Defendant McLennan'.

'There was no investigation, was there?'—'There was no further investigation after the correspondence.'

'You call writing a letter and getting an answer an investigation, do you?'—'That could be considered an investigation.'

And the same was true of other complaints 'investigated'.

Mr Gardiner put it to him that 'if the witnesses called for the Plaintiffs had been telling the truth', on the evening of December 24 there was a majority of 2,509 for Mr Byrne (Byrne 13,636, Haxell 11,127). Whereas if they were telling lies, then other figures would apply but there would still be a majority for Mr Byrne of 1,247.

'I suggest that you and Mr Foulkes and Mr Haxell, and probably Mr Frazer, must have known as well as Mr Humphrey how this election was going?'—'It's not true as far as I'm concerned,' said Mr McLennan. 'I can only speak for myself.'

'I suggest that you must have known when you went away for Christmas that Mr Byrne was leading by a substantial majority?'— 'I had no idea.'

'And that by the evening of the twenty-eighth the thing was virtually over and Haxell was out?'—'I had no idea.'

'And I suggest that it was on or about the twenty-ninth that you must have discussed with Mr Humphrey what could be done to get any late returns for Mr Haxell through the national scrutineers? And that the only way to deal with the Byrne branches would be to disqualify them for being late and send people out in cars to get envelopes posted to support that?'

'Entirely untrue.' And so it went on. Mr McLennan's long cross-examination ended with the Judge asking him about the occasions when so many complaining branch secretaries were called to Head Office and placated. They had all signed acknowledgments that an envelope then produced to them (by Mr McLennan) was in fact the envelope in which they had posted their ballot returns to Head Office.

'If any one of these visitors,' said the Judge, 'did in fact make it clear to you that he was not agreeing that the envelope produced was his own envelope—do you follow me?—'—'Yes?'

'And you thereafter suggested that he could nevertheless sign the document because it only meant that he had examined *an* envelope, that would have been a fraudulent trick on him, wouldn't it?'

Mr McLennan agreed.

'You've been in Court, you know, virtually the whole time in this case, haven't you?'—'Yes.'

'Was there ever any cross-examination on your behalf disputing the evidence of any one of those witnesses that he signed the form because he had been told it merely meant he had examined *an* envelope?'—'I can't remember.'

'But you must have been horrified when you heard witnesses saying: "Mr McLennan told me, 'There's no harm in signing this: it merely means that you have seen *an* envelope and you agree it has got such and such a postmark on it' "? Because according to you that was utterly untrue?'

'I think their recollection was wrong on that,' said Mr McLennan calmly. And as for its not being challenged by him before—'I'm disputing it when I'm being cross-examined by Mr Gardiner,' he said.

When Mr John Frazer, another Defendant, went into the witness-box on the thirtieth day of the evidence, it was generally realised that his story must inevitably be much the same as Mr McLennan's and the other co-Defendants'. The Court seats were noticeably less full, and the Press seats were affording elbow-room for the first time. But the absentees missed some excitement.

Mr Frazer said he had been an Executive Councillor of the ETU since 1954, and a member of the Communist Party since 1939.

His first denial was that there were any advisory committees of the Communist Party to deal with the affairs of the ETU. His next concerned the conversations he was said to have had at a TUC Conference with Mr Blairford, Mr Thomas, and others (see page

60) about ways and means of getting hold of spare ballot papers. Then he gave an account of his movements at Christmas-time in 1959 which would have made it impossible for him to go about the country posting fraudulent election returns: and he survived a gruelling cross-examination at the hands of Mr Gardiner, with the Judge joining in, about his inordinate drawing of free petrol during those few days—he had drawn enough petrol on ETU 'chits' to do 350–400 miles at least (the car he used being a Ford Anglia).

Like the others, he denied the existence of any 'advisory committee' of the Communist Party.

'We've been told,' said Mr Gardiner, 'by those who have been members of your Party, that the Party has both national and local committees with regard to every trade union'.

'That,' Mr Frazer said, 'is absolutely untrue'.

Mr Blairford and Mr Vetterlein, he was reminded, had said that 'the Secretary of the National Advisory Committee was a Mr Hendy, but Mr Frazer was really known as the actual secretary'.

'No, that's untrue,' Mr Frazer replied. 'I was not the secretary. It was not a committee.'

'Can you explain how your colleague Mr Hendy came to refer to you as the secretary of this committee at the time?'—'No, I can't explain what Mr Hendy has said. That's a matter for Mr Hendy to explain.'

But he explained later, in effect, that all the damaging references in Mr Hendy's long letter to Mr Cannon on November 23, 1951 (see page 183), were due to a kind of wishful thinking: Mr Hendy, with Mr Chapple, Mr Cannon and others, had 'worked very hard to get that type of committee but was unsuccessful'. Mr Hendy, he thought, did not understand the role of the Communist Party in the trade union movement.

Returning for a moment to the events of Christmas 1959 and the bogus envelopes in the Byrne-Haxell election, Mr Gardiner wanted to establish that the witness 'knew quite well that the election was virtually over and Mr Byrne had won'.

'Well,' said Mr Frazer tartly, 'your suggestion is absolutely wrong'.

'That was when you filled up with your ten gallons and went off and posted the envelopes?'

Mr Gardiner may have been guessing, but it made Mr Frazer furious. 'That is an absolutely scandalous suggestion,' he almost shouted, 'something I would not indulge in. I take strong exception' (his voice rose even higher) 'to you or anyone else implying that I would do such a thing.'

But there was no jury. There was only Mr Justice Winn: and he said:

'Don't behave like that. It's the duty of learned Counsel to put to you the case that is being made in this Court. It's no good waxing indignant about it. You are here to answer those charges, which are made in due form of law.'

The incident had not nerved Mr Frazer for the ordeal that was to come, a prolonged gruelling about all those branch secretaries who had come from all over Great Britain (at what expense!) to Head Office, Hayes, Kent, to be confronted with envelopes 'proving' that they had posted late. And at the end of it Mr Gardiner referred to the meeting of the Executive on May 14 and 15, 1960:

'If you were acting honestly, why didn't you say: "I think you ought to know that we have had piles and piles of letters from branch secretaries all over the country, all asserting vehemently that they posted their envelopes at quite a different date to the envelopes that Mr Humphrey has given me—Mr McLennan and I have seen a number of them. Most of them, as soon as they saw the envelopes, said 'That's not the envelope I sent my return in' "?'

'Because I didn't think of saying such a thing at the time. It's as simple as that,' replied Mr Frazer belligerently.

'But if you had been acting honestly, you couldn't have sat silently without telling the non-Communist members of the committee of this correspondence and of the interviews which you and Mr McLennan had had with the branch secretaries?'

'I was both honest and silent,' Mr Frazer said.

6   Mr Frank Foulkes

General President of the ETU for fifteen years, a member of it since 1915, and a member of the Communist Party since 1931, Mr Frank Foulkes was the Defendant whose arrival in the witness-box had been awaited with the most interest. A year or two before this case came into Court, the name of Frank Foulkes was spoken with something approaching affection throughout the Union—or throughout that problematical part of its membership that took any notice of the Union at all. The Press seats were full, and once more there was available in the public part of the Court standing room only for those prepared to use one foot at a time.

Mr Foulkes told Mr Neil Lawson that he was first elected General President in 1945, re-elected in 1950 (beating Mr Byrne), returned unopposed in 1954, and successful against Mr Blairford in September 1959. He agreed that he was Chairman of the Joint National Industrial Council for the electricity supply industry and Vice-Chairman of its Advisory Council, President of the Confederation of Shipbuilding and Engineering Unions, and 'a member of various bodies covering most of the industries of the country'. Nearly the whole of his time, he said, was taken up in negotiations with the 'employing interests'. He was far too busy to have anything to do with the preparations for the 1959 Byrne-Haxell election for General Secretary.

It was not surprising that, in denying the existence of any such body as the much-discussed 'National Advisory Committee' of the Communist Party, Mr Foulkes turned to the Judge and made this plea for indulgence:

'My Lord, I would like to say this. I have been sat in your Court for seven weeks, and some of the things I may say may have been collected in Court, as it were, rather than from my recollection.' But as for any committee whose function or hope was to control from outside the affairs of the ETU, 'you can be assured I would not accept their instructions'.

'Has anybody ever told you,' Mr Lawson asked him, 'what you have to do as General President of the Union, other than your own members?'—'Many people have tried—unsuccessfully, I would say.'

Speaking of the Executive meeting on February 6, 1960, when the importunate Mr Chapple wanted the names of the 112 disqualified branches read out slowly, Mr Foulkes admitted to having been vexed. 'I suppose I was vexed because of the things that had been said to me and the things that were in my mind. We're so used to

Mr Chapple taking copious notes now, that when he asked me to make special accommodation for him to take the notes that were going to be used against us in the Press the following day, I didn't feel justified in doing it. So I just told him' (i.e., Mr McLennan, the Assistant General Secretary) 'to read them in the normal way, and he did.'

When Mr Foulkes had completed his denials of the Plaintiffs' evidence that related specifically to him, and of a good deal of other evidence that did not, Mr Gerald Gardiner rose to cross-examine.

'Can you tell me,' he began, 'whether those Defendants who have not already given evidence—Mr Davies, Mr Feathers, Mr Cosby, and Mr Batchelor—are going into the witness-box?'

'I understood I was the last witness,' said Mr Foulkes, and he was nearly right. But it meant that Mr Gardiner would be asking him some questions that he would otherwise have reserved for the Defendants he had just named.

'Would it be right to say that, while Mr Haxell is feared, the members regard you with a good deal of affection?'—'They did until four years ago, I believe.'

'You remember the election in September 1957 between Mr Cannon and Mr Frazer?'—'Very vividly.'

'And various complaints were made, and enquiries as to whether certain branches should be disqualified?'—'I would say hundreds of complaints were made, not just "various".'

'I suggest this was the first election in which the Executive had sought to construe Rule 20(1), 1954 edition, as meaning that the members could not appeal against the acceptance of a scrutineers' report. Is that not right?'*—'No.'

From a discussion of the Rules which then ensued between Mr Foulkes, Mr Lawson, and the Judge ('I think you have a better understanding of our Rule Book, my Lord,' said Mr Foulkes; and 'from what I have heard from you, I would rely on your re-collection'), it then became apparent that the Rule relating to appeals was understood by nobody, inside or outside the ETU, in or out of the Court. But in 1957 Mr Foulkes had sent a circular

---

* There had been complaints that when the Executive Council should have disqualified certain branches for 'infringements' it had deliberately refrained from doing so because they had supported the Communist candidate.

letter to the branches (and to the Press) refuting the allegations being made in the newspapers. This contained the sentence: 'Normally the Executive of the Union would not engage in public controversy on matters which are of direct concern to the members only, and subject to the democratic processes of an appeals machinery.'

'If I was an ordinary member,' said Mr Gardiner, 'and I was convinced, rightly or wrongly, that the elections were being rigged, is there anything I could have done about it under your "democratic appeals machinery"?'—'Yes. You could have charged the General President of the Union, the General Secretary of the Union, or any of the members who you alleged were rigging the ballot.'

'Don't you know that the Rules expressly provide that, whatever you or the General Secretary does, no charge can be made against you?'—'We can be charged by the Executive Council,' Mr Foulkes answered blandly.

'Yes, but there's nothing the ordinary member can do?'

Mr Foulkes said that there were other people who could be charged; but after prolonged questioning it emerged (once again) that the Executive Council could prevent any appeal against a decision by the simple expedient of not recording that decision in the minutes.

In the 1957 circular Mr Foulkes had said that 'had all the votes of the branches mentioned' (i.e., the disqualified ones) 'been accepted then it would not have made any difference to the result of the ballot'.

'You made this statement, did you not,' said Mr Gardiner, 'to lead the members of your Union and the public generally to think that if none of the disqualifications which had been made had taken place, Les Cannon would not have been elected, anyhow?'— 'You mustn't put words into my mouth. We are dealing with the Press, my Lord' (Mr Foulkes turned plaintively to the Judge) 'and what *they* have said. Counsel is now trying to get me on another tack, and asking me what I wanted our members to think, and all I want our members to think is the truth.'

The Judge seemed unmoved. 'Don't be so pathetic and appealing all the time,' he said, 'as though you couldn't look after yourself.

You are fully capable, with all your experience, of hearty self-defence.'

'I would suggest,' Mr Gardiner went on, 'that it was this reported statement of yours which led a great many members at that time to say: "Well, what *does* it all matter? Les Cannon wouldn't have got in, anyway. What is he making all this fuss about?" '—'I suggest the members were not saying anything of the kind.'

'It is the fact, is it not, that if none of those branches had been disqualified, Mr Cannon would have been elected?'—'I don't know.'

But when he was shown the list again, and reminded of what Mr George Scott had said (see page 175), he agreed at last, but added that he had never intended to mislead.

Mr Gardiner came to the famous television interviews. He thought Mr Foulkes would be likely to accept the *Daily Worker's* version of what he had said to the interviewer on December 14, 1957 with Mr Norman Mackenzie. 'The *Daily Worker* is always very accurate and impartial?'—'If it was not impartial on my side, I would take it up with the *Daily Worker*.'

Mr Gardiner handed him a copy and read out: 'The Press myth about the "frightened" members of the Electrical Trades Union was shattered in an Independent Television interview last night by Mr Frank Foulkes, the General President. He did this by his simple straightforward answers.'

'It's about some of your simple, straightforward answers that I wanted to ask you. Is this right: "When Mr MacKenzie referred to the controversy which, he said, arose because of the defeat of Mr Les Cannon, a candidate in one of the Union's elections, Mr Foulkes replied that even if all the votes which had been invalidated in the election had been counted, Mr Cannon would still not have won the election." Did you say that?'—'I think I did. I was of that opinion at the time.'

'But it was untrue.'—'Was it?'

'You *know* it was now, don't you? You've seen the figures.'—'No, I don't know. I can't get the dates.'

'I suggest this was a deliberate untruth, done because you knew that your members, hearing it on television, would say "If Frank Foulkes says that it must be right, and what is the good of Les

Cannon making this fuss if he wouldn't have been elected anyway?" '—'I can assure you it wasn't a deliberate untruth. If I said
it, I thought it was true.'

'But these questions you had arranged with the interviewer
beforehand? I don't mean improperly.'—'That's not true.'

'This is not "Panorama", you know—this is ITV. You *had*
discussed with the interviewer the questions he was going to ask?'—
'No. MacKenzie was more co-operative than Freeman, but the only
thing that happened was that he gave me an idea of what the
questions would be.'

'Then you were asked: "Will you publish the voting figures?"
Did you say: "Voting figures will be published in full to the
members through the Executive Council's minutes within the next
fortnight or three weeks"? Did you say that?'—'If they said it in
the *Daily Worker*.'

'It was quite untrue, wasn't it?'—'No.'

Mr Foulkes didn't know himself what the voting figures were.
Nobody knew, he said.

'But are you wanting me to understand,' asked the Judge, 'that
when you said "if all the votes which had been invalidated had
been counted" you were including votes invalidated by the scrutineers?'—'I couldn't tell you what I thought at this moment, my
Lord. This was in December 1957.'

Then he said it was 'a newspaper report'.

'Are you now trying to say you were misreported?' asked Mr
Gardiner.

'No, I'm saying I may not have said it just exactly. Just let me
read it.' (He read it to himself again.) 'No,' he said, 'I can't imagine
me saying that'.

'You knew perfectly well, didn't you, that none of the votes of
the branches that had been disqualified would be published?'—
'Yes, but if he' (the television interviewer) 'had had the knowledge
that you and I have now, he would probably have said "And would
the *invalidated* votes be published?" And I would have said "No".'

'You said: "There is an appeals machinery, and we were responsible for introducing that appeals machinery into the organisation"?'—'Yes.'

'And "each member can go to his branch, and the branch can

appeal against any decision of the Executive Council at any time".
Is that true?'—'Yes, with the exception of the scrutineers' report.'

But there then followed a long colloquy with the Judge, the upshot of which (Mr Foulkes reluctantly agreeing) was that in the
1954 Rules, Rule 20(1) did *not* allow an appeal against a scrutineers' report.

'So that what you said on television,' followed up Mr Gardiner,
'was deliberately saying that which you knew was not true?'—'I
have never told a deliberate lie in the whole of my life,' was Mr
Foulkes' unique claim. 'Apart from the things that are said by the
people who are advising your clients, I am sure that there is nobody in this country who thinks that I would tell a lie deliberately.'

'I shall have to come to some other occasions, Mr Foulkes, when
you have said that which you knew to be quite untrue.'

'You prove it to me,' said Mr Foulkes confidently.

So Mr Gardiner went through the Jarrow story with him. In
that affair, said Mr Foulkes, it was the Branch Secretary who was
telling lies. Then came the September 1959 election for General
President—and here Mr Foulkes, unlike some of his co-Defendants,
admitted quite openly that he knew the election was going very
badly for him. He did *not*, at a meeting of the Stevenage Branch at
that time, say to Mr Joseph Thomas (because he had never even
met him): 'Joe, is there a pub in your area for sale?—it looks as
though I shall be out of a job very shortly'; though it *was* a
characteristic jest of his to enquire about pubs for sale. He did *not*
know that there were any surplus ballot papers at Head Office, or
that substitute envelopes had been posted ('and I don't think they
were, by us').

'You are one of the committee of three, are you not, responsible to
the Union and your co-Defendants for running this action?'—'Yes.'

'Do you agree that it was not until April the 21st, on the third
day of the action, when I called Mr Swift' (the printer) 'that any
admission was made by any Defendant that any one of these
twenty-six thousand voting papers had ever been at Head Office?'—
'I don't know whether that was the first time that any one of the
Defendants had said it or not.'

'If it was, do you want to offer any information about that, at
all?'—'No. I can only speak for myself. I didn't know.'

'You didn't know until when?'—'Until the solicitors told me.'

'When was that?'—'Last year,' disclosed Mr Foulkes.

Belfast Central was one of the election miracles of 1959. The branch nominated Mr Pike as its candidate for 'full-time official', giving him twenty-three votes (it was done by show of hands) as against Mr Brown's twelve and Mr Cosby's three. Mr Cosby probably sent up so few hands because he didn't belong to the branch— he came from Belfast Municipal. Yet at the election he got a hundred and nine votes from Belfast Central members as against Mr Pike's sixty—and got in. Similarly, for General Secretary the branch nominee was Mr Byrne, but in the election at the branch quarterly meeting he got only forty-one votes as against Mr Haxell's one hundred and twenty-seven.

'It's a most unusual thing for a branch to vote against their own nominee?' suggested Mr Gardiner.

'It used to be. In the last few years it hasn't been uncommon. I think I received about five hundred nominations. My opponent received maybe fifty—but he nearly beat me.'

'I suggest to you that on the rare occasions when they do vote against their own nominee, it is invariably the case that the opponent of their nominee is a member of your Party?'

'I can't tell you one way or the other,' said Mr Foulkes. He then offered an explanation of this overturn in the voting that was rather difficult to follow, but seemed to mean that an attendance of twenty was a good average at a 'nomination meeting', that the attendance of forty-seven on the Pike-Cosby evening was therefore high, that the more members there were to put their hands up at the nomination meeting the more likely it was that Mr Pike would be elected when the time came—but that somehow or other Mr Cosby got elected. 'Well, perhaps it would be more honest for me to say I can't explain it, my Lord, because I was not there.'

'So I would have thought in the first place,' said Mr Justice Winn tartly, 'instead of your making up what appears to me to be an entirely tendentious explanation which is quite plainly erroneous'.

'I thought I was assisting Counsel.'

Since Mr James Feathers, one of the Defendants, was not going to give evidence for himself, Mr Gardiner asked his General

President a number of questions about him. In particular, Mr Feathers had written a letter enclosing some notes he had made at a Communist Party meeting at King Street, Covent Garden, at which—Mr Gardiner suggested—Mr Foulkes had been the chairman. These notes contained some revealing phrases:

'*Necessity for only seventy-four resolutions re Vienna*' (referring to the Communists' 1953 Vienna 'Peace' Conference).

'*Must regularly attend to anti-EC branches*' (i.e., branches opposed to the Executive Council of the ETU were to receive 'the treatment').

'*Role of electricity: key position of Union. Must accept responsibility placed upon us. Party not yet big and strong enough to move the masses against RW*' (i.e., Right Wing?).

'*Up against rules of Labour Party. No such rules for TUC industrial affiliations. Our members must not sign documents.*' (Mr Foulkes agreed that this one might refer to the fact that in 1951 the TUC was reorganising the 'Trades Councils' and requiring members thereof to sign a document saying that they were neither Fascist nor Communist.)

'*May be necessary to modify our attitude as witch hunt develops; e.g., stooge TC*'—meaning presumably Trades Councils. (This one, thought Mr Foulkes, *might* have meant, 'Our members, being Communists, cannot sign that they are not. [Query: send stooge who is not a Communist and *can* therefore sign that he is not.]')

'But,' said Mr Foulkes, 'if that decision was taken at some meeting, it proves conclusively that I was not there, because I wouldn't stand for it' [*sic*].

'*Complete change in international situation. Will be followed through to the end. Concessions by USSR. Key importance of Party building. Key importance of DW.*' (Mr Foulkes agreed that '*DW*' here meant the *Daily Worker*.)

'*Attitude of General Council of TUC towards London Trades Councils and ETU, e.g., will attempt to isolate ETU and disaffiliate from TUC.*'

'*Alarmed to hear that positive moves had occurred in spite of the Advisory Committee.*' ('You've never heard of advisory committees of this kind?' Mr Gardiner asked the witness. 'I've heard a lot of them during this case,' he replied.)

Mr Foulkes' famous interview in the BBC 'Panorama' programme on February 22, 1960, with Mr John Freeman (of the
New Statesman) came under review next. Mr Gardiner reminded
him of the way it opened:

'Mr Foulkes, some pretty precise allegations have been made
about this election,' Mr John Freeman had said, 'by members of
your own Union, not only by members of the public; and the first
of them concerns the large number of branch ballots which
where disqualified. Now I want to ask you, how many were
there?'

'That,' said Mr Gardiner, 'was a very simple question, was it
not?'—'It was a simple question, yes.'

'Then did you say:

Well, first of all I would like to mention the fact that I am
not here to defend the innocence of myself or my colleagues.
You mention allegations. Well, I would just like to give
you a brief picture of the people who made the allegations.
You introduced them last week as members of good standing
within our organisation. I'll deal with Mr Reno first. Mr
Reno was introduced as being a well-known shop steward.
He's *not* a well-known shop steward: his tenure of that office
has been very brief wherever he has accepted it. Our members
have lost a lot of money through Mr Reno's activities, and one
of them is that he supports what we now popularly call 'wild-cat
strikes'. The other was Mr Marshall, who claimed that he didn't
know why he had been taken away from his branch secretary-
ship, and said the General Secretary had carried out an investigation which was worthy of the CID. Well, I'm sure our members will be delighted to know that he carried out such an investigation because there was £108 unaccounted for in Mr Marshall's
branch. Now obviously we couldn't have a secretary in a branch
having a position like that arising.

'That,' commented Mr Gardiner, 'was a very good way of not
answering the question, wasn't it—a very simple question: "How
many branches had been disqualified?" '—'Yes,' agreed Mr
Foulkes.

'You hadn't answered it?'—'Well, Freeman didn't take exception
to it.'

'It was done on purpose, wasn't it?'—'Yes.'

'To get out of answering it?'—'No.'

'Did you really not know on February the 22nd?'—'No.'

'When *did* you know? Perhaps you don't know now?'—'I *don't* know now. I think I've had a hundred and nine in my mind.'

Mr Gardiner asked whether he had said: 'There has been higher figures.' Mr Foulkes admitting saying that.

'I am talking about comparisons, when we had four hundred branches as against seven hundred and six now.' In 1941, said Mr Foulkes, there were ninety-three disqualified—out of four hundred.

'But just think from the point of view of anybody listening to this. Mr Freeman says: "If it were a hundred, and you don't deny it, would you agree that that was an exceptionally high figure?" You say "There has been higher figures". What on earth can that mean except higher figures than a hundred?'—'It means higher figures by a percentage of the branches that we have.'

'But he is not expressing the members disqualified as a percentage of anything, but as a number, one hundred?'—'I don't know *what* he's expressing, John Freeman.'

John Freeman, he added, 'didn't give you much time to say anything or think about anything.'

'Then,' went on Mr Gardiner, 'you were asked, "Now how do you answer those branch secretaries, and there are quite a number of them, who are prepared to swear that they posted on time?" Did you say: "Well, one swore on your programme last week, and since then he has been on the phone to me trying to get to know exactly when his envelope *was* posted. I checked on it today, especially before I came on this programme, and his branch can take my word for it that that envelope was posted and it was impossible to catch the date according to the Rules." What branch was that?'—'Eastbourne.'

Did Mr Foulkes think the secretary of that branch was telling lies when he said that he posted his envelope on December 19 (it was said not to have arrived until the 24th)?

'At this stage I don't know what I thought. Only what I said.'

'Then you were asked: "What about those branch secretaries who feared that this might happen, and posted in the presence of witnesses?" And did you say: "If they produce the witnesses or any evidence, then those witnesses will be heard by the Executive

Council, and the evidence will be considered?" You *knew* that was untrue, didn't you?'—'No, it's true. It's still true today.'

'There's no appeal against the acceptance of a scrutineers' return, is there?'—'I didn't say that. I said if they produced the witnesses—'

But the Judge interposed now. 'Just a moment,' he said. 'If you had wanted to mislead the audience and tell a downright lie about this, you might have said: "Well, they can always appeal against the scrutineers' report"?'—'They can't appeal against the scrutineers' report, my Lord.'

'But,' said Mr Gardiner, taking this up, 'you say: "There has been no appeal as yet—there could be under the Rules." That was a thoroughly dishonest statement, was it not?'—'No. Rule 21, Clause 70, gives the branch the right of appeal.'

'Against acceptance of the scrutineers' report?'—'No.'

'Against the disqualification of a branch by the scrutineers?'

Mr Foulkes agreed. But the Judge was now thoroughly puzzled, and throughout this long trial he had not allowed any puzzle to remain unsolved. 'I'm quite unable to understand,' he said, 'how the operation of that Rule could ever overrule a disqualification. Will you just take the Rule Book in your hand, and read to me the words under which it could possibly have that effect? I want you to tell me how you, with the intelligence that you possess, could possibly suppose that?'

Mr Foulkes read out Rule 21, Clause 70, which was very long but contained no word about the setting aside of a scrutineers' disqualification. 'That Rule,' said the Judge, 'contemplates only the possibility that after the scrutineers have allowed the vote, the Executive Council may disallow it. Isn't that obviously clear to a child, let alone a man of your intelligence and experience in the affairs of the Union?'

Mr Foulkes said he meant that the Executive Council 'would have the right to investigate, and rectify the position in the ballot vote'.

The Judge nodded rather grimly.

But Mr Gardiner thrashed it a little more. He reminded Mr Foulkes of another question from John Freeman—'So where a secretary *did* post in the presence of witnesses and all are prepared to swear, then an appeal can be heard, and what then?' And Mr Foulkes had answered, 'And the witnesses would be heard'.

'That's quite untrue, isn't it?' Mr Gardiner said.

'No.'

'Branch secretaries wrote in from all over the country, didn't they?'—'Yes, they wrote in.'

'Saying, "This must be a false envelope—it's not mine because I remember quite well posting it on such and such a date"?'—'Yes.'

'Did the Executive Council take any steps to hear them, or write a letter saying other than that there was no appeal?'—'No. No, they never took any action at that stage.'

'So this was a shockingly dishonest statement, wasn't it?'—'No.'

And so it went on, until at last—

'It's meaningless to me,' said Mr Justice Winn, 'if that's any help to you, Mr Foulkes. Would you like to try again?'

'I don't think so, my Lord, because I don't think I could describe it any different way.'

'Well, there it is,' said the Judge, and sat well back in his chair again. 'I can't force you to help us any more.'

Then Mr John Freeman was quoted again from the television interview—

'Mr Foulkes, you do realise, don't you, that these charges concern you personally? Now your own answers show quite clearly that these are not just charges of administrative inefficiency. You assured me this evening that you, yourself, presided over the scrutiny and so on. If they are not administrative inefficiency then they amount to charges of fraud and perhaps Communist conspiracy.' To which Mr Foulkes had retorted, 'I don't want anybody to prove my innocence, and I am quite well able to stand up to any charge of criminal conspiracy.' Mr Freeman then asked, 'Well now, why don't you do so? You have a very simple remedy. You can go to the Courts tomorrow morning and issue writs for libel against me, against the BBC, against all the papers that have attacked you, and against the four gentlemen who appeared in last week's programme.'

'That of course was true, wasn't it?' said Mr Gardiner.

'I don't know. I suppose I could.' But he thought that although you might get 'justice' from the Courts, 'your character may be spread all over the papers, and it's worth less when you come out of the Courts than when you went in'.

'You were against the TUC holding a judicial enquiry?'—'Yes. Do you want to know the reason?'

'If you wish to give it you may.'

'It was suggested that the Economic Committee of the General Council should carry out the enquiry. In the first place, I don't think the Economic Committee of Congress are able to carry out an enquiry into our organisation . . . A very important member of the secretariat, I'm informed from a very good source, wrote two centre-page articles for the *Sunday Times* under the name of "Trade Unionist", attacking our Union and suggesting that we were rigging ballots. I don't think the TUC were either capable of or would have given us a fair deal if they'd had an enquiry.'

But then Mr Foulkes made, almost involuntarily it seemed, and in answer to the Judge, the electrifying statement that 'the election *was* being rigged by somebody'.

'Do you care to say by whom?' asked his Lordship.

'I can't prove it, my Lord.'

'Do you care to say whom you *suspect* of having rigged your election, and if you like by what method?'

'I couldn't say the method. But I would say it has been rigged by Cannon and those people associated with him throughout the country.'

'Rigged so as to produce a Haxell victory?'

'Rigged to produce a null and void election. My theory is that Cannon and the other Defendants didn't want Byrne as the General Secretary . . . During the whole of the period that I've known the Defendants and all those people surrounding them they've never been very very friendly. Byrne decides to stand. They decide to adopt him, but they don't want him as General Secretary. What they want to do is to continue the atmosphere that has been prevalent in our organisation from four years ago, when Cannon was discharged from the College' (i.e., the ETU training college at Esher, of which he was in charge) 'because we had to close the College down on financial reasons. I have had reports from various parts of the country, from people who don't trust each other, that Cannon has made statements that he would spend every penny he had to smash Haxell . . . I personally think,' added Mr Foulkes, 'that somebody other than my colleagues has been guilty of late posting, in order to create a tremendous number of votes that were not valid in order to keep this atmosphere going. And they are my honest feelings. Only feelings—I can't prove a thing.'

As for the road itineraries covered by the enquiry agent who had posted all those late envelopes to the Plaintiffs' solicitors, that agent might have been the man who posted the original ones, said Mr Foulkes. 'I don't know—it may have been him that did it. If they employ him once they can employ him again, and he can do it—he has proved he could do it.' (This was an arresting thought, and it started some speculations among the Pressmen present. But they seemed to lead nowhere.)

In re-examination Mr Lawson managed to clarify Mr Foulkes' explanation of what he had said in 'Panorama' about the branches' 'right of appeal'. He had meant (though the Rule he quoted had nothing to do with this) that if the scrutineers were remiss in their work, the scrutineers themselves could be charged for breaking a rule of the Union.

Mr Lawson was also concerned, naturally enough, with the new suggestion that the other Defendants in the case, or some of them, had done the fraudulent posting.

'Is there anything in your mind that suggests to you one way or the other whether *any* of the Defendants in this action had anything to do with posting substituted envelopes?'

'Nothing in my mind at all,' said Mr Foulkes this time.

Then, in answer to the accusation that the witness had spoken dishonestly in saying that the disqualifications made no difference to the result, Mr Lawson read out a passage from a letter Mr Foulkes had written to Sir Ian Jacob, then Director-General of the BBC, about the 'Panorama' interview:

> Whatever figures other people may have, in this office we have the actual voting returns from each of the sixty-one branches in the No. 9 Division, and we repeat that if every branch *mentioned in the broadcast and by the Press** as having had their votes disqualified were to be included, then it would make no difference to the result.
>
> * Italics mine.—*Editor.*

And to this Mr Foulkes assented. He added that he had offered
to submit to an enquiry by the TUC, and he told the Judge that he
and Mr Haxell both 'thought it highly probable' that the Executive
Council, if asked by the TUC, would have taken legal action
against the Union's traducers.

'Mr Foulkes,' concluded Mr Lawson, 'have you personally, or
through anybody on your behalf, ever done anything dishonest in
relation to an election?'

Mr Foulkes said, 'No'.

Mr Lawson then recalled Mr Derek Warlow, of Head Office, to
throw doubt on the Plaintiffs' schedules of voting figures, infringements, late postings, warnings, and over-generous indulgences; and,
dealing with the three motor-car tours made by the private enquiry
agent, he appeared to satisfy the Judge (to use his Lordship's own
words) that 'a swindle could have been worked a different way—if
there *was* a swindle at all—more effectively'. And thus the
Defendants' evidence came to an end.

IV MR LAWSON'S FINAL SPEECH FOR
THE DEFENDANTS

IT was now June 13, and the trial had begun on April 17. Mr Neil
Lawson, QC, rose to make his final speech for the Defendants.

'The overall observation I would like to make about the Plaintiffs' case,' he said, 'is this: it has really pitched everything so high
that one is entitled to approach it with a certain amount of suspicion.' The main matter before the Court was the 1959 Byrne-
Haxell election. But the ETU had 'fallen into the pitfall of trying
to make almost every conceivable office elective, which involves the
Union in a persistent state of election, and having so large a membership they have got into the most fearful problems about how
you can actually organise your balloting'.

Therefore, for many years they had disregarded certain Rules,
building up a kind of practice for which, however beneficent its
intention, the Rules provided no authority. In this light, Mr Lawson went through the various stories that had come out in the
evidence, with the Judge occasionally offering highly significant
interjections. Of these, the following was typical:

'Here is an allegation,' Mr Lawson was saying, dealing with the
Jarrow election, 'which got into the Press, about ballot-rigging in
the Union; and that, I would submit, is properly a matter that
ought to be enquired into, particularly as the Branch Secretary was
the man in the middle of the problem, and was also the candidate
in whose favour these votes had been registered. I submit that one
would have been very surprised if the Executive had come to a
different view, other than that this was a matter which ought to be
enquired into on their behalf, and not left to the branch.'

'Enquired into promptly and vigorously,' said the Judge; 'not
in a fashion which produced a delay of well over a year and missed
the most obvious question. Mr Goldberg, at any rate, was a clever
man. I have to consider that case very carefully, to see whether it

demonstrates reluctance to get down to the truth of the matter, or the hope that it might all die down, or whether it is explicable by pressure of other business, or cupidity.'

From a speech which occupied almost two whole days it is not possible to do more than select, for the purposes of so short a book, a snippet here and there to show the ingenuity and indeed the brilliance with which Mr Lawson sapped the structure of the Plaintiffs' evidence.

On the question of the Communist Party 'advisories' he was more than usually (though, as it turned out, ineffectually) persuasive:

'Whether or not you call a thing officially a committee doesn't seem to me to matter very much. The question is: What was the nature of these bodies? What did they do? . . . One starts off with a long discourse, a general review of the situation by Mr Stevens, and then a general discussion, talking about the advisory committees and selling the *Daily Worker* and literature in branches, and so on. In my submission there is nothing at all improper in discussions of that character.' (No one, by the way, had suggested that there was.) 'Here are a group of people who share the same belief, who think that they ought to work for that particular cause within the organisation of which they are members' (i.e., the ETU). 'They ought, I suppose, to proselytise as much as they can within the organisation of which they are members. These are quite innocent pursuits, as long as, when you do come to the question of elections, nobody encourages the exercise by the individuals concerned of fraudulent practices.

'No one would desire to import into the concept of liability for wrongful acts any kind of theory of guilt by association . . . In relation to each of the individual Defendants the relevant enquiry is this: Firstly, what evidence is there of some specific act of participation, by the Defendant concerned, in the matters of complaint on the December 1959 ballot? And secondly, quite apart from those matters, how does that Defendant stand, on the evidence, in relation to his general trustworthiness and credit?'

Mr Lawson went through the evidence of his individual clients. Mr Haxell—'telling your Lordship the truth to the best of his recollection'; Mr Humphrey—'a pretty straightforward witness, again dealing with the questions frankly'; Mr McLennan—'there was no reason for him to be suspicious of these additional ballot papers requests—'

But here the Judge interrupted. 'He was in charge of the election. It ought to have been referred to him. How an Office Manager' (i.e., Mr Humphrey) 'can be allowed to deal with things like this in any properly regulated organisation I cannot imagine. It goes not to the management of the office: it goes to the security of the Union, in its reputation and survival. It's fantastic. It is one of the factors I have to weigh as to whether anybody' (i.e., Mr McLennan) 'could really leave such matters to an Office Manager.'

Mr Frazer next—'a good witness on whom one can place reliance,' said Mr Lawson; then Mr George Scott—'if one looks at the *Daily Worker* article written in December 1957, Mr Scott, in fact, was repeating something which had been said in a circular issued by Mr Haxell some ten days before—'

'My choice in this matter,' interposed the Judge again, 'is between convicting Mr Scott of dishonesty or crass error of judgment. He agreed with me that if you call your enemy a liar and then say the truth is so-and-so, you must be very careful that you are telling the *whole* truth. It can't be creditable to Mr Scott on any view.'

'He is much too keen,' Mr Lawson explained, 'to take up arms in the battle by writing an article of this kind, which is going to be a devastating reply to those who are attacking the chaps he believes in; and your Lordship may feel that he didn't act with the caution and wisdom that a more dispassionate consideration would have led him to adopt.'

The case against Mr Goldberg, Mr Lawson went on, was 'a very flimsy one'—it was merely that he 'sat by when this ballot was announced', and he didn't know about the surplus ballot papers (though he *did* know that the Jarrow secretary had 'diverted' ballot papers to his own use). He had nothing to do with any conspiracy.

Mr West (said Mr Lawson), 'from the point of view of intelligence and political experience', was 'not so ahead as Mr Goldberg' and was 'very much less likely even than Mr Goldberg to be involved in fraudulent acts of the kind alleged in this case'.

Mr Hendy was 'quite frank'. But, said the Judge, why was he

so ashamed of that letter he had written to Mr Cannon on November 23, 1951? Because Mr Cannon, an old friend, said Mr Lawson, in effect, was now a bitter enemy, and because the views Mr Hendy was renouncing were 'untenable on any basis of political morality'.

As for Mr Sell, there was 'nothing at all against him in this case'—the fact that Mr Rengert had been one of the scrutineers had 'gone a long way with him' (and Mr Rengert, it will be remembered, was already discharged from the suit). Mr Feathers—he was not now alleged to have been a member of the 'advisories', and as for the notes he had taken at the Stevens meeting in 1953, there was nothing there to convict him of ballot-rigging. Mr Cosby likewise, though an 'Area official', a Communist, and a man who had attended the Party meetings at which the ETU was discussed, was not the subject of any specific allegation about ballot-rigging. And it was the same, Mr Lawson maintained, with Mr Davies. The case against these last three (who had not given any evidence on their own behalf) was 'really pure suspicion'.

There was nothing against Mr Batchelor in relation to the December 1959 ballots (said Mr Lawson) except that he had had the use of an ETU car and received petrol and expenses at that time—and even so, other evidence showed that he could not have been on the itineraries (the 'rural rides') of which so much had been heard.

There were the allegations about 'getting hold of a branch stamp' (see page 64), but if the rigging was to be controlled from Head Office, there would be no difficulty in Mr Batchelor's getting all the stamps he wanted there.

And lastly Mr Foulkes. 'I wouldn't be surprised if your Lordship formed the view that he was a poor witness.' It was true that, at the Executive meeting on February the 6th, 1959, he ought not to have been 'vexed', and that he shouldn't have rushed things as he did; that he never took proper security measures about the ballots, although he knew what was being publicly said about them; and that his performance in the 'Panorama' interview (to say nothing of his preparation for that interview) 'fell short of the standards which it should have reached'. But Mr Foulkes had always been convinced that he and Mr Haxell were 'the subject of a very intense and, as he thought, unscrupulous campaign', and that was bound to influence his conduct. He had completely trusted his associates. His behaviour since his disillusionment about them had been 'completely defensive'. And as he had given his life's work to the ETU, he could not contemplate its grave difficulties with 'a sufficiently clear vision'.

And Mr Lawson ended with an anticipation that Mr Gerald Gardiner, in his speech, would repeat his complaint about the documents which the Defence ought to have produced but couldn't find. 'The burden on the Union,' he said, 'and on those advising it has been terrific . . . Any suggestion of deliberate suppression of documents does not really arise in this case.'

'I am therefore asking your Lordship to say on these grave charges there should be Judgment for the Defendants.'

'I should like to say, Mr Lawson,' his Lordship then said, 'that I am deeply indebted to you for your assistance throughout the whole of this trial'.

And Mr Lawson sat down.

V MR GARDINER'S FINAL SPEECH
FOR THE PLAINTIFFS

HALF-WAY through the morning of Thursday, June 15, therefore, Mr Gardiner began his second speech.

Mr Gardiner has a love for numbered, orderly lists of things. He had already said that there were over eighty separate issues for the Judge to consider (and, it was rumoured, could probably have recited them from memory). 'In my submission, my Lord,' he now said, 'the three things which matter most in this case are:

1. The substituted envelopes;
2. The additional ballot papers; and
3. The dishonest use of powers (real or assumed) of disqualification.'

For the purpose of his speech, however, he was going to put the case under five heads:

a The genesis of the action;
b Whether Haxell was elected by fraud;
c The relevance of the conspiracy charges in the Cannon election;
d If Haxell *was* elected by fraud, which of the Defendants had a hand in it; and
e What 'relief' the Plaintiffs were entitled to if they won.

Mr Gardiner recalled that the Courts had sometimes deprecated Court actions about disputes in trade unions 'if their own Rules give them a proper remedy'; but in this case the Defendants themselves had left the Plaintiffs no alternative but an action in the Courts to establish proof that the elections had been rigged. The monumental difficulty of establishing that proof was indicated in Mr Gardiner's next words:

'So on May the 10th' (1960) 'the writ in this action was issued

without the Plaintiffs even knowing which branches had been disqualified, let alone why, or the way in which they had voted . . .
the Plaintiffs were only told that fifty-six of those branches had
voted for Byrne, which is only about half. Of the fifty-six they
were only able to say in the case of thirty-one branches the date
on which they had had their quarterly meeting, and the date on
which they had posted their envelopes. All they could really say
was: "We allege that this election was rigged in the usual way or
ways." After a visit to a Judge in Chambers the Defence was
delivered, consisting in the main of a general denial. Obviously
everything depended on "discovery" ' (i.e., on the production by
the Defendants of the very evidence that would convict them).

The Defendants' solicitors had shown the Plaintiffs' solicitors a
'vast stack' of about 30,000 documents and said 'look at anything
you like'. And Mr Haxell had told them that the required documents,
contained in parcels or envelopes as dispatched from the branches
of the ETU, were 'estimated to number hundreds of thousands'.

'Informal discovery went on, my Lord, right up to the eve of
trial, and the problem for the Plaintiffs was to know what on
earth to look at and what on earth to ask for . . . This has been
an exceptionally difficult and messy case. A hundred and fifty-four
witnesses have been called. Three hundred and two exhibits have
been put in—of which even now I have no copies of a hundred and
twenty-nine . . . If, of course, the Plaintiffs could start again,
knowing what they know now, and knowing what the witnesses
called on subpoena were going to say, the whole case could have been
very much more streamlined and, I doubt not, very much simpler.'

Mr Gardiner had a long colloquy with the Judge about the 'rural
rides'. His Lordship thought that their implication could be much
weakened by mathematical comparisons and by a resort to the
laws of probability. Mr Gardiner, on the other hand, said that it
'couldn't be accidental that seventeen branches, from London up
to the west coast of Scotland, should post their envelopes in such
a time-sequence as would result where somebody driving a car
travelled north to post them'. He said he could 'only respectfully
adopt what Mr Foulkes said in his last answer to me, that it must
be the result of a plot'. As to the attack on Mr Cobbett, the fast-
driving enquiry agent, 'it would not be right,' said Mr Gardiner,

'that the Defendants in a final speech should suggest that Mr Cobbett was not telling the truth'.

'I think the point is,' the Judge observed, 'that Mr Cobbett, not doing it for the Defendants, had made such good time'.

But Mr Gardiner never really convinced his Lordship that a plot to post substituted envelopes would have needed to be carried out at such a break-neck speed, or that there would have been 'any need to rely on any particular route from A to B'. (He came back to the subject next day, with some fresh thoughts in support of it, but the Judge amiably and implacably told him that 'as one grows older one mistrusts the meretricious and the attractive'.)

Dealing with the additional ballot papers, Mr Gardiner commented on many of the branches' figures, but the cogency of his remarks about the Belfast figures may be selected as typical:

'It is at least suspicious that Mr McLennan' (as Assistant General Secretary) 'should go to Belfast. Of course, it would be no good posting Northern Ireland votes from England . . . The additional ballot papers had to be got to Northern Ireland, to Belfast. It's a remarkable coincidence that during the time the additional ballot papers were at Head Office, McLennan should fly to Belfast for twenty-four hours, and a legitimate inference that he was taking the additional ballot papers with him.'

As for the possibility that the papers were stolen from the printers—'Mr Swift, after an interview of some hours with the Defendants' solicitors (and it's fair perhaps to suggest that the Union are obviously valuable clients to him) rather leant over backwards to explain how bad his system was; but when one looks into it, it is not, in my submission, really as bad as all that—it's a perfectly reasonable system on the face of it.'

Mr Gardiner thought this trial must have been a record one for the number of witnesses who, like Mr Haxell, gave their evidence unsworn. 'It may be some people think that if they don't take an oath they needn't tell the truth.' And this, he thought, was important in relation to the 'affirmation of documents', which had been a prominent feature of the whole case.

'If I am to speak plainly,' he said later, 'I must submit that there are two lies which the Defendants have told on every possible occasion, including their appearance in the witness-box. The first is that the criticisms which have been made are malicious, vile insinuations made by unscrupulous people who want to break up the Union. Mr Scott and Mr Goldberg and Mr Foulkes—any witness who had an opportunity—made a little speech about these vicious attacks by the capitalist Press, who wanted to break up the Union. Far be it from me to say anything in defence of the capitalist Press, but this attack has not been on the Union but on the Defendants, a handful of Communists, who have got this Union in an iron grip. The second lie may be summarised in the phrase Mr Lawson made in his concluding speech when he described the whole thing as "a bitter feud between two groups". I utterly repudiate this.'

What had happened here, Mr Gardiner said, was 'the biggest fraud in the history of British trade unionism'. It would be a grave mistake to regard it as no more than a feud between two groups.

Then Mr Gardiner dealt with each of the Defendants in turn, beginning with Mr Humphrey—the man who ordered the additional voting papers, who held them at his office, who was the only man to open the envelopes, the only man who could have switched the branch returns into the 'All Right' file. Nevertheless, he was 'not a man of dominating personality', and Mr McLennan, after all, was his immediate superior 'and Mr Haxell the Big Chief'.

Then Mr Haxell, who 'told deliberate lies to his own Executive Council in order to conceal a fraud committed in the interests of the Communist Party', and gave such evasive answers (with a 'large, nervous grin') concerning his whereabouts between December the 30th, 1959, and January the 4th, 1960, when the bogus votes were being posted.

Then Mr Frazer, 'employed whole-time by the Union in some capacity or other, although he hasn't been elected to it', a man high up in the Communist Party, 'just the sort of man who would drive a car fast', and after Mr Haxell 'probably the ablest and most dominating personality'. When all those suspicious branch secretaries travelled to Head Office at Hayes to challenge the fradulent envelopes, it was Mr Frazer who was chosen to see them with Mr McLennan.

Then Mr Batchelor, who hadn't been in the witness-box to give any evidence—about, for example, such matters as Mr Thomas and the branch stamp (see page 64). Mr Batchelor had a duodenal ulcer, and nine days before he was due to go into the witness-box he consulted his doctor, who went to Court and said that giving evidence would make the ulcer worse. Any jury (said Mr Gardiner) would say, 'After all, this man is charged with fraud. It isn't going to kill him to go into the witness-box. A lot of people have duodenal ulcers.'

Then Mr Foulkes, 'a very old and close associate of Mr Haxell—they have been running this Union together for many years'. As his performances on the ITV in 1957 and on 'Panorama' in 1960 showed,* Mr Foulkes was 'a man prepared to say or do absolutely anything if it helped the cause'. Whether or not he knew about the substituted envelopes (and Messrs Haxell, McLennan, Frazer and Humphrey *might* have kept it from him, though he maintained in evidence that he was omniscient about the Union's affairs), his position in the Union's history was such that he *must* have known the election was being rigged, even if the exact means were unknown to him.

Then came the Defendants Cosby, Hendy, Feathers, Davies, and Sell, the other Communist members of the Executive Council. Their position was important, said Mr Gardiner, for two reasons. First, no one must be found guilty of fraud if he was innocent. Secondly, members of the ETU were entitled to know the truth about all these individuals, so that no man who was a party to the fraud would be able afterwards to go round the branches saying: 'I've been acquitted—nobody can say anything about me.' These five men, said Mr Gardiner, were 'not dishonestly exercising powers of discrimination like Mr McLennan, nor driving cars like Mr Frazer and Mr Batchelor: their task was one of at intervals raising the right arm; but it was a very effective one and an essential one in the fraud'. Mr Hendy, in particular, was 'a man of considerable attainments, and it's all very well' (said Mr Gardiner) 'for Mr Haxell to sneer at the intellectual attainments and the bourgeois traits of a man who, to his credit, nine years ago was disagreeing with elections being rigged. The trouble is that since

* Mr Foulkes' experience on television led to an exchange of letters in the *Times*, in which those who deplored the TV interview as a new and unfair pillory for public men were out-numbered by those who welcomed it as a new searchlight on public business.—*Editor.*

then he has thrown in his lot with the others'. Not one of them
would have remained long on the Executive Council if he had
started putting awkward questions to Mr Haxell. They were all
involved in the fraud.

The non-Communist Defendants, Goldberg and West, Mr
Gardiner described as 'stooges'. ('It is, after all, the word to be
found in Mr Feathers' notes.') They were very different from each
other: 'Mr Goldberg was quite obviously a highly intelligent man;
as to Mr West, one doesn't want to be offensive, but your Lordship may have wondered whether Mr West could really be as
stupid as he seemed to be.' They both knew the part they were
playing, and the impression it was designed to make on the TUC—
this support for the ETU's policy by two solid Labour Party men.

Lastly, Mr George Scott—'perhaps the most dangerous witness
in the case'. The harm that such a man could do (Mr Gardiner
said) was much greater than what the openly avowed member of
the Communist Party could do. 'He was, in my submission, much
the best witness of anyone who was called.' Mr Haxell had always
chosen him to conduct Head Office 'investigations' into complaints
of ballot-rigging because he could rely on him for a report suitable
for the purpose of presentation to the TUC. And it was Mr Scott
who acted thus in the case of the Southend Electronic Engineers'
minute book, which was 'the most barefaced fraud perpetrated
in all the matters which have been enquired into in the course of
this long and protracted hearing'. Mr Scott had been in Court
almost throughout the trial. He had heard many witnesses, his comrades, telling what he must have known to be the truth. He had
heard Mr Humphrey and other witnesses admit, in substance, that
the thing was a fraud. But 'he doesn't come here' (Mr Gardiner
went on) 'and say: "Now that I've heard this, sooner than continue
to serve those who are obviously determined to maintain their
stranglehold on this Union by fraud, if necessary, I'm leaving—
and I shall try and get employment somewhere else." Not at all.
He continues to back up the Party line in the biggest fraud in the
history of British trade unionism'.

The whole action, Mr Gardiner concluded, was not launched
on the instance of any 'group'. 'In order to establish the existence
of Communist advisory committees I had to call a group of

members who had formerly been but are not now members of the Communist Party. They have no other connection with this case at all. The only other group which has been referred to was referred to by a branch secretary, who said: "The only group I'm a member of is all the members who were getting tired of the elections being rigged." They are entitled to be so tired. Ordinary branch secretaries had become more and more annoyed at the rigging of elections, and had "gradually come to the determination that this is a thing which ought to be stopped". It is for that purpose that this action has been brought.'

Mr Gardiner concluded with a plea that, if the Plaintiffs succeeded, the Judge grant (*a*) an injunction restraining Mr Haxell from acting as General Secretary of the ETU, (*b*) a declaration that Mr Byrne was validly elected to that office, and (*c*) an award of damages to Mr Byrne for loss of the salary he had been entitled to since the election.

The evidence and speeches were over. 'I must reserve my judgment,' said Mr Justice Winn; and it was generally expected that it would take him at least three weeks to compile it.

VI   THE JUDGMENT

THERE had in fact been an interval of only twelve days when, on Wednesday, June 28, 1961, the Court reassembled, this time in the Lord Chief Justice's Court in the Queen's Bench Division, the Court room normally used for the Court of Criminal Appeal. In those twelve days Mr Justic Winn had compiled a judgment of over 40,000 words, which he proceeded to read at a pace that soon demonstrated, to the men in the Press seats, the need for some new system of shorthand. At the end of the first hour only the official shorthand writer was still at work. The following is a greatly condensed version of his Lordship's masterly statement.

1   The ETU Rules

'The litigation has been extremely bitter and represents the culmination, in a public battle, of an internecine struggle which ever since 1957 has rent and troubled the membership of this great Union . . . It was, in fact, inevitable that such matters as the Plaintiffs believed required investigation should be submitted for determination by a Judge.

The Rules of the Union* provide: By Rule 10(7)(a), that 'a member shall not send any circulars relating to the conduct of the Union or its business, or to the conduct of any of its officers or members, to other branches or members except by permission of the General Council.'

By Rule 38(7): 'No charge shall be laid against any Executive Councillor or Area Committee member, or any full-time official alleging a breach of or failure to carry out his duties in his office . . . except by the Executive Council.'

By Rule 38(8): 'Any allegation that a member . . . has committed an offence at a meeting . . . of the Executive Council shall be reported to and be dealt with by the Executive Council. The

* His Lordship was citing the 1958 edition of the ETU Rules.

Executive Council may in its discretion decide whether or not a charge is to be made on any such report.'

By Rule 38(13): 'If, by decision of the Executive Council, a charge is made against any member under this Rule, the Executive Council shall deal with the charge.'

'Further,' the Judge went on (for only by citing the principal Rules would the stage be set), 'there was a prohibition against standing for election on any programme involving a contention that elections had been "rigged", or should in the future be more strictly controlled, because the Executive Council exercised a censorship of election addresses. It would not permit the Plaintiff Byrne to include, in one which he desired to circulate to branches, the following passage:

> A perusal of the Executive Council minutes shows that the returns from ballot voting have fallen off, and that at almost all ballots there is a surfeit of complaints about the conduct of the ballot. This is not a happy state of affairs; and I would advocate the scrapping of the present system and its replacement by a postal ballot where each member entitled to vote would receive a stamped return form, which would be subject to scrutiny by independent scrutineers.

'This exclusion was an exercise of the power given by Rule 21(3), which, though its primary object may be excellent, plainly enables the Executive Council to stifle criticism of proposals, however well justified, for protecting the sanctity of the franchise of members.'

2   The Crux of the Action

'The action,' the Judge went on, 'raises (apart from the essential issue, upon which its outcome must turn, whether the December 1959 election was fraudulently conducted: and, if so, which, if any, of the Defendants was a party to an agreement to employ or facilitate fraudulent methods) a myriad of collateral issues, the majority of which cannot be ignored because they impinge with varying degrees of directness upon the main issue. In particular, it has been necessary and right that the Court should consider and assess a considerable body of evidence about the relationship of the ETU to the Communist Party of the United Kingdom. This is so, not because the Plaintiffs chose to introduce that topic into the action, nor because there is any basis for supposing that a link between those two bodies could itself constitute any cause of action; but because it has been urgently submitted to the Court that if indeed there was fraud in the election the true motive for it was not material gain or personal ambition, but desire or obligation to serve the Communist cause, and to avoid such a loss of prestige for the Communist Party, and such a set-back in the development of its influence in the trade union world, as would, in my judgment, have been involved in the defeat and removal from office of such a prominent protagonist as the Defendant Haxell.

'Whatever be the assessment which the Court should rightly make of the degree of Communist influence in the only trade union whose affairs it has had to investigate, there are some relevant facts to which the epithet "startling" may without over emphasis be applied.

'Of these, the one least widely known before the trial was as follows:

'The membership of the ETU is about 240,000—possibly as many as 250,000. The number of Communists in the whole country is, according to the evidence of Mr Hendy—a student of matters of political and economic interest and a keen supporter of the Party— about 25,000, that is, about one-tenth of the membership of the Union.* Not all of those 25,000 would be in trade unions but probably 24,000 would be. On a straight numerical distribution this would mean that about 2,000 would be found among the 240,000 men belonging to the ETU. In fact, Mr Hendy did not think there would be so many.'

From that one per cent of the membership, Mr Justice Winn pointed out, the bulk of the Executive Council and the national officers were drawn. Normal voting, he said in effect, would never produce such a result.

'It is of relatively slight importance, and certainly did not lighten the action, that at the outset of the trial the Defendants formally

* This figure presumably represents formal membership of the Communist Party: an unknown number of people call themselves Communists without belonging to the Party.—*Editor.*

admitted by their Counsel that the validity of the election could not be sustained by reason of various irregularities.'

3 The Communist Committees

'Communism,' the Judge continued, 'is not illegal in this country. Nor are Communist gatherings proscribed, provided they are not aimed against or calculated to subvert the State. In this action I have heard no evidence of gatherings or activities of that character . . . If, as the evidence emphatically suggests, the assiduity in branch offices of Communists is greater than that of those whose political and economic aims are different, it would not be surprising to find candidates for office *favoured* by Communists (whether or not themselves Communists) achieving successes in the ballots. Nor could that afford any cause of action to a defeated candidate.'

The Judge was not shocked, he said, by the evidence he had heard indicating 'obsessive delusion' about ends and means. People to whom 'truth' and 'justice' are merely relative terms (owing to 'lack or loss of any other faith' than Communism) will not always feel bound to obey rules. 'To assess such witnesses is a very much more difficult task than to detect the lies of wholly dishonest rogues. It involves a closer and perhaps more sophisticated study of momentary changes in demeanour, voice and expression.'

On the question of Communist control through 'committees' of the Party, his Lordship found that 'not only was the ETU managed and controlled by Communists and pliant sympathisers, but it was so managed in the service of the Communist Party and the ideas of the Party. In my judgment it is nothing but what has sometimes been called "double talk" to speak of serving the ETU by aiming to achieve for its members the aims and objects regarded as optima by Communists. Simplified, that means rallying the Union in the Communist struggle for those objects.

'In my judgment, in 1959 the Communist Party controlled the ETU . . . through the allegiance of Mr Haxell, and of other Communists in the Union, whom he directed.'

As for the existence or non-existence of the Communist 'advisory' and other committees, it was important to have in mind the provisions of Rule 10(4) of the 1958 Rules:

A member shall not divulge outside the Union any Union business.

In the 1954 Rules a corresponding provision in Rule 9(4) had been qualified by the words 'to the detriment of the Union'. Some witnesses would have had the Court believe that, whereas before the change discussions of Union affairs with strangers who were Communists could not, in the subjective view of a Communist member, be detrimental to the Union, obedience to the new and more absolute prohibition was in and after the year 1958 complete. I reject all such evidence.

'Mr Chapple described the body to which he belonged as a committee of the Communist Party formed to direct the activities of the Communist members of the ETU. There was an interesting exhibit which was described as an agenda of the East London Area Committee of the Communist Party. It comprised the following item: "Election of officers . . . Comrade responsible for Advisory Committee . . . Electricians, Frank Chapple".' (There were other committees concerned with building, transport, clothing, teaching—and women.) 'In my judgment such committees were not maintained for the giving of advice to the Communist Party about women, but for a greater efficiency in disseminating Communist Party advice, exhortations to the various categories of workers.

'Mr Chapple stated that the committee which he attended summoned its members by "written notice to those who could be trusted to destroy" such a notice; to others by word of mouth. This statement, which was not consistent with other evidence, has the appearance of picturesque embroidery.'

His Lordship accepted the evidence of Mr Blairford that at meetings of ETU members which were, in fact, committees of the Communist Party, 'policies were imparted to us and it was our responsibility to have them implemented throughout the branches and trades councils', and pending ETU elections were discussed and support for Communist candidates organised. The Judge, in this way, went through the evidence (as to the Communist committees) of Messrs Townsend, Moss, Tuck, Sullivan, Vetterlein, and Thomas; and thus arrived at Mr Hendy.

'He is a man,' said the Judge, 'who is inspired, if not possessed, by a fervent faith that the Communist creed is the ultimate Truth, an appeal to which will afford an answer logically solving any problem of behaviour, or choice of action. I judged him to be a man of intellectual honesty as well as intellectual power, personally honourable to the extent that he would not adopt any course of conduct which seemed to him to be unjust to an individual, unless the demand of loyalty to Communist tenets left him no choice. In his mind, as I judge his personality, no loyalty to the ETU or any other body or individual could be allowed any influence adverse to unswerving duty to the Communist Party and its ideals.

'When Mr Hendy was asked whether he remembered Mr Allison saying at a meeting that the Communists in each ETU branch ought to fix a figure of pro-Communist votes to be obtained and obtain it, by hook or by crook, he replied, "I don't remember Mr Allison saying anything as—", then caught himself up and finished "anything like that". But he agreed that Mr Allison had made a suggestion, to which he himself took exception, that as many votes as possible ought to be got without undue regard to the Rule Book. It may be coincidental that Mr Hendy acquired the nickname of "Honest John".

'Mr Hendy was tense and apprehensive when he was cross-examined about the existence of committees called "Advisory Committees". He expressed the view, which I too formed from the evidence, that there is room for differences of nomenclature, but what he felt constrained dutifully to deny was that there ever existed for the purpose of influencing the affairs of the ETU any "special committees of the Communist Party".'

The Judge thought it probable that those committees were neither *appointed* by the Communist Party nor authorised to call themselves 'advisory'. But 'Mr Hendy, knowing that he was about to be confronted with a letter of his own, written in 1951 (see page 183) to Mr Cannon, then a close friend and supporter, said in self-accusatory confession that his "group" was indeed called a committee, but that that was his sole responsibility, not that of the Communist Party. Throughout his evidence Mr Hendy gave a wonderful performance of adroit side-stepping and circumlocution; but the letter rather pinned and cribbed him.'

Mr Haxell's evidence, too, had to be considered in relation to the 'advisories'. He had denied explicitly that he had been either chairman or member of 'a body called a national advisory committee, being a committee of the Communist Party consisting of Communist members of the ETU'. He said that he did not know of any such committee. In his Lordship's judgment this answer was an instance of 'swearing by the book'. 'The substance of the matter, which he was endeavouring to conceal, is that a committee of Communist members of the ETU met, often with him in the chair, to consult with an appointed representative of the Communist Party and with one another in order to foster Communism in and by means of ETU activities.'

Neither Mr McLennan nor Mr Frazer had changed the Judge's way of thinking about this, the latter having told him a 'palpable lie', to the effect that the meetings 'had nothing whatever to do with the ETU'.

'It is as pertinent to the general discredit of Mr Frazer as to that of Mr Haxell that they put forward such puerile mendacities.' On this topic, his Lordship said, 'none of the Defendants was frank or truthful: all of them incurred discredit by their evidence about it'.

4   The Powers of Scrutineers

The Judge pointed out that under the ETU system of elections, both under the 1954 and the 1958 Rules, 'every vote counted irrespective of majorities in branches'. He decided that the Rules gave power to the 'national scrutineers' to rule a ballot out of order, and to determine how many votes had been cast for whom; but they could not decide upon anyone's eligibility to vote. They could be compared, he implied, with a Returning Officer in a Parliamentary election.

'At any rate, one national scrutiny was conducted very much in accordance with my view of the scope and the function of the national scrutineers under the 1954 Rules. Mr Edward Nash, an accurately precise man, told me that when he acted as national scrutineer for six elections in 1956, the process occupied between two and three hours; that it was "an accountancy procedure"; that the scrutiny proper had taken place at the branch; that all that happened at Headquarters was just a collation of voting figures for the national scrutineers, who saw nothing but the branch scrutineers' returns and the collated figures. His duty, he said, was merely to check the collated figures with those on the branch scrutineers' returns. He was in no position to check whether any return had been sent in later than the Rules permitted. The crucial effect which may be produced by the rejection of the votes of some branches is well established by the statement of Mr Nash that he observed during his scrutiny that four branches had out-voted twenty-two others. The important question is thus posed: Where, if anywhere, did any power reside under the 1954 Rules to reject the votes sent in by an individual branch? I think the answer is that those Rules did not give any such power.'

5   Appeals by Branches

As to the right of a branch to appeal, Mr Haxell had said that ever since 1946 'the view was always held that there was no appeal against a report of the scrutineers'. If it were assumed for the moment that the Executive Council had any power to decide whether to accept or reject the votes of a particular branch ('which in my judgment,' said his Lordship, 'was *not* so') any such decision would be a quite different matter from the mere acceptance by the Council of the report of the scrutineers. Mr Foulkes, who 'had a far clearer understanding of the position' than Mr Haxell, had said: "It has never been my view that there could be an appeal against the actual scrutineers' report." '

This was perhaps an understandable difference of opinion between the two men. 'It is distinctly more startling, and more difficult to accept as consistent with *bona fide* obedience to the Rules, that Mr Haxell should have taken it upon himself to impose disqualifications . . . In my judgment that practice was a rank usurpation of power by the General Secretary. It is trite that usurped power corrupts even more absolutely than power duly conferred . . . The question arises whether Mr Haxell believed that he had such powers. On the whole, I do not feel constrained to disbelieve his assertions in this respect, though I think it con-

sistent with his character that he should have been so arrogant as
to take for himself, without any precedent, such virtually un-
controlled power. I am convinced that Mr Haxell knew that
branches believed that rejections of their votes for breach of rule
were imposed by the Executive Council or perhaps by the national
scrutineers, and deliberately induced this belief lest his practice in
the matter be challenged and his *de facto* control abrogated.'

6   Disqualification on Technicalities

Under the 1958 Rules the Executive Council acquired an express
right to 'declare void the return of any branch guilty of a breach
of Rule', so long as it might *materially affect the result of the
election.*

'This,' said the Judge, 'seems to me to preclude its exercise on
the ground of merely technical breaches, such as a delay of a few
days in the arrival of the branch scrutineers' returns; whereas
there might be good reason to apply it to a case where the election
had been held on a meeting-night other than the prescribed
quarterly night, without adequate notice to members'. But there
had been cases in which the Executive Council had applied it
without even considering whether the election might be 'materially
affected'. Such rejections, said the Judge, were *ultra vires* and
void. 'There was nothing in the evidence I heard to suggest' (for
example) 'that a delay of a few days, of the order of anything up
to ten days, would be of any serious consequence.' And the words
'posted to reach' an address 'not later than first post on the fifth
day' meant 'not later than the time at which the first post, if any, is
delivered on the fifth day after the meeting'. This construction
would have saved many branches from disqualification; but 'a
failure properly to apply such a set of Rules as this Union has
inflicted upon itself, of a complexity scarcely commensurate with
the grasp of some (at any rate) of its members, is no evidence,
standing alone, of fraudulent motive'.

Nevertheless, 'it was most regrettable, as well as quite unauthorised by the Rules, that Mr McLennan should have taken it on
himself to decide in what cases there should be investigation, upon
material which no Court would consider sufficient. Inevitably he

thereby incurred suspicion of favouring branches which voted for Haxell, seeing that, in fact, out of seven complaints against such branches none produced an investigation or disqualification, whereas ten branches which voted for Byrne and *were* the subject of complaints were disqualified. After careful consideration of these matters,' the Judge nevertheless decided, 'they do not seem to justify any more severe condemnation of Mr McLennan's conduct than I have expressed'.

7   *The Cannon-Frazer Election*

Referring to Mr George Scott's article in the *Daily Worker* of December 14, 1957—'The Press and the ETU—What Are the Facts?'—the Judge found that it was 'literally and barely true' when it said that even if the disqualified votes in the Cannon-Frazer election had been included the result would have been the same. But it was true by suppression; 'and in my judgment,' said his Lordship, 'Mr Scott is not the kind of man who would make such a statement in a serious Press article without checking what he believed to be the relevant information. He was plainly horrified when his error was demonstrated to him in the witness-box. He had sought permission from Mr Haxell to write the article; and I unhesitatingly infer that Mr Haxell gave him only partial facts and misled him.'

On Mr Foulkes' statement on television, that voting figures would be duly published, the Judge said, 'he must have known that the votes of disqualified branches were *never* published, and I regard this important public statement as a lie'. So was Mr Foulkes' television assertion that branches could appeal against Executive Council decisions at any time. 'My assessment of both Mr Foulkes and Mr Haxell as men who are prepared to prefer expediency to truth was materially influenced by their behaviour in sending out circulars and by Mr Foulkes' answers on television.'

8   *'Rules Revision'*

In 1957 Mr Goldberg had proposed that decisions of the national scrutineers (to void ballots) be placed beyond the possibility of any appeal. This step was to be taken at a Rules Revision conference, though its advance agenda showed only financial proposals, and delegates would therefore have little or no warning of what was coming.*

'Had the complete reference been inserted,' the Judge said, 'any delegate who received the Agenda, and all the Executive Council, would have had several days in which to consider its effect. In the incomplete form in which it was issued, the reference could not do more than arouse curiosity about the manner in which it would be completed by a supplementary *errata* sheet'. He continued: 'It is passing strange that, after appreciating that the reference required the addition of a letter, he should not only have failed to insert the one which he says was intended, but should have put in the one letter, (*o*), which would frustrate the instructions allegedly given to afford an appeal about boundaries.

'I find that Mr Haxell and Mr Burns deliberately contrived this method of inserting the exclusion of appeals against action taken under 11(2)(*i*), and I reject the evidence of each of them that the last-minute alteration was to correct an error and give effect to an amendment adopted by the Executive Council. Mr Haxell was contriving an advantage from the Rules Revision Committee, to secure a weapon for future use to exclude appeals about election results.

'After the Conference Mr Burns prepared and Mr Haxell sent out a circular to branches which was silent about the matter of appeals, as too was the condensed report of the Conference. I think that was deliberate.

'I find that Mr Haxell, to his discredit, did, with the help of Mr Burns, slip before the Conference a provision which had not been approved by the Executive Council, and procured, by the device of attracting attention from it, the unwitting, unreal but ostensible approval by the Conference of that sub-Rule, as well as of the grant of a right of appeal against boundary decisions which I hold to be no less null and void than the purported exclusion of Rule 11(2)(*i*) from appeal. This was a wicked fraud upon the members of the ETU.'

* The proposed amendment would add a new clause to Rule 11(2), which defines the powers of the Executive Council in twenty-one Clauses, lettered (*a*) to (*u*). Clause (*i*) is about scrutineers' powers, and Clause (*o*) about fixing the boundaries of 'Areas'.

9 The 'Jarrow Affair'

'In my judgment, the vote at this branch was undoubtedly rigged, with the motive of securing the choice of a Mr Carr, who was then the Secretary of the Jarrow Branch,' said Mr Justice Winn. He then recounted the story of the surplus ballot papers, the inordinately high postal vote, the 'whitewashing' enquiry conducted by questionnaire to members, and the thirteen months' delay in doing anything else about it. 'In my judgment, not only Mr Haxell and Mr Goldberg and Mr West ostensibly conducted this enquiry and delayed it for the improper purpose of covering up a fraudulent attempt by some person or persons, whom I cannot identify, to increase the votes credited to Mr Carr, a supporter of Communist principles. It is significant that the chosen signatories of the Report should be those two members of the Sub-Committee who were not avowed Communists . . . The Jarrow matter does not, in my judgment, form an integral part of any conspiracy directly affecting the December 1959 election, but its implications are relevant to that issue.'

10 The 1959 Byrne-Haxell Election

Necessarily the Judge first re-examined, in this context, the arrangements made in September 1959 with Mr Norman Swift, of the Express Printing Company, Manchester, for the printing of 'estimated' requirements as to quantities of ballot papers and the decision to mark them with branch code numbers (which made it easier, or at least more convincing, to pass off faked ones as genuine).

'My judgment of this matter, expressed with full appreciation that it involves a grave finding against Mr Humphrey, is that he deliberately ordered substantial excess quantities of ballots for branches where he expected that fraudulent votes could be registered, if need be, for Mr Haxell, intending that the excess quantities would be sent to Head Office—or could be caused earlier to be sent to branches. Mr Haxell, Mr Foulkes and Mr McLennan all denied having any knowledge that surplus ballot papers were to be sent, or were sent, to Head Office—until the Plaintiffs' "particulars" of January the 17th, 1961, were received.

'The Court was asked to accept that, apart from Mr Warlow, no one at Head Office became aware of these clandestine movements of ballot papers or of their being in store: this passes credulity.'

His Lordship turned to Mr Blairford's conversation with Mr Haxell 'in a bar' in 1954 or 1955 at a Trades Union Congress (see page 60), when Mr Haxell had advised him that he should tell the secretaries who were Communists that 'if they wished to indulge in this, all they had to do was to send a memorandum to the General Secretary saying they were short of ballot papers—would he please send maybe a hundred ballots'.

The Judge believed Mr Blairford. Mr Haxell, on the other hand, 'denied that any such conversation took place, in a firm, well-controlled voice and with steady eyes. Unfortunately, practice and will-power can produce these appearances, though not always maintain them. He was asked: "Do you say that no such conversation took place at all?" He replied: "I do: I wouldn't be so foolish." I was watching Mr Haxell very closely when he gave that last answer, which is as odd as it was spontaneous. I distinctly saw on his face an expression not of indignation or repudiation of the idea that he could lend himself to the suggested malpractice, but of self-satisfaction over finding the supposedly convincing materialist answer, that is to say: "I am not such a fool that I would speak to anyone about it." On that plane of mere argument it is to be remembered that Mr Blairford was, at the time of the alleged conversation, an ardent Communist. I have no doubt that on this issue Mr Blairford was telling the truth and Mr Haxell was lying.'

His Lordship then began going through the branches which had had additional ballot papers. Much of this part of the case, he said, rested on suspicion only, and he found that at some of the doubtful branches there was no actual fraud. 'Mere suspicions, even when piled one upon another, cannot amount to proof. Zero multiplied by even an infinite number remains zero. At the same time, it is rational to note anomalies and departures from norm or average, and their number, when considering whether all are satisfactorily accounted for by explanations acceptable for a relatively few instances. The proverbial saying, "The exception proves the rule", means that a substantial number of departures from a given rule or norm postulates the existence of another rule.'* Even Mr Haxell recognised that it was a valid test of the genuineness of a branch ballot to compare its vote at one election with the general level of voting for the same branch at other elections.

Of the 'Southampton complex' his Lordship said that fraud was established. He had thought over Mr Lawson's theory that some-one ill-disposed to Mr Haxell had done the extra postings, 'with the deliberate intention of their being detected and taken as evi-dence of ballot-rigging by him'; and he rejected it. 'I find without hesitation that a true explanation is that a fraudulent supporter of Mr Haxell intended, by their use, to increase his vote in each of these Branches' (i.e., Hythe, Woolston and Southampton Central) 'but acted prematurely in posting what may well have been only the first batches of forged ballots. Further, I find that these ballots were obtained from Head Office. I reject the suggestion that they were stolen from the printers.'

11   The December 1959 Scrutiny

The Judge then exhaustively examined the evidence about the Head Office arrangements for the opening of envelopes, the accept-ance and rejection of branch votes, the exercise of indulgences and concessions, and the issue of warnings for 'breach of Rule'. Much of the clerical work here, particularly in relation to previous 'de-faults' by branches, fell upon Mrs Higgs, 'a competent and careful young woman who gave her lengthy evidence patiently'; but the Judge, before summarising her important evidence, took occasion to rule that it was 'quite irrelevant to consider whether a non-conforming branch had made default previously in a like or unlike respect', and that consequently a great deal of Mrs Higgs' work was futile.

'I am satisfied,' the Judge said, 'that the national scrutineers formed *bona fide* judgments in those cases which they considered on such material as they had supplied to them; but it was, of course, a quite unjudicial and unsatisfactory form of determination,

* Columella's *exeptio probat regulam* seems to have had the meaning (perhaps more suitable to the Judge's purpose) that exceptions prove there is a rule, since otherwise there could be no exceptions.—*Editor.*

in the cases where there had been complaints and denials. I think they might just as well have spun a coin.*

'Mr Humphrey stated in evidence that he did not gain any knowledge of how the two candidates were progressing in the election. I reject this evidence of Mr Humphrey. I thought the way in which he gave it was unconvincing and that his voice and face betrayed tension.

'If anything was fraudulently done to mislead the national scrutineers by misplacing voting returns in the files prepared for them, or by presenting to them faked material, it is unlikely that it would have been done before the need for drastic measures had been revealed by the incoming returns, all of which went, unopened (by force of Mr Haxell's direction dated August the 26th, 1959), to Mr Humphrey. Study of the returns date-stamped as received on or before December the 24th establishes that, if all possible grounds for disqualification by the scrutineers are ignored, there had come in:

For Byrne, 12,060   For Haxell, 10,813

So Byrne then had a lead of 1,247. The Head Office appears to have been closed, and it is not known that any Defendant attended there between Thursday, December the 24th and Monday, December the 28th. On the latter date, on the same footing, the votes which had come in then totalled:

For Byrne, 20,363   For Haxell, 19,385

So Byrne then had a reduced lead of 978.

'I do not entertain a shadow of doubt that this situation was fully known not only to Mr Humphrey, but to Mr Haxell and Mr McLennan. Its obvious implication of disaster threatening the power of Mr Haxell, the position of his two myrmidons, and the prestige of the Communists in trade union circles, produced, in my judgment, not only a temptation but a compulsion to adopt such measures as could be hastily devised without opportunity for cool, intelligent planning. After anxious thought and considerable doubt, I do not feel compelled by the logic of the situation which

---

* It will be remembered that the two national scrutineers for that year (1959), Mr Rengert and Mr Shipman, had already been dismissed from the case.

then existed at Head Office to convict Mr Foulkes of possessing the same knowledge at so early a date.'

12   The 'Substituted' Envelopes

'Subject to what has been said about the likelihood of an emergency breeding panic, the expedient of such a process of substitution is manifestly almost as improbable as it would be criminal. When considering these forty cases of straightforward but difficult fact, I have had in mind the Court of Appeal judgments in the case of *Hornal v. Meuberger Products Ltd (1957)* (1 Queen's Bench, p. 247). I have had regard to the words of Lord Justice Denning at page 258: ". . . the standard of proof depends on the nature of the issue. The more serious the allegation, the higher the degree of probability that it requires; but it need not, in a civil case, reach the very high standards required by the criminal law."

'Accordingly the standard of proof must be very high and the onus wholly on the Plaintiffs. Before a Judge of trial, sitting without a jury, decides such an issue as this one of "substitution", he has the lonely task of debating it with his conscience. Of the forty cases of alleged substitution into which the Court enquired, I find that twenty-seven were established to my complete satisfaction and beyond any doubt which I can regard as reasonable. A further four cases seem on balance of probability to be made out.'

Mr Byrne's lead 'was reversed, in the result as published, so as to become a victory for Haxell by a majority of some one thousand votes, a shift over of the order of two thousand'.

'A hundred and nine branches were disqualified, but a hundred and six of them had produced a majority for Byrne; and the remaining three, as a group, on balance contributed for Haxell no more than three votes majority. Neither Mr Haxell, nor Mr Foulkes, nor Mr McLennan could think of an explanation consistent with honesty. I cannot.

'Therefore it is established, in my judgment, that the scrutineers were caused, by devices which can only have been fraudulent, including some forged votes, to make their return in favour of Haxell in their brief one-and-a-half-hour scrutiny. But for them, Byrne would in my judgment have had a majority of at least one thousand one hundred and fifty, but probably of the order of fifteen hundred.

'It is not possible to determine who must, for certain, have known contemporaneously of the plan to post substitute envelopes. I am prepared to believe that neither Mr Foulkes nor Mr McLennan participated in that. Their temperaments are, I think, too prudent and (if the word is not inapt) squeamish for so harsh a crime. It has, in my judgment, the hallmark of Mr Haxell and Mr Frazer, both of whom I judge to be blunt, unsubtle, and ruthless. Agents must have been used whom it is impossible positively to identify.'

13   Cobbett's 'Rural Rides'

The car journeys of Mr Cobbett, the enquiry agent, though they had not greatly influenced his Lordship, remained now to be dealt with. He said they 'afforded a remarkable demonstration of the fact that it was physically possible for the driver of a car on each of those routes to have posted envelopes, as he went along, which would successively have received such postmarks of towns and times, progressing in the same order as his own distance/time schedule, as are to be found among the alleged substitutes bearing dates of the 30th and 31st of December, 1959 and the 1st and 2nd of January, 1960.' In this Mr Cobbett had 'achieved virtually complete success, though he had to drive very fast on certain sections'.

The Judge still thought it *possible* that the laws of chance (being what they are) might 'afford the same phenomena'. The Defendants had proved that other branches—Byrne branches—near each of the routes could have been more easily eliminated. There was no time for a careful plan. Mr Foulkes *had* said that chance could not explain what had happened, but he thought the idea of the plan (evolved by the Plaintiffs, not the Defendants) was to hold back envelopes so that they arrived late and then allege substitution. The Judge disbelieved this because he thought many of the branch secretaries were truthful witnesses. Mr Haxell had said that there was nothing odd about the time/distance sequence; but 'he would be bound to do so if he was involved in bringing it about'.

On the whole, his Lordship thought Mr Cobbett had produced evidence which had '*some* corroborative significance'. And once the Judge's mind was made up about substitutions at the twenty-seven (out of forty) branches, he found that seventeen of those twenty-seven were branches on Mr Cobbett's routes.

It was 'not inconsistent with the general probabilities that the aid of the Communist network was invoked' in getting substitute envelopes posted. Although Mr George Scott drove to Scotland at the material time, the Judge did not think he did any of the posting (and neither, for that matter, did the Plaintiffs). Mr Haxell, on the other hand, was 'unconvincing to the point of seeming a sorry figure in the witness-box when he was asked where *he* had been at the material time. I noticed,' said the Judge, 'a nervous grin and shifts of stance. Of course, he *may* have been embarrassed for domestic reasons; but certainly he was ill at ease, though he must for a long time have foreseen that the topic would be raised.'

Similarly with Mr Frazer—'no less likely than Mr Haxell to have posted some of the envelopes: to do so would not have been alien to his character as I assess it. He gave a thoroughly unsatisfactory account of having gone on Saturday, January the 2nd from Head Office to the London office, to work there on correspondence (which he did not produce) in a room next to that in which was held an Area Committee which he ought to have attended. He had an ETU car at the time, into which a not inconsiderable amount of petrol was placed during the material period.'

As for Mr Batchelor, he drew six gallons of petrol on December 23, six on December 30, and seven on January 3; also 'delegation fees' of £12 10s. for the fortnight ending January 4, 1960. And he made an expense claim for another nineteen gallons (this was thirty-eight gallons in all). 'I refrain from finding against him, in his absence' (Mr Batchelor was the man with a duodenal ulcer), 'more than that he may well have had opportunity to post some of the envelopes—and that there was evidence from a Mr Thomas that some years ago, when ballot papers had to bear the stamp of the branch to which they were sent, he told Mr Thomas that he would like to be able to use his branch stamp on a hundred or so ballots.'

14   The Announcement of the Byrne-Haxell Result

'Mr Rengert and Mr Shipman had signed a document,' his Lordship said, 'declaring the election result to be: Byrne 18,577, Haxell 19,611. In this they further stated: "The following branches failed to comply with the provisions of Rule 21 and their scrutineers' forms were therefore rejected"; and they listed a large number, including Hythe and Woolston. Mr McLennan read out the votes as ascertained by the scrutineers and added, what they had *not* said, "F. L. Haxell elected". The Defendant Frazer at once said, "Move". The Defendant Sell seconded—this was his first appearance at an Executive Council meeting: he was a new recruit to the Communist Party. Mr Foulkes asked: "Those in favour? Against?" and then recorded the voting even before Mr Chapple had said, "We are entitled to have a scrutineers' report which includes . . ."'

'No doubt he was going to say "includes the disqualifications". That was, of course, right. I have no doubt of any of the following facts, all of which I find to be irresistible inferences from the evidence as a whole and from my assessment of the characters and motives of the men involved:

'(*a*) that Mr Foulkes deliberately put the motion prematurely in order to stifle discussion of the disqualifications.

'(*b*) That he did this not merely for the reason which he gave in evidence, that he was tired of the troubles Mr Chapple caused in the Council meetings, but because he already knew that the disqualifications were wholly abnormal in number, and either knew or deliberately shut his eyes to the explanation.

(*c*) That when he learned there had been such a number of disqualifications, the approximate extent of which must have been already apparent to him from what he heard and saw at the scrutiny, whether or not he played any fraudulent part there himself, he must have appreciated that the situation was wholly anomalous and symptomatic of rigging.

'(*d*) That both Mr Foulkes and Mr McLennan knew perfectly well that the established practice, never varied in normal cases, was that the whole report of the scrutineers be read out before its adoption was considered.

'(*e*) That Mr McLennan made a deliberate pause after announcing the voting figures, and did this by prior arrangement with Mr Foulkes. He inserted the unusual statement, "Haxell elected" in order to afford a proposition on which a motion could be moved. He would not have read the rest of the report had he not been compelled.

'(*f*) That the defendants Frazer and Sell knew in advance that such an opportunity would be afforded, and had agreed to seize it by moving the adoption of the statement provided for them; and that the Defendant Haxell knew of the plan and aided it by remaining silent.

'(*g*) That even when Mr Chapple had demanded that the rest of the report be read, Mr McLennan said, "You've had the usual report", knowing that to be a lie, in the hearing of Haxell, who, although he admitted in evidence that it was untrue, made no correction and thereby associated himself with the attempt to suppress information, if in fact he was not involved at an earlier stage —as I am certain that he was.

'(*h*) That the refusal of Mr Chapple's request for a slow reading of the names of the disqualified branches was not only contrary to the Rules but a further attempt to hush up the facts. So too was the delay which occurred in publication of the minute concerning the accepted voting.

'(*i*) That the Defendant Sell made a speech in order to divert attention and obstruct Mr Chapple; but it would not be justifiable to assume that such a raw hand was *fully* in the confidence of the others.'

15   The Individual Findings

'The Defendants Cosby, Davies, Feathers, Goldberg, Hendy and West,' said the Judge, 'were also present as Executive Councillors when the scrutineers' return was adopted. But their position is somewhat different. It was rightly said by Mr Gardiner that the election of Mr Haxell was accomplished by the resolution of the Executive Council, and that these Defendants all raised their hands or otherwise signified that they supported it. It was submitted that I should find each of them to have been a party to the conspiracy alleged in this action. After careful consideration and considerable doubt I have come to the conclusion that, in each of these cases, as well as those of Mr Scott and even Mr Batchelor, by contrast with those of the other Defendants, the evidence and the inferences to be drawn therefrom do not come up to the standard required to establish so grave a charge.'

Eight of the remaining fifteen personal Defendants were thus exonerated, though more equivocally than would have been effected by a jury's verdict of acquittal. Especially was this so in the cases of Mr Goldberg and Mr Hendy.

'The cases of Goldberg and Hendy,' said his Lordship, 'have caused me particular trouble, because each of them has such intelligence, and so much experience of Union affairs, that it is contrary to the balance of probability that he was ignorant of the rigging. Had that been the proper criterion I would have found each of them guilty. Each gave materially untrue evidence to the Court, and Goldberg I regard as a not very scrupulous henchman of Haxell.

'I find, for reasons which I have endeavoured to state, that the Defendants Foulkes, Haxell, McLennan, Frazer, and Humphrey acted between September 1959 and February 1960 in their several capacities as officers or servants of the Defendant Union, and on its behalf, in breach of the Rules of the Union; also that they conspired together to prevent by fraudulent and unlawful devices the election of the Plaintiff Byrne in the place of the Defendant Haxell as General Secretary of the Defendant Union; and thereby caused him monetary loss. That loss I assess at £380 to date, less income tax, continuing at an annual rate of £306 until such time as Mr Byrne may begin to receive the salary of General Secretary.'

There were other matters still to be cleared up—applications for 'further relief', including the safeguarding of future elections—but the trial, after eight weeks, was essentially over. Mr Byrne's supporters crowded round him as the Judge left the Bench (the first to shake him by the hand being his co-Plaintiff Mr Chapple), and those who could not reach him across the intervening Court benches cried 'Good luck, Jock!' from outer circles of excitement.

The Defendants, turning away from this spectacle, left the Court silently.

VII THE IMMEDIATE OUTCOME

On Monday, July 3, the Court again assembled to deal with questions of costs, appeals, and the way in which future ETU elections might be more satisfactorily run.

The Plaintiffs were asking for a number of 'declarations' from the Judge, which were consequential on his findings against the Defendants. The first of them concerned Rule 39(6)(j) of the ETU Rules, which was about the branches' right of appeal against Executive Council decisions. The right of appeal did not apply to:

any decision of the Executive Council under Rule 11(2)(i).

And Rule 11(2)(i) said that the Council had power to 'receive the scrutineers' report in connection with the result of any ballot,' and to 'take such action as is required arising out of such report'. This virtually unlimited power, without right of appeal, was the one conferred upon the Executive by the provision which (the Judge had held) Mr Haxell had 'slipped before the Conference'.

The Judge granted a 'declaration' which, in effect, overruled it. He then, after hearing Mr Gardiner and Mr Lawson, granted a declaration that

the purported election of the Defendant Haxell as the General Secretary of the ETU was contrary to the Rules of the Union, was and is void, and was brought about by fraudulent and unlawful devices by the Defendants Foulkes, Haxell, McLennan, Frazer and Humphrey.

In the form in which Mr Gardiner asked for it, this had ended with the words 'acting in their several capacities as officers and servants of the said Union'. Mr Justice Winn would not have this, although (as Mr Gardiner reminded him) it followed the wording of his delivered judgment. 'I don't wish my decision in respect of that finding,' he said, 'to be understood as meaning that this was pursuant to an official resolution of the Union. I have in mind the provisions of the Trade Disputes Act, 1906' (by virtue of which a trade union cannot be sued 'in tort').

'Then I will delete that, my Lord,' Mr Gardiner said; and in its thus modified form it was granted.

The third of the declarations asked for by the Plaintiffs was that 'at the said election the Plaintiff Byrne was validly elected, and now is, General Secretary of the ETU'.

Mr Lawson strongly contested this one. Quite apart from fraudulent conspiracy, he said, there had been breaches of rule by the scrutineers about posting, and the dates of branch membership returns. Any other members of the ETU could now challenge the validity of the election of Mr Byrne; as the Plaintiffs had (successfully) challenged that of Mr Haxell. The Judge, said Mr Lawson, must not be 'put in the position of conducting a scrutiny of the election returns'. Mr Byrne's only legal remedy was damages, not a declaration that he was the elected General Secretary.

'But I've a very strong impression,' his Lordship replied, 'that there has not been an election in this Union within human memory which was conducted in perfect accordance with the Rules. I think that as good and sound and real a result of this election will be achieved as is possible if I now declare—and I *do* declare— that Mr Byrne was elected General Secretary of this union in the December 1959 election.'

Mr Gardiner went on. He next wanted an injunction to restrain Mr Haxell from 'using the name or style of, or directly or indirectly acting as, or doing any part of the work of *any other office* in the Union unless he shall have been duly elected thereto'.

Mr Lawson urged that this ought to be confined to 'any other *elective* office', so that Mr Haxell might now be usefully if harmlessly employed in non-elective jobs by the ETU, whose affairs he so thoroughly understood. The Judge agreed. 'I don't think it would be right to deprive the Union of the services of Mr Haxell if he can do some work as an employee. I don't yet know whether the members may take a very different view of him from that which I have taken, and one may still find him back as the elected General Secretary. Certainly I think it should be "the work of any other *elective* office", in that form.'

The next point was who was to pay Mr Byrne's arrears of salary as General Secretary—the guilty Defendants or the long-suffering ETU funds. Was it to be the Union? Mr Lawson said that he had gone into the question of 'the permissibility of causes of action against the Union under the Trade Disputes Act, 1906'.

'You remember my raising the point?' asked the Judge (see page 106).

'Yes, I do,' Mr Lawson said.

'It was when you were speaking on the fourth day of speeches— and if I may say this, certainly not intending to be in any way unkind, still less offensive, I was amazed at the lack of reaction which followed my observation, because it was for that reason I intervened.'

'I have throughout been dealing with the matter,' said Mr Lawson, 'upon the basis that there was no such claim'.

'Yes, I fully understand . . . I think it would be wrong in law for me to award damages against the Union for fraudulent conspiracy—which, after all, is plainly a tort.'

There remained the question of *costs* against the Union, but the Judge came back to that later.

Meanwhile Mr Gardiner wanted an order from the Judge —

> that the ETU do hold the forthcoming elections for the offices of Executive Councillors in accordance with the directions scheduled hereto, and that the Defendants Foulkes, McLennan, Davies, Feathers, Frazer, Goldberg, Hendy and Sell do all such acts and things as may be necessary to comply therewith.

'As your Lordship knows,' he said, 'the whole of the Executive Councillors are coming up for election in September; and my friend Mr Lawson agreed that it would be proper that consideration should be given to the question how that election ought to be conducted. The Plaintiffs have suggested that the election should be conducted by the Electoral Reform Society, which conducts elections of some of the largest trade unions in the country.'

Mr Gardiner explained that the Electoral Reform Society would arrange for the printing of election addresses, ballot papers, and business reply envelopes addressed to the Society, and send them all out to the members entitled to vote, each of whom would then mark the ballot paper with his branch number and sign it.

'Branch number?' said the Judge. 'What does branch number mean?'

'His branch membership number—each member has a number.'

'Curiously enough, I don't think I ever heard that in the course of the hearing.'

(His Lordship was right: the fact had never come out.)

Each candidate, Mr Gardiner continued, would be entitled to nominate not more than three members (including himself) to attend the 'count' by the Society. And the Society would have an absolute discretion to reject ballot papers arriving late, or spoilt, or from someone not entitled to vote. 'This is not the only trade union, my Lord, which has had some difficulty with its elections; and a number of them make use of this Society. The ballot would be by post, so that all the members could be assured that the scrutiny of the votes would be conducted by a wholly independent body.'

Mr Lawson opposed it on the ground that the ETU Rules did not provide for it. 'Your Lordship just can't be invited to sweep away the whole of the Rules in relation to particular elections in this Union and replace them by something which the members have never agreed to—and which any member who is not a party to this action might object to. But the Union has had under consideration,' Mr Lawson said, 'the proposal that the Union's auditors, a prominent firm of chartered accountants in Manchester, should be appointed (so to speak) as delegate on behalf of Executive Council, to be responsible for the arrangements in relation to the printing and dispatch of ballot papers. But the members of the Union have the right to the observance of the Rules until such time as those Rules may be altered and some different ballot method adopted.'

The Judge conceded that there was a great deal in all this. 'But the ground is cut right away,' he went on, 'if you tell me that you are about to challenge the rulings that I have given (and I assume that that's what you *are* going to say ultimately). Because it would be just farcical for you to say on the one hand: "You can trust the members of this Executive Council, of whom, with few exceptions, you have said that their conduct is quite disgraceful, and they will abide loyally by the rulings and constructions that you have given to the Rules": and then on the other hand say: "I am going straight to the Court of Appeal to say you are wrong about the whole thing." It's just farcical.'

Mr Lawson reiterated that the next election ought to be carried out according to the Union's own Rules, even if it was 'administered by some outside person'.

'Unfortunately,' his Lordship replied, 'you are addressing someone who no longer has an unprejudiced and open mind about the individuals on trial before me. I regard the whole lot of them with the greatest suspicion, personally; and I don't think it right that the fortunes of a most important organisation of working men, forming one of the healthy cells in the body of this community, should be left for a forthcoming election in the hands of these individual men. I think the Court must take drastic measures here. It surprises me that your clients' (i.e., the ETU) 'do not say at once: "Yes, of course we'll agree to have independent control of our next election." '

'What I was indicating to your Lordship, I hope, was that in so far as the administrative arrangements were concerned—'

'It's not administrative arrangements. It's the psychological atmosphere and the dominance of individuals carrying out the arrangements. I wouldn't trust *anyone* at the Head Office virtually now, to conduct a straightforward election. That's my state of prejudice against the whole organisation.'

Mr Lawson persisted that they must stick to the Rules: otherwise the Union would be exposed to claims in litigation. 'Your Lordship has no jurisdiction to make an Order which would involve a wholesale disregard of the Rules of this Union—something which hundreds of thousands of the members have never agreed to.'

'Tell me, Mr Lawson, what are *you* proposing should be done? *You* say bring in a firm of chartered accountants. Where do the Rules provide for that?'

There was a perceptible pause. Mr Lawson was in a corner. The Executive Council, he said, *could* appoint someone to do the 'administrative work' in an election—Rule 21 allowed it. There was no reason why branch officials should not be required to double-check parcels coming from the printers, and go to the post office two or three at a time so as to witness the posting off of ballot results. 'Those are the sort of administrative arrangements one has in mind . . . The alternative is that your Lordship is really being asked to write a new Rule Book.'

The Judge smiled; but for the occasion, one would have said that he grinned.

'You know me well enough,' he said, 'to know that I was driving you into a corner. And now you're there; and you are offering me an undertaking, are you?'

'Would your Lordship give me a moment to take instructions?'

'I am really not prepared to be trifled with,' his Lordship said by way of anticipating those instructions. 'The Court recognises the value of trade union control of their own affairs. I think that I should require the appointment by the Executive Council of a firm of chartered accountants—at, of course, the expense of the Union.' And he adjourned the Court for twenty minutes so that a proposition could be worked out.

The proposition Mr Lawson then submitted was that Messrs Foulkes, McLennan, Davies, Feathers, Frazer, Goldberg, Hendy and Sell would 'use their best endeavours to cause the Executive Council to appoint an independent chartered accountant to be responsible for the administration of the ballot, and to supervise the dispatch of the ballot papers from the printers and the destruction of surplus ones. Branch secretaries would be told that parcels from the printer must be opened only in the presence of two other members, and that the branch committee must check the ballot material for dispatch to members and witness the posting of it. The national scrutineers would have to open the envelopes in the presence of the chartered accountant. And (as an afterthought, prompted by the Judge) the chartered accountant would be responsible for destroying the kind of left-over ballot papers that, in the 1959 election, had gone to St Pancras Station.

The Judge seemed satisfied with this, but asked Mr Gardiner what he thought.

Half a loaf, Mr Gardiner thought, was better than no bread. But 'with regard to the forthcoming election, there has been immense activity by the Defendants in procuring their own re-nomination by large numbers of branches . . . There are two spheres of fraud in these elections. One is at the branches and one is at Headquarters. The arrangements proposed do not, in my submission, preclude fraud in the branches. The first and vital thing is to secure that the branch secretary sends to every member entitled to vote a ballot paper, and that he doesn't take one out of six out of its envelope and keep them in reserve, so that he can then pass them on to himself. If there is an order that the branch committee are to sit there night after night while the branch secretary sends out the envelopes, they won't in fact do it, and indeed they can't be made to do it—they have, of course, other things to do . . . What is really important is that the member should be certain of receiving his ballot paper, which can be done only by his being sent it by some independent person, and that he should be then entitled to send it by post *direct* to that independent person.'

'I will say no more about this matter,' said his Lordship, 'than that I would prefer to do that which Mr Gardiner has asked me to do. If I had been a caliph under a palm tree, I should have done precisely what he has asked me to do. I am not. In my judgment I should be acting illegally, and therefore should produce no effective result.'

Mr Lawson's undertaking was therefore accepted, once he had removed a final anxiety of the Judge's about the proposed chartered accountant's political impartiality; Mr Gardiner's last word on it being that it didn't mean that 'Mr Byrne was in the least satisfied that if the steps which the Defendants say they will take are taken the Communist branch secretaries will not rig the election as in the past'.

Finally, the question of liability for costs was, after prolonged argument, settled in this way: Mr Rengert and Mr Shipman were awarded costs of £25 each, just 'for the sake of their reputations', against the Plaintiffs (Mr Gardiner having unsuccessfully urged that these be paid by the five unsuccessful Defendants). Mr Goldberg and Mr Hendy were not allowed costs against anybody. The other 'successful' Defendants were to recover their costs, if they could, from the unsuccessful ones. The Plaintiffs were granted costs not only against the individual Defendants found guilty of fraud but also against the Electrical Trades Union (which thus, in due course,

found itself at least partially reimbursing the Legal Aid Fund). And
his Lordship refused a stay of execution.

Mr Justice Winn's unique task was over: the democratic
machine had been shown, after years of misgiving and frustration
on the part of its operators, to have after all a master-switch. If
the machine went wrong or was so mishandled as to work like an
irremovable despot, the Law could switch it off, call in a tech-
nician, and start it up again. It had taken a long time and had all
gone fairly quietly, but the Judge's watchful serenity may have
concealed a dynamo running at full capacity. At the Annual Conference of the Law Society in 1961, Lord Justice Pearce had used a
different metaphor. 'If a Judge seems to float along on the Bench
with effortless serenity,' he said, 'like a swan upon the mirrored
surface of the lake, it may be wise to remind the litigant that the
Judge, like the swan, is paddling madly underneath.'

INDEX

N.B. (P) denotes a witness for the Plaintiffs and (D) for the Defendants.

Twickenham Branch. *See* Brodie, Clifford

Varty, Jack, Secretary of Kendal Branch (P), 33
Veitch, Ernest, Secretary of Billingham Branch (P), 33–4
Vetterlein, Thomas, member of ETU Executive Council (P), 59, 66–7, 69, 121, 190
Vincent, Thomas, formerly of the ETU Executive Council (D), 130–1

Walker, Colin, Secretary of Greenock Branch (P), 85–6
Walker, Mr, member of ETU Executive Council, 73, 74, 79
Wallingford Branch. *See* Thomas, Wilfrid
Ward, Mr, 69
Warlow, Derek, of ETU Head Office (D), 145, 206, 231
Warwick, John, Secretary of Central Branch (Scotland), 61
West, Harry, of Stratford Branch (D), 114, 130, 138, 153, 209, 217, 230; in the witness-box, 155–6; exonerated, 238
White, George, Secretary of Neath Branch (P), 49
Widnes Branch. *See* Fazakerley, George
Will, John, Secretary of London Station Engineers No 2 Branch (P), 91
Winn, Mr Justice, 17, 26, 27, 30, 39, 49, 57, 58, 63, 68, 69, 79, 84, 87, 88, 94, 95, 103–4, 108, 112, 113, 118, 119, 120, 121, 125, 135, 137, 152, 169, 174, 218; on making 'jury points', 34; refuses application to amend the Defence, 21; on pejorative use of 'Communist', 36–8; on branch secretaries, 38, 91; on secondary evidence, 42; on the missing ballot papers, 43, 44; on the rule of evidence, 45–6; on the late arrival of envelopes, 46–7, 52; and postal votes, 47–8; on preparation of certain documents, 49–50; on Mr Blairford as a witness, 61;

rebukes Mr Reno, 63–4; and superfluous evidence, 65–6; and advisory committees, 67, 80; and 'probative material', 67–8; and branch voting, 76–7; on fringe matter, 80; and national scrutineers, 83; and the Jarrow election, 85, 207–8; and Cobbett's 'Rural Rides', 94, 95, 96, 214; rebukes Mr Lawson, 96; rebukes Mr Byrne, 98; and Mr Byrne's salary, 101; on the Secretaries of the Southampton branches, 104; on 'estimated numbers' of ballot papers, 104–5; and liability of ETU to pay damages, 106; and Mr Haxell, 122, 126; and Mr Burns, 127; and disqualification of branches, 132, 133, 134; and Mr Humphrey, 137–8, 139, 140–5; and missing documents, 147; and pleaded issues, 148, 149; and Mr Rengert, 150, 151; and Mr Shipman, 151; and Mr Goldberg, 151, 155; and Mr West, 156; and party membership, 156–7; remarks on adjourning for Whitsun, 161–2; and Mr Francis Fraser, 162–5; and London Electronic Engineers No 2 Branch, 160; and Mr Sell, 169–70, 173; and Mr George Scott, 175–9; 209; and Mr Hendy, 182, 183–4, 209–10; and hearsay evidence, 185–6; and Mr McLennan, 186–9, 209; and Mr John Frazer, 191; and Mr Foulkes, 194–5, 197, 198, 202, 203; judgment, 219–39; Plaintiffs seek 'declarations' from, 240–6; and costs, 246–7
Withecombe, Stanley, Secretary of Southampton Dock Branch (P), 80–2
Woolston Branch, 115, 116, 118, 232
   See also Saunders, Charles
Wright, Denis, of London Station Engineers No 5 Branch (D), 166

Yate Branch, 92
Yeovil Branch. *See* Sparkes, Harold
Young, Mr, Chairman of Finch Branch, 72, 93, 130